T0284039

Advance Praise for *The* ⅃

"Michael W. Higgins, a brilliant writer, scholar, and reporter, gives us a tantalizing read of Pope Francis's revolutionary papacy in *The Jesuit Disruptor*. Quirky, quizzical and even occasionally quixotic, his approach is accessible and the style entertaining." —James Martin, SJ, author of *The Jesuit Guide to (Almost) Everything*

"An essential guide to one of the most consequential figures in the history of the church. What makes this pope such a surprising 'disruptor' is shown not just in the consistency of his pastoral vision, but in his unusual capacity to listen, learn, and evolve in response to events and encounters." —Robert Ellsberg, Publisher, Orbis Books

"Higgins gives a thorough and erudite treatment of the Jesuit pope's record … contextualizing Francis with thinkers who have inspired him … and diagnosing with remarkable precision and nuance Francis's modus operandi." —Colleen Dulle, Associate Editor of *America Magazine* and host of the podcast *Inside the Vatican*

"Who knew that academic rigour and intellectual subtlety could come with such energy, humour, and craic? … A profound personal portrait of Pope Francis, which is both accessible and entertaining … Exhilarating." —Gerry O'Hanlon, SJ, author of *The Quiet Revolution of Pope Francis: A Synodal Catholic Church in Ireland?*

"Michael W. Higgins has given us a picture of the pope that illuminates the complexity of his struggle for a church that is both more merciful and more adult. Anyone who reads this lively account will come away with a clearer understanding of the immensity and importance of the task that the Jesuit disruptor was called to accomplish." —Paul Lakeland, Emeritus Professor of Catholic Studies, Fairfield University

"With passionate wit and perceptivity, this astute observer of Vatican affairs paints a deeply personal portrait of the Argentine outlier pope." —Catherine Clifford, Professor of Systematic and Historical Theology, Saint Paul University, Ottawa

"A very accessible academic, yet deeply personal examination of the pontificate of Francis thus far … Written in agreeable and erudite prose, this book will be welcome reading for those in the pews, and those outside of the church." —Dr. Mark G. McGowan, Professor of History, University of Toronto

"Higgins is a deeply thoughtful writer who hasn't lost the skills to engage and delight … Francis is indeed a disruptor, an actual inspirational disruptor for a time in need of great disruptions." —John Fraser, author of *The Secret of the Crown: Canada's Affair with Royalty*, and Executive Chair of the National NewsMedia Council of Canada

"A clarion call for a fresh way of seeing the Gospel, urgently reminding us both of the critical need to respond to God's Mercy and that the church is not a refuge for the saved, but a field hospital for the wounded—a timely message for our confused, distempered times." —James Clarke, retired Ontario Superior Court judge and poet

"Sagacious and lucid … Higgins illuminates Francis's recovery of the original animating spirit of the church." —Douglas Roche, former senator and author

"Michael W. Higgins manages to carve out some fresh space in a crowded field. What a joy to read such punchy and elegant storytelling." —Brendan Walsh, Editor, *The Tablet*

"Higgins's narrative is fresh, candid, solidly grounded, and insightful—a delight for discerning readers." —Richard Yanikoski, President Emeritus, Saint Xavier University, Chicago, and President Emeritus, Association of Catholic Colleges and Universities

"Higgins reveals to us a pope convinced that the church must urgently reform itself, by accompanying ordinary people in the struggle to believe, in our dangerously polarized world." —Brother Mark O'Connor FMS, Pope Francis Fellow, Newman College, University of Melbourne, Australia

"Higgins is a prolific writer … whose turn of phrase, succinct descriptions, and wealth of experience will delight the reader with a readable, provocative synopsis of the bridge-building pope." —John Dadosky, Professor of Theology and Philosophy, University of Toronto

THE JESUIT DISRUPTOR

A Personal Portrait of Pope Francis

MICHAEL W. HIGGINS

ANANSI

Published in Canada in 2024 and the USA in 2024 by House of Anansi Press Inc.
houseofanansi.com

28 27 26 25 24   1 2 3 4 5

Library and Archives Canada Cataloguing in Publication
Title: The Jesuit disruptor : a personal portrait of Pope Francis / Michael W. Higgins.
Other titles: Personal portrait of Pope Francis
Names: Higgins, Michael W., 1948- author.
Description: Includes bibliographical references and index.
Identifiers: Canadiana (print) 20240353587 | Canadiana (ebook) 20240353579 |
ISBN 9781487010058 (softcover) | ISBN 9781487010065 (EPUB)
Subjects: LCSH: Francis, Pope, 1936- | LCSH: Popes—Biography.
Classification: LCC BX1378.7 .H54 2024 | DDC 282.092—dc23

Cover design: Greg Tabor
Cover artwork: iStock.com/Kokkai Ng
Book design and typesetting: Lucia Kim

*House of Anansi Press is grateful for the privilege to work on and create from the Traditional
Territory of many Nations, including the Anishinabeg, the Wendat, and the Haudenosaunee,
as well as the Treaty Lands of the Mississaugas of the Credit.*

Canada Council Conseil des Arts
for the Arts du Canada

ONTARIO ARTS COUNCIL
CONSEIL DES ARTS DE L'ONTARIO
an Ontario government agency
un organisme du gouvernement de l'Ontario

With the participation of the Government of Canada | Canadä
Avec la participation du gouvernement du Canada

*We acknowledge for their financial support of our publishing program the Canada Council for
the Arts, the Ontario Arts Council, and the Government of Canada.*

Printed and bound in Canada

MIX
Paper | Supporting
responsible forestry
FSC® C103567
www.fsc.org

This book is printed on FSC® certified paper.

CONTENTS

INTRODUCTION

IT IS A DRAMATIC disjunction to think of Jorge Mario Bergoglio, the tireless and people-focused Pope Francis, as someone associated with a thinker who could write that a human is "a novelty, a monstrosity, chaotic, contradictory, prodigious, judge of all things, feeble earthworm, bearer of truth, mire of uncertainty and error, glory and refuse of the universe."[1]

And yes, a reed, if a thinking reed, as this author quoted by the pope is famous for saying.

The early seventeenth-century French polymath Blaise Pascal is not, on the surface, a natural spiritual and intellectual companion of the Argentine pope. But it appears on a careful reading that, in fact, he is.

Pascal—originator of the prototype of the calculator, mastermind behind the first public transportation system, a mathematician of astonishing genius, and a theological thinker of arresting insight—was not a Jesuit lover, and Francis is, well, a Jesuit.

So, what gives? Why is Francis so taken with Pascal that he writes an apostolic letter—*Sublimitas et miseria hominis*—on the occasion of the fourth centenary of the French thinker's birth? And what does it mean for this book, a personal portrait of a pontificate?

Long before I had even heard of Jorge Mario Bergoglio, and decades before he became the Successor of Saint Peter, I was commissioned to write a documentary on Blaise Pascal and his tender (if occasionally tortured) relationship with his sister Jacqueline. My CBC producer John Reeves[2] wanted a dramatic exploration of this relationship that would capture their respective voices through their letters and the correspondence of their sister Gilberte, all framed by a narrative situating time, place, and background.

Although I had studied Pascal in a third-year undergraduate philosophy class taught by a Glaswegian of fierce logical disposition, I needed a refresher. So, I sought the help of a senior French professor and colleague whose love of the three Pascals—Blaise, Jacqueline, and Gilberte—was as touching as it was informed. And a huge boon for me.

What I was able to unearth in the correspondence was the "heart." For all Pascal's success as an abstract thinker—a man who would spend countless hours in private conversation with his esteemed contemporary René Descartes, a man who would take on the formidable French Jesuits in his polemical broadside, the *Lettres provinciales*—he was the very same man whose mystical and fiery night of revelation of November 23, 1654, his *Memorial*, confirmed the limitations of reason and that his God is the God of Abraham, the God of Isaac, the God of Jacob, the God of Jesus Christ, and *not* the God of philosophers and scholars.

Pascal discovered that *le coeur a son ordre*, the heart has its order, and it has its own reason that reason does not know. This resonates with Pope Francis's own practical mysticism and pastoral sensibility, as seen in his apostolic letter on Pascal:

> Neither the operations of geometry nor philosophical reasoning permit us, of themselves, to arrive at a "very clear view" of the world or of ourselves. Those enmeshed in the details of their calculations do not benefit from the view of the whole that enables us to "see all the principles." That is the task of the "spirit of finesse" which Pascal extols, for in attempting to grasp reality, "one must immediately take things in at a single glance." This intuitive vision has to do with what Pascal calls the "heart." "We know the truth not only by reason but even more by the heart."[3]

Pascal knew that reliance on the ratiocinative alone was a straitjacket. Human yearning cannot be reduced to the machinations of the mind. There is a deeper truth that holds us all, and access to that truth cannot be manipulated by the "operations of geometry."

Pope Francis, who taught chemistry when young and has retained a lifelong interest in the natural sciences, has never subscribed to the shibboleth that science is the enemy of religion, that reason is inimical to faith. Pascal validates Francis's conviction—a conviction that has gathered strength during his papacy—that

> "reality is superior to ideas." Pascal teaches us to keep our distance from "various means of masking reality," from "angelic forms of purity" to "intellectual discourse bereft of

wisdom." Nothing is more dangerous than a disembodied reason: "He who would act as an angel, acts as a beast." The baneful ideologies from which we continue to suffer in the areas of economics, social life, anthropology and morality, keep their followers imprisoned in a world of illusions, where ideas have replaced reality.

And reality for Francis is the field hospital, the place where the balm of mercy is applied to the wounded, where hope is generated, healing effected, spiritual equilibrium restored. He shares Pascal's detestation for a disincarnate reason, for the easy seduction by the latest gadgetry, for the "idolization" of the truth with its fake omniscience.

Humanity is a thing of grandeur as much as it is a thing of misery, *sublimitas et miseria*.

There is a sweet irony in the pope's special affection for a figure so opposed to the French Jesuits. Pascal castigated the Jesuits for their casuistry or sophistry and for what he perceived as their laxity in the area of grace and salvation. Debates with the Jesuits and his support for the community of Port-Royal—a hotbed of resistance to Cardinal Richelieu, chief minister of France—were not politically astute choices on his part. Port-Royal was a locus for what was nervously deemed by Rome and Paris as a real threat to orthodoxy: the Jansenist[4] movement. This put Pascal at odds with majority opinion in the country. In addition, his sister Jacqueline was a nun in the community, and although he was initially opposed to her taking her vows, he came to accept her decision and became Port-Royal's principal advocate. But he backed the wrong party—both ecclesiastical and political.

For Francis, Pascal may have been on the wrong side on

some issues—although history nuances these things in ways that blur the victor's confidence over time—but his patience, "evangelical radicalism," and breadth of spirit and mind make him an inspirational model for all times.

In summary, what Pascal taught Francis was that (a) ecclesial rules and regulations have their limitations; (b) works of mercy are primary because "the sole object of Scripture is charity"; (c) attention to the suffering of the poor is critical to a life of faith; (d) understanding the limits of reason does not diminish the dignity of reasoning itself; and (e) the existential and the personal take priority over the abstract, as "reality is superior to ideas."

Although Francis alludes to Pascal's sisters, Gilberte and Jacqueline, only a couple of times in his apostolic letter, the role they played in his life—Jacqueline in particular—underscores the centrality of love and fidelity. As Gilberte said of Jacqueline and Blaise: "Their hearts were ever as one heart … They knew what it was to love and to be loved in utter confidence … each with the other abundantly content, never apprehensive of possible division … He did well to love her … She was in all things his confidante."[5]

In Pascal, Francis found a mystic, a poet, and a scientist—a lay Christian—who lived in the "now," recognized humanity's innate grandeur and its misery, and placed himself in the service of the Infinite Mercy. Like Pascal, whose God is not the God of the philosophers, Francis understands that an encounter with the God of Abraham, Isaac, Jacob, and Jesus is an encounter not circumscribed by the canons of reason: "Only one who has encountered mercy, who has been caressed by the tenderness of mercy, is right with the Lord … the privileged place of the encounter is the caress of the mercy of Jesus Christ."[6]

More than any pope in the last century, Francis reminds us that he is a sinner in need of the caress of mercy.

In his ministry as pope, as Universal Pastor, he has made mercy his byword. And mercy, too, *he* will need as he helms the Barque of Peter through, in the inelegant phrasing of German novelist Ernst Jünger, the *Scheisskrieg* or shit war he inherited.

THE POPES AND ME

A Personal Obsession

WHEN I WAS AN undergraduate at St. Francis Xavier University in Nova Scotia in the 1960s, I had a column in the university newspaper, the *Xaverian Weekly*, in which I would indulge my penchant for pontificating. One of the English professors, who had decamped to Colorado but read the paper religiously from that safe distance, was especially irritated by my oracular pontifications and dubbed me "the church basement pope." I was an instant celebrity, if a quickly fading one.

I have always loved popes, whether pontificating or otherwise—ever since I developed prereflexive consciousness. It is not piety that drove me into their elaborate court, their special sphere in Christian history, but something more constitutive of my nature: the allure of drama.

And drama and the popes, theatre and the papacy, are the pre-eminent reason why the world—Catholic and non-Catholic alike—is mystified by the goings-on in that rarefied sovereignty on the Tiber. It is not just me.

When popes die, the globe stands still. Well, the media globe at least. The protocols around election, the rites and ceremonies associated with the passing of one pope and the arrival of his successor dominate our screens for days (weeks if the election is a particularly contentious one). The personalities of those who elect the next pope are the subject of popular press profiles and seasoned critical analyses by professional commentators, becoming in the process that most strange of media concoctions: cardinal celebrities. The world is simply agog with curiosity and fascination. I am sure the devout are in there somewhere but, by and large, the world is transfixed by a panorama without precedent.

It is high drama with the trappings of sacrality.

But I had the papal bug early. I was bitten and smitten. And the bond lasts to this day. Having said that, and connecting this abiding interest with both scholarly and journalistic forays into the papal orbit, I can still align with the wise and balanced judgment of my coreligionist and contemporary the historian Eamon Duffy, who remarks in the preface to his *Saints and Sinners: A History of the Popes*: "For Roman Catholics, of course (of whom I am one), the story of the popes is a crucial dimension of the story of the providential care of God for humankind in history, the necessary and (on the whole) proper development of powers and responsibilities implicit in the nature of the Church itself."[1]

Personal faith, theological conviction, affective attachment, and an intellectual predilection for the historical combine to sustain my enduring attraction to the institution of the papacy but more particularly to the colourful characters who have exercised the ministry of the Bishop of Rome from its inception—especially during that comparatively short duration when I accompany in time whoever sits on the Chair of Peter. Not that there is any causal or consequential connection.

Historian P. G. Maxwell-Stuart reminds us that the seduction of scandal is fully operational in the world of the papacy but that it would be a great distortion to reduce the papacy to nothing but its legion of scandals:

> Say "Borgia," and inevitably the word poison leaps to everyone's lips. There are, alas, many such associations. Formosus (891–896) is considered to be a pattern of vanity for calling himself "Handsome" (*formosus*) when he became pope: but who recalls that he was a highly intelligent man and a preacher of the Gospel? ... there is no lack of material for those who enjoy mere titillation. But scandal, of course, does not define an institution.[2]

But it sure makes it more interesting.

My own engagement with things papal has not been governed by a taste for the salacious nor, for that matter, driven by a pious motivation. It began early—in secondary school, to be precise—when I happened upon *The Church in the Age of Revolution (1789–1870)*, by the French historian Henri Daniel-Rops, and learned that Napoleon had some hefty troubles with popes Pius VI and VII that resulted in some pretty tricky manoeuvres on the Corsican's part. Bonaparte was calling the shots. He even corralled Pius VII by having him travel to Paris for his own and Josephine's coronation in Notre-Dame Cathedral, although in the end the pope merely blessed the crowns: the actual crowning was commandeered by Napoleon himself. Pius was second fiddle. Didn't seem quite right: blasphemous, even.

And so, I started to read about other popes as well, partly to shore up my faith in the Petrine ministry but also because the papacy seemed to have lasting power. Adolescence is a time of hyper flux, with unsettling new things happening to your body and psyche, and so you crave a bit of order and predictability in your life. For me, the papacy provided that intellectual grounding. Kingdoms, regimes, and governments come and go, but the popes will always be there.

Not quite so simple, really, as I began to read more widely and outside the Catholic spectrum. It was around this time that I had a mini trauma, a disconcerting awakening. My school, although public and not private, was predominantly Jewish in its composition. The children of European Jews who had fled the continent post-1945 and who lived in my area of Toronto introduced me to a world well outside my tribal Catholic orbit. I became aware of raw feelings—fear, isolation, suppressed memories, unspoken truths—that hitherto I knew nothing about.

I read Guenter Lewy's *The Catholic Church and Nazi Germany* shortly after its publication in 1964 and was gobsmacked. Shortly after that—with its comprehensive indictment of church timidity, if not complicity with National Socialism's hold on Germany, specifically in relation to the plight of the Jews—I read *The Deputy*, the more disturbing and highly controversial play by Rolf Hochhuth, and I followed closely the riots and protests that attended its North American premiere, including its Crest Theatre iteration in Toronto. In recent years, although closer examination of the Hochhuth play has revealed aspects of its genesis, historical accuracy, compromised authorial intention, and problematic political attachments, it was *the* popular catalyst for provoking discussion over the perceived, if not comprehensive, indifference the reigning pontiff felt toward the Shoah. That pope, Pius XII (Eugenio Pacelli), the august embodiment of an imperial papacy and the perfect product of Vatican training over decades in the service of the church at head office, was also papal ambassador to Berlin in the 1930s during the ascendency of the Nazi party. But he was a much more complex, anguished, and indeed competent figure than Hochhuth allows in his drama. Still, for me, at the time that I read *The Deputy*, I was enraged. I felt betrayed. And in a moment of high, real, but misplaced dudgeon, I ripped up my paperback copy of the play and self-righteously deposited it in the garbage can in the garden. I purged myself of any complicity. My morality was intact. But then, years later, I had to purchase a new copy, so I paid an economic price as well. I wasn't so keen on that.

I would later write: "a play of nearly Wagnerian length, suffused with post-war German angst, polemical, in turn both historically sound and recklessly speculative, emotionally incendiary, prey to the worst features of intellectual reductionism and callow melodrama, *The Deputy* may well be, in the words of Justus George Lawler, a third-rate literary effort comparable in its impact to *Uncle Tom's Cabin*."[3]

That's how I situated the play in a book on the politics of creating saints that I researched and wrote in the first decade of the twenty-first century while examining the ever-unfolding debate over Pope Pius XII's silence—its diplomatic calculus, its divisive consequences, its deleterious effect on the reputation of Eugenio Pacelli personally and of his pontificate; it constitutes a more detached view in contrast to my teenage outrage. Pius's controversial "silence" in relation to the plight of European Jewry was in great measure the product not so much of his personal temperament or his theological thinking but of his policy of diplomatic engagement:

> That meant attenuating in public the profound anger and anxiety experienced in papal circles over the start of the war. Even though the years of diplomatic protest and thinly veiled critiques of Nazi policies had failed to achieve Pacelli's objectives in the Vatican's relations with the Hitler state, the operating principle of papal diplomacy remained constant: to avoid doing or saying anything in public that might provoke the Germans—or the Italians for that matter—into ramping up policies that the church had for years been working to mitigate. This approach called for supreme rhetorical constraint, a careful measuring of every word and sentence so that papal disapproval was couched in ways that allowed for the preservation of the Vatican's formal diplomatic relations with the belligerent powers.[4]

The consequences of such a policy and style are with us still in terms of Pacelli's politically fraught candidacy for sainthood—a candidacy not likely to be processed through to canonization during the Francis pontificate—and an intelligent corrective to my adolescent self-righteousness. A reminder that in the court of scholarly opinion, though never as objective as some historians would have us believe, matters are more complicated and nuanced than fervent advocacy allows.

By the time I entered the seminary in 1966, my interest in popes strangely abated, but only for a bit. The publication by Pope Paul VI (Giovanni Battista Montini) of the divisive encyclical *Humanae vitae* (On Human Life), reaffirming the ban on all forms of artificial birth regulation and deemed necessary because of the enormous popularity of the easily available and portable birth control pill, created a firestorm in the Catholic world. I was in the kitchen of the seminary helping the nuns clean up after our lunch when the news of the encyclical was relayed by radio, rising over the clamour of the dishes and the warm and animated chatter of the Franciscan Sisters of St. Peter of Alcantara. I was startled and distraught. Not that I knew a great deal about contraception, oral or otherwise. In fact, I was hopelessly innocent about such things, but I had followed the heated debates in Catholic circles—lay and clerical—over the possibility, indeed the great likelihood, of change in the traditional Catholic banning of all means of artificial birth regulation. I was as disappointed as millions of other lay Catholics, even if my inexperience made that outrage more vicarious than personal. As I would later write, at a time when I was a father of four children, Paul VI's efforts "to affirm the authority of the church by disallowing any possibility of deviation from previous papal teaching, had seriously undermined that authority."[5] I can now better appreciate the complexities around Paul VI's decision-making, although I remain convinced that the encyclical was misguided, blinkered, and damaging in its effects.

If the publication of *Humanae vitae* and its subsequent aftershocks created all kinds of dilemmas—immediate moral ones over family size, with all their psychological and economic determinants, arguments around the "reception" of such teaching, the role of individual conscience, the public disagreements among theologians and bishops—I retain a soft spot for him personally in spite of my youthful rage.

He is the first pope I met. Well, not really met. I was in a room with him, a big room, the hall in his summer residence in Castel Gandolfo, the papal palace and gardens south of Rome. Until Pope Francis, it was the papal residence during the heat of a Roman summer throughout the national vacation phenomenon known as the *Ferragosto*. But retreat from the Vatican does not mean the absence of work. Popes traditionally hold public audiences in Castel Gandolfo for pilgrims, tourists, papal paparazzi, and souvenir collectors. So, there I was in the hall waiting, along with a multitude of others, for the pope to arrive. And when he did, carried aloft on his *sedia gestatoria* (a ceremonial throne on which the pope is transported on the shoulders of devout hefty men)—a practice no longer in use— the gathered audience broke out into a robust, if musically discordant, rendition of the *Pater Noster* (Our Father) from the *Missa de Angelis*. It was quite moving, as well as surprising. The full-throated Jewish couple beside me from Brooklyn didn't miss a beat.

It was my first on-site encounter with the papal mystique. But earlier encounters—remote, but no less real—peppered my late undergraduate education. I wrote my senior year BA thesis on a figure Harold Bloom called an "eccentric genius," with the emphasis on the eccentric part. His name was a multi-barrelled arrangement—Frederick William Austin Lewis Mary Rolfe— and God forbid you got them out of sequence. Father Rolfe, or Baron Corvo, as he dubbed himself, was a fin-de-siècle decadent, aesthete, dandy, and deeply disgruntled Catholic convert who felt that the ecclesiastical and publishing authorities were out to destroy his priestly and writerly vocations. His imagination, his very personality, thrived on phantasms of paranoia: out of this whirligig of emotional conflict, he produced works of stunning vituperative power. One of the fictional volumes of his autobiography-tinged tetralogy, *Hadrian the Seventh* (1904), reappeared as *Hadrian VII* with theatrical flourish in the 1960s, accommodated for the stage by playwright Peter Luke.

It was a stellar financial and critical success, with performances in London, New York, and at the Stratford Festival in Ontario. I was bewitched by the production—expensive sets, extravagant costumes, glorious music—and especially by the lead actor, Hume Cronyn, who played Hadrian VII with the appropriate blend of sympathy, righteous fury, and misplaced valour.

Corvo recidivus.

But he is an admittedly acquired taste.

I acquired it from an eminent literary authority—the Reverend Brocard Sewell of the Order of Carmelites of the Ancient Observance—a priest with a taste for the outlier, the untoward, the recondite, the minor figures ignored by the taste-makers of establishment culture, both literary and religious.

Sewell had written a letter to the *Times* of London protesting *Humanae vitae*, arguing in favour of Eastern Orthodoxy and its primacy of love over the dominant Roman approach with its emphasis on the monarchic primacy of jurisdiction, suggesting a course of action not typical of obedient Catholic clergy: "The present pope a few years ago made a significant pilgrimage to the tomb of San Celestino. If he would now resign his See, as did Saint Celestine, and make it possible for one of the Oriental patriarchs to succeed him, the Latin Church might yet be saved from an ignominious dissolution."[6]

Unsurprisingly, both Rome and the English hierarchy didn't follow up on the letter's suggestion, if for no other reason than because the said Pope Celestine V, the hermit pope, was forced to abdicate by more politically minded prelates, and Pope Paul was likely familiar with that fact. Instead of heeding the

Carmelite's suggestion, they chose to censure Sewell and to dispatch him to suffer the pains of isolation in the stunning Black Mountains of Wales, where he wrote his justification, his apologia, fittingly titled *The Vatican Oracle*. Prior to its publication, his Carmelite superiors, with Sewell's ready concurrence, decided on a period of exile to a remote place on the planet, where the editors of the *Times* might have some difficulty contacting him: Antigonish, Nova Scotia, Canada.

He was lured to the country by R. J. MacSween, a priest, English literature professor, poet, and essayist who was familiar with Sewell's work as editor of the *Aylesford Review*. MacSween was looking for a founding editor of what would become— and still is—a leading literary platform in Canadian letters: the *Antigonish Review*. And so, Sewell joined the faculty of St. Francis Xavier University. Unfortunately, the two priests had a falling out; Sewell was dispatched for a second time, in this instance to Niagara Falls. But prior to his relocation to the Falls, he was my thesis supervisor and Corvo was my subject.

Hadrian the Seventh is a rococo entertainment, all pomp, style, and Byzantine ornateness, a phantasmagoria typical of the author's obsession with the minutiae of rite and ritual. It is also insightful, psychologically penetrating amid its wordy perversities, as is evidenced by this especially prescient passage from the pope's bull *Regnum meum*:

> We use worldly things till they are wanted by the world: then we relinquish them without even so much as a backward thought. For we are all clearly marked to get that which we give. Nothing is irrevocable on the orb of earth. Nothing is final: for, after this world is the world to come. Therefore, let us move, let us gladly move with the times, really move. God always is merciful.[7]

Pope Francis prefigured? This non-fictional Pope of Mercy, as he has been called?

But long before the cardinal archbishop of Buenos Aires, Jorge Mario Bergoglio, was elected pontiff on March 13, 2013, I had been building my papal credentials for years. *Hadrian the Seventh* was fantasy, after all. Getting to know the inner workings of the papacy—without being a full-time *vaticanista* or amateur Vaticanologist—meant I had to move beyond reading the histories and commentaries to actually being on-site (even if only periodically), cultivating some reliable Roman contacts, insinuating myself into the corridors of power, providing analyses for both scholarly and general-interest publications as well as for radio and television outlets, and just being present for things as they happened in the Vatican City State, the Holy See, St. Peter's Basilica, the place where the pope can be found.

A constellation of good fortune ensured that that would unfold: that I would go to Rome regularly, that I would meet and, in some instances, befriend key figures in the Vatican orbit, and that I would get the kind of professional exposure essential for covering the papacy with more than a modicum of savvy, knowledge, and feverish interest.

This constellation consisted of many parts, all aligning nicely over a two-decade period. There was my appointment first as associate editor, and then as editor, of *Grail: An Ecumenical Journal*, a university-based publication that was the brainchild of my colleague and friend Douglas R. Letson. Work for *Grail* allowed for many Rome-based assignments for the two of us— principally as accredited journalists covering the Roman synods of the 1980s and 1990s—and this in turn opened up avenues for exploration that would be helpful in the years to come.

Most importantly, while attending the 1985 Extraordinary

synod, we met and bonded with two gifted observers of the Vatican scene: John Wilkins, editor of the *Tablet: An International Catholic Weekly*, a Cambridge-educated former BBC producer; and the illustrious papal biographer, Oxford lecturer, and former Jesuit Peter Hebblethwaite. Both of these men were crucial in providing background, historical context, personal contacts, and the collective wisdom of just being survivors of the papal machinery.

Hebblethwaite in particular—a polyglot, shrewd observer of Roman follies, and voracious reader of all things Catholic—managed as a papal scholar to navigate the rough shoals between the Scylla of cynicism and the Charybdis of piety with astonishing deftness. He remained, up to the time of his death in his early sixties, a Catholic of solid intellectual integrity and spiritual fidelity. Whatever his personal view of the popes that defined his years as a writer—John XXIII, whom he loved, Paul VI, who generated strong feelings of conflict in him, or John Paul II, the pope whose totalist manner disturbed him greatly—he was scrupulously fair in his assessment of their respective pontificates.

He became the model for me of the conscientious, if not acidic and fearless, Vatican commentator whose judgments, even if occasionally wrong or reckless in their timing, set the highest standard in his profession. He loved what he did, and I found that infectious as I began to whet my own emerging expertise on the Vatican—its personalities, conflicts, and intrigues.

As a result of my synod trips to Rome, I became a resource for the Canadian media—the public secular media, mainly. Courtesy of the work of CBC *Morningside* producers Richard Handler and Peter Kavanagh, I provided numerous commentaries for host and interviewer Peter Gzowski, whose personal interest in the papacy was at the bottom of the list of his professional news priorities but whose fondness for John Paul II allowed him to connect with his own Polish roots.

Handler was particularly keen on my tracking the numerous controversies associated with Joseph Ratzinger, the future Benedict XVI, and used every stratagem at hand to ensure that I got access when I could to Roman events that featured the formidable cardinal prefect of the Congregation for the Doctrine of the Faith, once tagged the Holy Office of the Inquisition. Kavanagh, who accompanied me to Rome at one point and who was my co-author for the award-winning *Suffer the Children unto Me: An Open Inquiry into the Clerical Sex Abuse Scandal*, made sure that when he was assigned to work with Michael Enright, host of the CBC's *Sunday Edition*, Vatican and papal matters did not disappear from the national broadcaster's radar screen. He didn't need to worry. Enright shared both our interest and our Catholic sensibility—firmly rooted but not devout, skeptical but respectful, anti-doctrinaire but fuelled by intense intellectual curiosity.

These qualities also defined my relationship with Damiano Pietropaolo, the cosmopolitan producer of CBC Radio's flagship intellectual affairs program, *Ideas*. We collaborated on a series called *Catholics* that allotted one segment to the mind of John Paul II and once again provided the support necessary to do some on-site interviews and research.

But the most unexpected development—welcome, propitious, and credential enhancing—and one that landed me squarely in the midst of the Vatican—its history, colourful rogues, and saints—was the ambitious six-hour television series *Sir Peter Ustinov's Inside the Vatican*. I was approached to be one of the consultants by the producer-director John McGreevy, whose work includes an award-winning documentary on and with pianist Glenn Gould as well as an earlier collaboration with the Russian-born English polymath, *Sir Peter Ustinov's Russia*.

In time I became the chief consultant, not by dint of skill or learning but because the other three died during production and I was the only one left standing. The job of a consultant, McGreevy reminded me, is basically to keep litigators at bay by ensuring historical accuracy, avoiding all forms of defamation, smoothing feathers when needlessly ruffled, and providing a patina of credibility.

It was an unusual, eclectic, and highly original series bearing the distinctive mark of the McGreevy style, which was basically to insert invented dramatic bits into the point-of-view perspective of the host. What you got in the end was a historical narrative—largely written by the arts and culture writer Gary Michael Dault—interspersed with dramatic cameos featuring veteran actors in dialogue with Ustinov. These actors, portraying such figures as Charlemagne, Martin Luther, Julius II (the pope who hounded Michelangelo to finish the Sistine Chapel), and Cardinal Pietro Gasparri (Pius XI's principal negotiator for the Lateran Treaty signed in 1929 with Count Ciano and Benito Mussolini that created the Vatican City State as we now know it).

These conversations were erudite, subtitled (Ustinov's interlocutors spoke in their native tongue while the host kibitzed, probed, nuanced, and charmed in English), and were done, naturally, in full dress costume. Every effort was made to guarantee verisimilitude. But it wasn't really conceived or executed as a strict history series. It was entertainment: Ustinov the major attraction, an eccentric series, a hodgepodge of witty asides with travelogue commentary, a peregrination that spent more time out of Rome as it sought to survey the reach of the papacy, its persistent appeal, its wayward history.

It was a quirky series that sat comfortably between fact and invention, was driven mostly by the sophisticated personality of its occasionally quixotic but always witty host, and managed to stake out an approach that was distinctly different from its numerous peers: history-laden documentaries of high seriousness, cinematic narratives with an overlay of piety, and eye-appealing travel flicks with a mighty dollop of the byways of papal history.

My role was very small, but the opportunity, however marginal, to work on the series deepened my appreciation of the artistic dimension of the papal legacy and solidified my conviction that the broad mystique the papacy continues to hold for the devout, the skeptical, the curious, and those delicious malcontents who find so much evil resident in popery remains undiminished by scandals, declining religious attendance in the Western world, and aggressive secularization.

Popes are simply damn interesting, with their deaths more so than their reigns, the political squabbles within their administrative units more compelling than their countless edicts, and the mechanics and rituals around the election of their successors media fodder for the multitudes and gold for the lottery impresarios.

Research involving numerous interviews with key players of the Vatican governance apparatus courtesy of letters of introduction by Toronto's rock star archbishop and Order of Canada Companion Cardinal Gerald Emmett Carter—Douglas R. Letson and I were his official biographers—meant that we were ushered into the private chambers of curial luminaries, taken into the corridors of power outside the limited itinerary of places for tourists, pilgrims, and media mavens, and got access to the nooks and crannies, literal and metaphorical, of the Vatican kingdom and its denizens.

Subsequent trips to Rome for research on *Power and Peril: The Catholic Church at the Crossroads*, as well as other writing assignments—scholarly and general interest alike—provided me with the opportunity to shore up my contacts, to cultivate my own Deep Throat (Sir John MacPherson, Gentleman to His Holiness, a member of the Sovereign Council of the Military Hospitaller Order of St. John of Jerusalem of Rhodes and of Malta, and a retired academic who spent most of his mature years roaming in the Vatican empyrean), and to familiarize myself further with the Byzantine patterns and protocols that define an institution two millennia in the making. It is easy, especially in the early stages of courtship, to become besotted with this alternate reality, to fall sway to the magic of *romanità*. But then you move on. Or should do.

Films, novels, biographies, and historical studies of popes and the papacy are more numerous than the body parts to be found in the four-hundred-plus church reliquaries scattered throughout the Eternal City. The oldies like Morris L. West's *The Shoes of the Fisherman* (with Anthony Quinn as Pope Kiril in the film adaptation) up to more recent imaginative concoctions like *The Two Popes* (with Anthony Hopkins as Pope Benedict and Jonathan Pryce as Cardinal Bergoglio) speak to the inexhaustible interest not only in the office of the papacy but in the personalities who occupy that office.

And it is the personality of the current occupant of that office that is the primary reason for this book.

The cradle Catholic Irish novelist and essayist Colm Tóibín has little truck these days with Catholicism, particularly its Hibernian brand, but the Catholic Church, its characters, machinations, institutional hypocrisies, and heroic outliers continue to fascinate him. In a lengthy essay for the *London Review of Books*, he labours to situate Bergoglio in the scheme of things:

> The fact that Bergoglio had spent so little time in Rome before he became pope had its advantages. He didn't climb the Vatican ladder while picking up lurid information about the private lives of cardinals. He didn't become part of a whispering circle or feed on innuendo. But his distance from all of this also meant that he seemed to believe, at the beginning of his papacy, that there could actually be robust and sincere debate among cardinals and bishops about the private sexual lives of others, including divorced people and homosexuals. All that winking, nodding, subterfuge and underhand knowledge, all those interlocking networks and double lives, are hardly in line with the transparency and clarity of purpose required by the Heavenly Father, who is invoked regularly by even the most reprobate prelates. Bergoglio's power comes from the fact that he doesn't belong to this world.[8]

It is true that Bergoglio doesn't belong to *this* world, but he does understand *this* world, and it is a mistake to think otherwise. His detractors, critics, and intractable in-house opponents do very much understand that he grasps who they are, what their vision of the church is, and why they have so much invested in perpetuating an older model that secures their identity and their power.

For some of his more fringe critics, Francis is the Antichrist, sundering the church from within, playing with dogma, more pap and mush than rigorous orthodoxy, playing to his fans, weakening his authority, allowing the gates of hell to prevail against the church.

Strong stuff.

But they are right in seeing him as the disruptor because he is that—and not just any disruptor. He is the Jesuit disruptor, and that defines him more than anything else in his biography.

What follows now is not a biographical narrative, neither a hatchet job nor a hagiography, and I am not engaged in replicating the fine work that has already been published covering the details of his life from birth to the See of Peter, the diverse influences on his life as an Argentine and as a Jesuit priest, the politics of his election as pope, his global challenges, et cetera, although I will be drawing from the well of such information to craft this papal portrait. Because that is what it is: a portrait of a pontificate, part polemic, part contextual probe, and part a veteran papal watcher's personal essay.

As Corvo would say: a gallimaufry. The mutterings of a church basement pope.

"THEY DON'T KNOW MY JORGE"

The Early Years

IT HAPPENED DURING A hitherto mild, cordial, and collegial conversation with a close friend of Pope Francis: the Argentine rabbi and scientist Abraham Skorka. We were dining together on the occasion of his visit to Sacred Heart University in Fairfield, Connecticut, where I was vice-president of Mission and Catholic Identity at the time. The university was forging a relationship with the rabbi as it moved to firm up its support of the Francis pontificate. Subsequently, we would open and dedicate the first university building in the United States to the Latin American pontiff (the Bergoglio) and celebrate his hand-chosen nuncio to Washington, the experienced Breton diplomat and Francis ally Christophe Pierre, with an honorary doctorate.

And then suddenly, as I queried the rabbi on the growing perception in certain conservative circles—Catholic and otherwise—that Francis is out of his depth in the Vatican, that he will be sidelined by the curial bureaucracy, that his ambitions for change will be squandered by internal disputes, and that he will be dismissed as a lightweight by the old guard keen on securing a deferential continuity with both the John Paul II and Benedict XVI papacies—that's when it happened. He put down his fork, mid-munch, stiffened his stature, firmly slapped the table and thundered, "They don't know my Jorge."

He was right. They didn't at first, but they do now know his Jorge.

But where does he come from, this whirlwind of Latino energy and new thinking? As in the case of every pope since Adrian VI in the sixteenth century—with the revolutionary exception of the Polish John Paul II and German Benedict XVI—Pope Francis has deep Italian roots, roots that in many ways define him, his piety, his aesthetic sensibility, his devotion to family. Yet, Jorge Mario Bergoglio is also Argentine to the core: born in Flores, a suburb of Buenos Aires, on December 17, 1936, the first of five children. His mother, Regina María Sivori, was born in Argentina, and his Italian foundation was laid by his father, Mario José Bergoglio, an immigrant from Portacomaro, near Turin.

There are always great stories—real, apocryphal, hagiographical, or fantastical—told about future popes. Premonitions, forebodings, prophecies, supernatural adumbrations, and a vision or two outlining the future pontiff's divine election surface in both serious biographies and the more devout variety. One of these stories attached to the beginning of the Bergoglio narrative is the story of the ship not taken. The emigrating Mario José, accompanied by his parents, Giovanni and Rosa, embarked from Genoa on an astonishingly long six-month trip to Argentina on board the steamship *Giulio Cesare*. Had it not been for the intervention of Providence, or the family's dilatoriness, they would have been on the doomed *Principessa Mafalda*, their liner of choice that didn't make it.

The sinking of the *Principessa Mafalda* has a place of ignominy in Italian maritime history because of its combination of faulty engineering and cowardly crew members, panic and chaos on the ship as it listed, with several lifeboats launched without full complements, the captain drowning, the chief engineer suiciding, and many of the hundreds of perished to be found in steerage (the third-class accommodations the Bergoglios would have purchased). Unnerving parallels with the *Titanic*, but with a lesser death count.

This is one of the historical items you find in papal biographies: the *what would have happened if?* Not quite the stuff of counterfactuals or pious mythmaking, but a presaging of the special destiny of the future pope. The beginning of the drama.

At its inception, the Bergoglio clan was matriarchal. Jorge's paternal grandmother was a formidable figure in the family compact and unafraid to exercise her influence. She instilled in him the rudiments of the faith, served as his primary conduit to the history and culture of Italy, and inspired him with the confidence born of a secure faith. His zeal of steel manifests early in his formation, as biographer Paul Vallely notes in *Pope Francis: The Struggle for the Soul of Catholicism*. When young Jorge inquired of his fellow senior school classmates whether they had yet made their First Communion, and in so doing discovered that a minority had not done so, he undertook their immediate catechizing. No slacker, our Jorge.[1]

But it wasn't all rigour and cocky righteousness that defined Jorge's youthful Catholicism as Grandmother Rosa, no enthusiast for any Protestant heresy, had a soft spot for the Salvation Army. My own British-born paternal grandmother had a similar affection and respect for this sturdy Victorian expression of faith in action. By making an exception for the Salvation Army, Rosa, in an unostentatious way, prioritized Gospel-generated action over dogmatic correctness. It is very unlikely that Rosa thought seriously about the "salvation" of the Salvation Army officers and recruits, moved by their compassion for the poor and disadvantaged and uninterested in debating the finer points of doctrine, and it is even more unlikely that she would have communicated this to her grandson. However, simple declarations of affection for a group committed to living a faith of service was sufficient for Jorge to remember, decades later, Rosa's approval of some women in the Salvation Army that she knew.

It is the little gestures and sayings that constitute the gold of memory.

But Rosa's fervour wasn't alone in shaping Jorge's early sensibility. He was schooled by the Salesians of Don Bosco. It was a Salesian priest, Enrique Pozzoli, who baptized him in the Basilica of San Carlos Borromeo. It was Salesian nuns who educated him when he was a student at San Juan Bosco school on the Calle Varela. And it was a Salesian priest, Lorenzo Massa, who founded the local football club whose matches Jorge would frequently attend and where his lifelong love of football was nurtured. The Salesians are a nineteenth-century Italian order, one of the largest in the world, and their special charism remains education—in its genesis, education dedicated to the needs of street children and the marginalized. They retain a strong presence in Latin America; during the pontificates of John Paul II and Benedict XVI, they were often the preferred order, supplanting the Jesuits in papal trust and esteem, their numbers increasing in the global hierarchy, in the College of

Cardinals, and in the Roman Curia. They became a force to reckon with, and their inclination was staunchly conservative. Among their more controversial members are such figures as Cardinal Miguel Obando y Bravo of Managua, Nicaragua, and Tarcisio Cardinal Bertone, Vatican Secretary of State. Their influence was greatly augmented with pontifical favours lavished on their seminaries and publications by popes John Paul II and Benedict XVI.

But not all the Salesians who rose to prominence at the same time that the Jesuits declined in influence were reactionaries. For instance, Cardinal Oscar Rodriguez Maradiaga of Tegucigalpa, Honduras, is not only a leading Latin American progressive prelate whose thinking is congruent with that of Papa Bergoglio, he is also one of the initial members of the pope's reforming Council of Cardinals. In fact, Francis has adroitly managed to level the cardinalatial playing field by striking numerical equivalence: there were the same number of Salesians as there were Jesuits in the College in the first half-decade of his papacy.

If his early education was defined by Salesian spirituality and pedagogy, it was not to the Salesians that he would turn in his pursuit of the priesthood. That pursuit was more delayed and elliptical than direct and uni-focused. His desire to be a priest had to be weighed in his mind with competing futures: his interest in medicine, his studies in chemistry at the industrial college Escuela Nacional de Educación Técnica, his attraction to women (at one point he was prepared to propose an engagement), his eagerness to placate his father's enthusiasm for a priestly vocation and his mother's coolness to the idea, and, of course, his natural disposition to seek guidance and wisdom from his grandmother. The resolution of his dilemma—priesthood or not priesthood—came with a peculiar encounter that not only proved determinative in his decision-making but has now, evoked by Bergoglio and his numerous biographers alike, entered fully into the papal narrative.

As it has been recounted in interviews with Pope Francis himself, the young Bergoglio was still debating the pros and cons of a married life as opposed to a celibate one, a lay life against a clerical one, when en route to a picnic with friends he opted to go to confession in the church of San José de Flores. He spoke with a priest-confessor he had not met before; out of that conversation came the rock-hard conviction that he needed to, that he must, test a vocation to the priesthood. Bergoglio considered his encounter with the priest, Carlos Duarte Ibarra, providential, no chance connection or fortuitous coincidence but an epiphany.

Flowing from this confessional encounter would come a new direction—not immediate but four years in the making—that would bring him to the archdiocesan seminary of Immaculada Concepción and his formation and studies as a priest of Buenos Aires.

But he would later change direction and not be ordained for Buenos Aires.

Rather, he would elect to join the Jesuits, the Society of Jesus, drawn to their command of discipline and order, their educational apostolate, and their missionary roots.

On March 11, 1958, he began his Jesuit journey, first in Córdoba, Argentina, and then off to the novitiate in Santiago, Chile. His studies would follow the standard curriculum of the time for priestly formation—courses in philosophy, the humanities, theology—but the Jesuit signature, differentiating his formation from that of a diocesan priest, would be its twofold emphasis on Ignatian pedagogy and Ignatian spirituality.

Of the former, there is no better description of why the Jesuits are committed to the educational enterprise and of what that commitment consists than this summary by the Jesuit historian John Padberg:

> Diego de Ledesma, one of the original sixteenth-century Jesuits, and our great educational theorist, when asked why we had schools, responded that there are four reasons. First, they provide a way in which people can effectively earn a living. This is the *practical* reason. Secondly, they provide for the right governing of society and the proper making of law and public affairs. This is the *social* reason. Thirdly, they provide the "ornaments of splendour and perfection" of the rational human. This is the *cultural* reason. And, fourthly, there is the theological dimension helping to lead men and women to their last end, their eternal destiny. This is the *religious* reason.[2]

Ignatian spirituality is the cornerstone of Jesuit life. Robert Drinan, one-time Democratic representative in the US Congress, an accomplished lawyer with lots of political connections, a law dean, and a passionate Jesuit up to the time of his death in 2007, identified the defining mark of the Jesuits, the perduring signature of the Companions of Jesus, in that enchiridion or spiritual manual written by the founder of the order himself, *The Spiritual Exercises of Saint Ignatius Loyola*:

> It is remarkable that they have the power to guide you, almost like the *Imitation of Christ* [a medieval spiritual handbook attributed to Thomas à Kempis and widely used for centuries

throughout the Catholic world]. You pick up the *Exercises* of Ignatius at any point and you will find out what you need at that very moment. The *Exercises* gives you the foundation, but I think that, like St. Ignatius himself, we need to move beyond the basics. He was a mystic for most of his life, his spirituality deepened as he matured, and I think that you can say that for most Jesuits. They deepen their own spiritual lives by going back to the things of Ignatius, to the first thirty-day retreat, and then to the second thirty-day retreat that we do during our tertianship [a stage in Jesuit formation]. The concepts of the *Exercises* have a way of getting into your soul in such a manner that you may not be able to articulate them, but they are there—real, pervasive and determinative.[3]

When Bergoglio entered the Society of Jesus to begin a decade-long formation, he moved into a world that would shape and define him—his personal life, his priestly life, and his life as the first Jesuit in the history of the papacy. Once sealed as a Jesuit, he would carry within him the ethos, the heart, of the founder's vision of service to the world rooted in service to Christ. What is especially important to note is something that the young Bergoglio—a Jesuit-in-training—would discover only in time: being a Jesuit alive to the world is not a univocal, unalterable, fixed reality. The order that admitted him to its ranks would undergo seismic adjustments in the years following his entry: internal debates and factionalism would tarnish or invigorate the Jesuit brand, depending on your ecclesial view; popes would be wary of Jesuit leadership and direction; Jesuit theologians, social scientists, editors, and political activists would be silenced or hobbled; a radical rethinking of Jesuit spiritual and educational priorities would create fresh and revolutionary changes; and the nightmares of Jesuit history—persecution by hostile political regimes and monarchies, to say nothing of suppression for four decades by the papacy itself—often left the Jesuit leadership in compromised positions.

This was all yet to come, and Bergoglio was not immune to the institutional upsets. In fact, he would be found at the centre of some of them in his native land. But for now, on March 11, 1958, it is only the beginning.

He finished his philosophical studies, taught literature and psychology during what Jesuits term the "regency," and then pursued theological studies, culminating with his ordination on December 13, 1969. Further studies in Spain were to follow after being priested, with his final profession as a Jesuit secured on April 22, 1973. Then, in rapid and surprising succession for a freshly minted "full" Jesuit, he began a series of short-term in-house administrative appointments—novice master, theology professor, provincial consultor, and then rector of the Colegio Máximo's Faculty of Philosophy and Theology.

And then, on July 31 (the feast day of Saint Ignatius Loyola) in 1973, his ecclesiastical career was set on a life-changing trajectory: he became the provincial[4] of the Jesuits in Argentina.

This coincided with a turbulent time in the life of the nation: political repression by a nervous state that witnessed the Chilean coup that toppled Salvador Allende just a couple of months after Bergoglio's election and that ensured the rise of Augusto Pinochet, compounding the fear in much of neighbouring Argentine society over the dangers of Marxist insurgency and right-wing military retaliation. After all, Argentina had its own history of political instability and uprisings. The guerrilla tactics of the leftist Montoneros, the cultic hegemony of Juan and Evita Perón and the political movement they spawned known as Peronism, and the power and mystique of the generals all shaped the political and social landscape of the country for decades. Tensions were never far below the surface and the mounting acrimony and instability generated by increasingly aggressive Marxist groups. In addition, numerous groups were unpersuaded by Communist ideology but committed to the goals of a more equitable society unshackled from its dependency on the United States with their corporate and political interests. All of them were pitted against the established moneyed powers and their military enablers, a traditionalist church, and a national attachment to *caudillismo* (strongman leadership). But Jorge Mario Bergoglio, at this point in his life, was not be found in the ranks of the politically charged dissidents.

The new provincial was not a liberationist, a priest-rebel drawn to leftist activism. He was, in many ways, the scourge of politically liberal Jesuits, and he moved quickly to right a ship he was convinced was foundering. Jimmy Burns, author of *Francis: Pope of Good Promise*, catalogues the numerous instances of Bergoglio's take-charge approach when dealing with leftist Jesuit sympathies, including cleaning house of radical Jesuits in the University of Salvador, imposing community living as the norm, and mandating traditional clerical wear in the seminary of San Miguel, establishing through all these measures his firm and authoritative leadership style.[5]

During his tenure as provincial, Bergoglio betrayed his unhappiness with the politically progressive tendencies of the Society of Jesus—although he barely disguised his misgivings before his election—seeing markers of a widening disunity in the divisions that erupted in the order regarding its prioritizing social justice and service to the poor over the more classical components of faith that included a hyper-attention to the spiritual health of the faithful.

He would bring about sound discipline, good governance with an emphasis on the traditional vow of obedience, a distancing from the activism that threatened the neutrality of the order, and a clear delineation of priest versus lay vocations with a concomitant respect for, and attention to, the devotional life of the faithful unencumbered by ideology and elitist theology. As a Jesuit priest and former rector/educator, Bergoglio now held the true reins of power over the Jesuits of Argentina, and he was prepared to exercise that power with hard authority.

If he found himself out of sorts, non-sympatico, with many of the brethren, there is little indication that he was moved to change his mind because of this disjointment. Particularly with his country now enmeshed in what would come to be known as the Dirty War, the military employing brutal tactics of intimidation, incarceration, mass arrests, and savage torture—their primary tool of terror being the "disappeared," the *desaparecido*, those victims who were executed, their bodies often unloaded while still alive from helicopters flying over the Plate River or the ocean. It was the darkest of times.

Bergoglio did not come out of this period unscathed. His doctrinal rigour and traditionalist piety that had put him at odds with many of his fellow Jesuits in Argentina saw him out of sync with his confreres throughout the Latin American continent. Inspired by their 32nd General Congregation (the supreme governing body of the Society of Jesus that is convened periodically to elect a new general of the order or to address issues of institutional correction, discipline, new vision, and directions), the Jesuits identified social faith and justice as their priorities in 1974–75. Michael Campbell-Johnston, a British

Jesuit, economist, past provincial of the British Jesuits, and a contemporary of Bergoglio's, outlines the lineaments of the new thinking in a 1991 interview in his London office:

> The Superior-General, Pedro Arrupe, convoked the Congregation to try and *re-define* what a Jesuit is in *today's* world. We came up with a definition of a Jesuit as someone who works for the service of faith, but the promotion of justice is an absolutely indispensable part of that; you can't separate one from the other. This is a re-definition but not a new departure. If Ignatius Loyola were alive today this is the sort of thing he would be saying.[6]

But when Campbell-Johnston, then serving in the Social Secretariat of the order in Rome, was sent by Arrupe to Latin America to assess how the Jesuits were faring with the implementation of the new thinking on the turbulent continent, he found himself in sharp disagreement with the Argentine. The disagreement was around Bergoglio's method of implementing the decrees emerging from the 32nd Congregation, his reluctance to take the forceful, if not adversarial, path adopted by his Latin American peers as they wrestled with military regimes, with their corruption, with their reliance on complicity by church leaders in their shared life-and-death battle with atheistic Communism. In the name of the Gospel, in the name of the Society, confrontation, not timidity, was imperative. It was not violent confrontation that was being advocated but a pastoral and spiritual confrontation with the oppressive powers of the state—government, business, the military, and co-opted bishops.[7]

It is not that Bergoglio was opposed to the 32nd Congregation—he was obligated as both a Jesuit and especially as a provincial to implement the new vision—but that he sought a moderate approach, a *via media*, that allowed for both his more conservative cultural and theological instincts and for the reality of the Dirty War.

The most dramatic challenge to his leadership in this regard came three years into his tenure, following the military coup in March 1976 when the decadent triumvirate of Admiral Emilio Massera, Army Chief Jorge Videla, and Air Force Brigadier-General Orlando Agosti began their reign of terror. The following May saw two Jesuit priests who had been working for years in the slums and shanties in Buenos Aires arrested, incarcerated, abused, and threatened with death. Unlike the others who worked with them—six laypersons—the Jesuits were eventually released, in great part because of the intervention of Bergoglio.

The freed Jesuits, Orlando Yorio and Francisco Jalics, were distressed by their provincial's *modus operandi* when dealing with the security forces and felt betrayed. Eventually, Jalics came to understand, if not approve of, Bergoglio's tentative, ethically firm and persistent but strategically conciliatory approach, but Yorio went to his death unconvinced that Bergoglio had acted with moral integrity.

In numerous interviews in subsequent years, Bergoglio explained his point of view: Yorio and Jalics were never involved in "subversive activities" as described and feared by a military that saw subversion everywhere, and when he first heard of their capture, he moved immediately to find ways to press for their release. It is not that he was unaware of the cost in blood being shed by those who, in the name of religion, stood with the oppressed and paid the ultimate price—clerics like the beloved and charismatic Jesuit Carlos Mugica and Bishop Enrique Angelelli. But he preferred an alternate route, navigating the shoals of political authoritarianism, personal Christian witness, and accountability as a religious leader.

During the Dirty War in Argentina, Bergoglio opted to stay below the radar, eschewing either martyrdom or collaboration as options. Biographer Burns notes that in electing a strategy of pragmatic accommodation when necessary, Bergoglio would be haunted for years by his conscience, knowing that what he did was never enough.[8]

Without sounding glib, one could say that this was his Pacelli [Pius XII] phase and that we would need to wait awhile before we have his Roncalli [John XXIII] phase.[9]

When his tenure as provincial ended—a controversial and divisive tenure, as we have seen—he was not out of office yet. He became rector of the Colegio Máximo, was at one point elected procurator (a position of importance within the governing structure of the Jesuits), and, although no longer the supreme player, held sway in both administration and leadership. And there were many Jesuits, those previously at odds with him and those disciplined by him, who were unhappy with his post-provincial residual influence.

In fact, the order was polarized: there were *bergolianos* and *anti-bergoglianos*. An unnerving adumbration of the pontificate, save the divisions then won't be among the Jesuits—less tribal and more global. Still, that is to come, and no one, not even Bergoglio himself, could see that scenario unfolding.

Frustrated by his intransigence, his failure to curb his authoritarian tendencies, his outsize modelling for archconservative clerics, and his unfashionable fondness for folk piety or religiosity, his superiors decided on a correction for the recalcitrant padre: Córdoba.

Time in Córdoba was not time in foreign parts—it was

certainly *not* the great city of Moorish legacy in Spain but the Argentine city with which he was already familiar, as he had spent a couple of years there during the early period of his Jesuit formation. But this time it would be different. He was in exile, not in formation; censured, not tutored.

The authorities forbade his movement among different Jesuit houses, he had his mail under surveillance, his phone calls required advance permission, he could celebrate Mass but only under certain restrictions limiting public exposure, and he was under instruction to work on his doctoral dissertation, work that he had neglected for some time. These two years in the city were two years of isolation, ostracization, and, as the Jesuits like to think, desolation. But they were also years of consolation as he submitted meekly—surprising most of his confreres, complained mildly of the boredom but abided obediently by the strictures, prayed and discerned deeply, and matured with a deeper understanding of the art and virtue of humility.

In an interview with his fellow Jesuit and close ally Antonio Spadaro, after becoming pope, Bergoglio spoke frankly about his Córdoba experience:

> My style of government as a Jesuit at the beginning had many faults. That was a difficult time for the Society: an entire generation of Jesuits had disappeared. Because of this I found myself Provincial when I was very young. I was only 36 years old. That was crazy. I had to deal with difficult situations, and I made my decisions abruptly and by myself. My authoritarian and quick manner of making decisions led me to have serious problems and to be accused of being ultra-conservative. I lived a time of great interior crisis when I was in Córdoba.[10]

Chastened, disciplined, and removed from regular social and intellectual intercourse with his brother Jesuits, Bergoglio was thrown back on his own resources, spiritual and emotional. He probed his spiritual heart in new and penetrating ways, he cultivated a greater sympathy for and identification with the poor, and he turned his attention to the subject of his doctoral work, the Italian theologian and seminal thinker Monsignor Romano Guardini. Both faced political and social turbulence in their priestly lives, and both saw in a philosophy of dialectics a possible hermeneutic for ecclesial reform.

There will be much more to say about this later on. But for now, Bergoglio's detailed rereading of the primary sources, although illuminating and persuasive, and in many ways subtly appropriated, would not result in the completion of the doctorate. His preparatory work during a few months at Sankt Georgen Graduate School of Philosophy and Theology outside Frankfurt, although augmented by his closer reading in Córdoba, would not result in a formal academic project, any more than his weeks of learning English at Milltown, a Jesuit enclave and graduate institute in Dublin, would result in fluency in the language.

What the Jesuit superiors, and indeed Bergoglio himself, had in mind following the "purification" in exile is of no consequence. His next career move would take him out from under the authority of his order and into a new power accountability relationship: he was named an auxiliary bishop of Buenos Aires. He had new bosses.

The cardinal archbishop he served as a suffragan was a hierarch of a specific school and style: traditionalist, much enamoured of his perks and ecclesiastical entitlements, caesaropapist in orientation (seeing religio-political alliances as good things as long as that religion is Roman Catholicism), and a strong supporter of Pope John Paul II's vigorous opposition to all things that have a Marxist tinge. Antonio Quarracino, archbishop of Buenos Aires, Primate of the Church in Argentina, was an able leader of a certain mould: orthodox in teaching, with a firm grip on the clerical troops to prevent softening of dogma or collaboration with politically subversive movements, and a reliable conduit for Vatican authorities, nuncios, and curial heads keeping an eye out for institutional stability in the broad Catholic world.

But for all his behaviour as a princeling, Quarracino was not corrupt; rather, he often proved naive in relation to diverse swindlers and advisors whose counsel and directives in relation to a major bank provided ample fodder for a money scandal that besmirched his reputation and compromised the financial health of the archdiocese. Nothing particularly theological in all of this. Just bad oversight as an administrator. No reason for Rome to remove him. Simmering scandals are not unknown to the Vatican.

But with failing health, and with an unshakeable confidence in Bergoglio, whose trust, administrative competence, and obedience he could rely upon, Quarracino deftly stickhandled Bergoglio's appointment as his coadjutor, thereby ensuring his successor. It worked.

On February 28, 1998, Bergoglio became the archbishop of Buenos Aires.

He began his new duties in earnest: his clergy would have ready access to him, he established a commission to investigate the financial scandals that plagued his predecessor, and he built on his personal relations with the large Jewish community in the city—a relationship he had assiduously cultivated for

some time, especially with his soon-to-be lifelong companion in the search for interreligious harmony, Rabbi Abraham
Skorka. He distanced himself from the perks of office by living
outside the episcopal palace, he appointed skilled clerics to
curial positions and relied on their counsel and independent
judgment, specifically Guillermo Marco, and he assumed the
mantle of leadership among the Argentine hierarchy negotiating the difficult politico-cultural terrain post–Dirty War. He
became a presence in the corridors of power in a way that was
quantitatively different from when he was Jesuit provincial or
auxiliary bishop. He was now a player in a different orbit: the
premier prelate in a divided Catholic country with rising cries
for retribution, if not reconciliation, by aggrieved families who
suffered the loss of loved ones during the reign of the generals;
accusations of complicity levelled against the Vatican's nuncio
during the years of acute turbulence, the seasoned Pio Laghi
(later nuncio to Washington); and the endless waves of financial
upheaval following the collapse of commerce and the devalu-
ation of the country's currency.

The qualities of the earlier Bergoglio leadership style—
certitude, stolidity, firmness—were no longer the qualities
required for this higher and more public ecclesial post. The
lessons learned from his Córdoba exile were kicking in.
Authoritative leadership, for example, especially in light of
the shifting sands of Peronist, post-Peronist, and anti-Peronist
political iterations—some seeking to co-opt the church, some
seeking an unholy alliance, and some manifestly hostile—
required a leadership *exercised* in a different way. Michael
Collins, author of *Francis: Bishop of Rome*, observes that
Bergoglio's often severe judgment of priests was tempered by his
good-natured fun deflating pompous clerics by likening them

to peacocks, all resplendence up front but telling a different story from the rear.[11]

He would have plenty of opportunity to distance himself from peacock ministry: he was created a cardinal on February 21, 2001, by Pope John Paul II. Cardinals are not the hyper-ordained; they are not super apostles; their rank and status have neither biblical nor patristic origin. They constitute the cabinet for the pope, trusted counsellors, "princes of the church," electors of a new pope, and dicasterial prefects for key Vatican offices. Traditionally, many of them come by this elevated role in the governance of the church by way of their residential Sees. In other words, if they happen to be archbishops or metropolitans of large dioceses that have a history of cardinals, then it is more than likely—barring some disapproval of a sitting incumbent by the pope (and only popes "create" cardinals)—that such a prelate will be given the "red hat."

Buenos Aires is such a See, and Bergoglio was not seen as inimical to the Wojtyla papacy.

And so, at a consistory—the gathering in Rome where the new cardinals are formally inducted into the College of Cardinals, feted, and pledge loyalty to the pope who created them—Bergoglio became part of the upper echelons of ecclesiastical governance. He became part of the club of princes and by virtue of that a potential *papabile*, a serious candidate in a papal election. In fact, when it comes to electing a pope, the cardinal electors are not bound to the membership of their college—abbots, monks, and bishops have been plucked from obscurity and chrismed in Rome. But such instances are rare and, in recent centuries, as likely as a safe vehicular intersection in the Eternal City.

Cardinals engage the public imagination in a way ordinary

prelates do not. The rituals associated with their duties, their unique honorific (Eminence), their formal wear of vermillion and silk, their proximity to the highest authority in the Catholic Church, and their role as consultors to the papacy have long made them the subject of numerous novels and films: from a reverential treatment (Henry Morton Robinson's 1950 novel *The Cardinal*, subsequently filmed by Otto Preminger in 1963), to the seriously accurate portrayals coupled with the playfully ahistorical (the villains in red that people the series *The Borgias*), to the fantastical similitudes you find in George Lucas's *Star Wars* saga, where they are the prototype for the Emperor's praetorian guards.

But reality, for those cardinals in charge of large dioceses balancing the many pressures that constitute their managerial mandate, tends to dull the lustre of their office. Or at least diminish the romance and augustitude associated with its exercise.

I recall a conversation in the kitchen of Gabriele Niccoli, an Italian studies professor at St. Jerome's University, between a Canadian Supreme Court justice, Frank Iacobucci, and a university president and future governor general, David Johnston, neither of whom is Catholic. They were arguing with full forensic fury their respective case: the justice thought the College of Cardinals the greatest assemblage of intellect on the planet, with the president countering vigorously that such a proposition was outlandish. As I feared, they turned to me as the presumed expert on the matter, as I had had many dealings with the men in red, and I managed as Solomonic a response as could be expected under the circumstances: there can be, and indeed are, some men of very high intellect in the College, but the majority are not stellar intellectuals as it is not a requirement for the job. After all, the College of Cardinals is not the Vatican's version of the Académie française.

I have met many cardinals. Some I have interviewed and written about, some consulted with, some jockeyed with, and some critiqued, and their character and gifts vary as widely as they do in other cross-sections of the Catholic clerical world: the saint (Paul-Émile Léger of Montreal and latterly Cameroon, George Flahiff of Winnipeg, Joseph Bernardin of Chicago, and Franz Koenig of Vienna); the pastoral educator (Marc Ouellet of Quebec City and the Congregation of Bishops); the academic (Aloysius Ambrozic of Toronto and Joseph Ratzinger of Munich and the Congregation for the Doctrine of the Faith); the politician (Gerald Emmett Carter of Toronto and Sebastian Baggio of the Vatican diplomatic corps and other dicasterial bodies); the manager (Paul Grégoire of Montreal and Édouard Gagnon of the Pontifical Council for the Family).

They could be self-disclosing when prompted, fiercely secretive when they judged it necessary, mixing ambition with service (not without calculation), combative when trusted, possessed of the occasional eccentricity and lapse into befuddlement that made them, if not endearing, more than pedestal occupants.

Now a cardinal, Bergoglio had enhanced profile, prestige, and influence. But his day job remained much the same— running a populous archdiocese during a precarious time, dealing with uncertain political mandarins, addressing fiscal irregularities (a leitmotif that runs consistently right up to the papacy), and helping to shape a Latin American voice and presence in the global church.

As a cardinal and younger than eighty, and therefore not retired and obligated to forfeit his right to vote in a papal election, he held one of the most coveted prizes in any democracy—in this rare instance, the Roman Catholic Church acts democratically—and could vote for a candidate to the papacy once the position was declared empty, the *sede vacante*.

Within four years of being created a cardinal, he was off to his first conclave—that convocation of papal electors who gather in Rome to name a successor of Saint Peter after the death of a pope and do so in a setting that is basically a high-level sequestration with key, *cum clave*. He was reputed to have been *the* runner-up, but the electors chose continuity over innovation, Old World as opposed to New World culture, a prelate with extensive Vatican experience coupled with international status as a theologian as opposed to a Jesuit pastor. They chose Joseph Ratzinger, dean of the College of Cardinals, prefect of the Congregation for the Doctrine of the Faith, former archbishop of Munich and professor at the University of Regensburg: the man who knew well the recently deceased Pope John Paul II, shared his ecclesiology (with significant but non-dogmatic differences), and was instrumental in staffing the Vatican governance offices with like-minded clerics.

Back in Buenos Aires, seemingly unfazed by his near election, Bergoglio set about his pastoral administration. The greatest achievement of his years as Benedict's successor-in-waiting, a status there is no evidence he ever considered possible or legitimate, was the key role he played in contributing to the drafting of the closing document of the Fifth General Conference of the Latin American Episcopate (CELAM) in Aparecida, Brazil, in 2007. CELAM's position on the contentious issue of globalization clearly delineates the high points of Bergoglio's own critique to be found in several of his writings as pope:

In globalization market forces easily absolutize efficacy and productivity as values regulating all human relations … A globalization without solidarity has a negative impact on the poorest groups. It is no longer simply the phenomenon of exploitation and oppression, but something new: social exclusion. What is effected is the very root of belonging to the society in which one lives, because one is no longer on the bottom, on the margins, or powerless, but rather one is living outside. The *excluded* are not simply "exploited" but "surplus" and "disposable."[12]

Rooted in the *conscientization* around the oppressive condition of the poor characteristic of liberationist thinking throughout Central and South America, preoccupied by the worsening plight of the poor in a time of growing economic disparity in his own country, and committed to a leadership role among the bishops on the Latin continent on social justice matters, Bergoglio had little time for the machinations of Roman careerists, the heightening problems around the credibility of the Ratzinger papacy, and the media nightmare unfolding on the Tiber as scandals small and big mushroomed to dangerous levels.

And then …

The bombshell:

On February 10, 2013, Benedict XVI addressed the prelates gathered for a regular meeting to discuss three canonizations. They did not suspect that there was another item on the papal agenda for that day and so were unprepared for what they were to hear—that following diligence in prayer and discernment, the Successor of Peter was announcing his imminent departure. Shock, numbness, incomprehension. Who would think such a thing possible? Clearly, Joseph Ratzinger did, and now he was acting on it:

> After having repeatedly examined my conscience before God, I have come to the certainty that my strengths, due to an advanced age, are no longer suited to an adequate exercise of the Petrine ministry. I am well aware that this ministry, due to its essential spiritual nature, must be carried out not only with words and deeds, but no less with prayer and suffering. However, in today's world, subject to so many rapid changes and shaken by questions of deep relevance for the life of faith, in order to govern the barque of Saint Peter and proclaim the Gospel, both strength of mind and body are necessary, strength which in the last few months has deteriorated in me to the extent that I have had to recognize my incapacity to adequately fulfill the ministry entrusted to me. For this reason, and well aware of the seriousness of this act, with full freedom I declare that I renounce the ministry of the Bishop of Rome, Successor of Saint Peter, entrusted to me by the Cardinals on 19 April 2005, in such a way that, as from 28 February 2013, at 20:00 hours, the See of Rome, the See of Saint Peter, will be vacant and a Conclave to elect the new Supreme Pontiff will have to be convoked by those whose competence it is.[13]

Immediately, the Vatican machinery for election began its well-practised artistry, but not before those in attendance struggled to understand the *why* and the timing of this most unconventional of decisions, although a papal resignation was not entirely without precedent—remember Celestine V. Still, supremely rare. And *now*? If those who first heard Benedict's decision—delivered not in his native German or in Italian, the lingua franca of daily business in the Vatican, but in Latin, as if to underscore its gravity and the solemnity it deserves—were stunned, the rest of the Catholic world would be electrified.

Much has been written trying to uncover the reasons for the resignation—not that those proffered by Benedict were considered disingenuous, only that they were considered incomplete—and there is much ground for speculation. That the pontiff's strength was no longer sufficient for the task, we have much evidence for—although the years of his retirement saw him active, with many scholarly undertakings and publications (he lived to the grand age of ninety-five), the administrative duties had become overwhelming.

But more germane are the plethora of missteps, ecclesial crises, media gaffes, dramatic instances of myopic governance, numerous revelations of sexual impropriety and scandal in the Vatican itself, and personal betrayals by close aides (including his personal butler), all of which combined in the end to seriously hobble Benedict's effectiveness. He was simply no longer in charge. When he ran the Congregation for the Doctrine of the Faith, there was no doubt who called the shots—even John Paul II could bend to the Grand Inquisitor's will—but as the head of the church and the Vatican City State, he was dealing with different realities, and his management skills were wanting. He knew that, and his resignation speaks to a degree of self-honesty that is edifying.

And so, a new papal election began. The date for the conclave was set; the cardinals (electors as well as those over eighty who forfeit a vote but can still attend the numerous ceremonies and rituals outside the conclave scrutinies and exercise a diminished but potentially determinative role via personal influence) all gathered in Rome. The cardinals listen to each other—at presentations called general congregations—mingle among themselves, check out the talent, as it were, do a lot of praying, listen to solemn addresses by the dean of the College of Cardinals and sundry other curial and papal household dignitaries charged with seeing to the right governance during the interregnum, and finally get accustomed to their temporary digs (once awful and cramped but now more spacious) for when the conclave proper—the sequestering and voting—begins.

These centuries-old conventions and rituals are updated periodically to take into account contemporary expectations, deal with enhanced communications possibilities (cardinal electors using cellphones and social media conduits while in conclave pose greater challenges for control and secrecy compared to quill, parchment, and under-the-cell-door delivery), and see to the health needs of an older demographic in a timely manner.

Once they are confined to the Sistine Chapel—under key— the serious business of election begins. The time for speeches is over. They vote and continue to vote until they have their choice.

The politics of a papal election, the secretive nature of the voting results, the ever-shifting tallies of the candidates as they are slowly eliminated through several scrutinies until the requisite number of votes for election is secured, are not conducted under media coverage. There is no access to the secret unfoldings, only speculation by pundits, commentators, experts, anchors, and the interested public. Or, at least, that is the theory.

In practice, there has long been a range of subterranean, in-house sources who chronicle the proceedings of the conclave and then discreetly leak their observations via diaries or journals, but especially by means of prudential and targeted revelations,

conversations, and elliptical asides delivered to trusted journalists: journalists who will ensure anonymity, who exhibit a
benign disposition toward high ecclesiastics working in the
Vatican machinery, and who can be relied on to protect their
sources (sometimes aggrieved electors, sometimes ecstatic ones).

That's how we come to know the kinds of things that are
presumed veiled, beyond our right to know, above suspicion
and gossip. It is the journalists who open up that vista. The
scholars come later.

The often-preferred mode of expression by the confided-in
journalist is the daily diary, covering events as they trot or saunter
by, attending to the ceaseless murmurations not of starlings or
Jesuits but of competing reporters and players, the essential fodder
of the diaries dependent on the whisperings that often make up
the livelihood of the seasoned Vatican correspondent. That is why
solid reportage is critical, the credentials of the reporter tried and
proven, the diary less speculation—although there is plenty of
that—and more a space for insiders to seek a safe platform.

For the 2013 conclave, the most dependable record is that
provided by Gerard O'Connell, a long-serving scribbler on
Vatican matters, generally deferential to church authority,
inclined more to piety than cynical deconstruction, safe in
his calibrations but trustworthy. If his fervour occasionally
borders on the ecstatic, his journalistic instincts are right and
his perspective coherent.

Cardinal electors, by his own admission, shared memories
with him, provided data, deliberately and perhaps sometimes
unintentionally disclosed voting scores, opined on the quality of
candidates, indulged rumour, recorded rancour, sifted through
the spasms of adulation, and did it all by pledging anonymity.
The product: *The Election of Pope Francis: An Inside Account of*

the Conclave That Changed History. A formidable exercise in autobiography-laced reportage.

In spite of the marketing hype of the subtitle—the elections of John XXIII and John Paul II were similarly epoch-making events—O'Connell faithfully tracks the chronology leading up to and including that culminating moment when the new pope is revealed to the world. He captures the competing priorities of the voting cardinals, the behind-the-scenes intrigues, the squabbling and the rivalries, the fake humility and the genuine self-effacing, the fears that accompany an awesome task upon which so much depends, the need for deep prayer and wise discernment.

It is all there, and more, in O'Connell's diary, replete with a gentleness of tone that speaks to the diarist's devoutness. He does not use the text to settle scores, personal or institutional, and he takes clear delight in being at the centre of things. And along with his wife, Elisabetta Piqué, also a Vatican correspondent and one whom he quotes extensively in the diary, he delights in being vindicated for past prognostications. But diaries, of course, are by their very nature self-referential, and the voice we hear is principally that of the author. Still, much more appealing than a dry sociological tract, for all its insufficiencies.

In past conclaves there were three distinct ways of proceeding: the *via acclamationum* (the way of acclamation), the *via compromissum* (the way of compromise), and the *via scrutinium* (the way of the ballot), but in 1996, John Paul II eliminated the first two ways and decreed that following three weeks without a candidate who had secured two-thirds of the cardinal electors' votes, a simple majority would suffice. Following *his* election, Benedict XVI had a different view about the process and, as church historian Alberto Melloni makes clear, set a different stage for what would be the Bergoglio election:

In June 2007, Benedict XVI made a small but surgically precise adjustment to the rules. Perhaps because he had seen Cardinal Jorge Mario Bergoglio of Buenos Aires receive a third plus one of the votes in one ballot in the 2005 conclave, to free his successors from the insinuation that they had been elected only because their opponents realized they didn't have enough votes to prevent it, he reinstated the requirement that a two-thirds majority would be required for the election of a pope, regardless of the number of ballots needed.[14]

And so, the stage was set for a reprise. Bergoglio was number two in the last election, and now he was a contender again. A more serious contender for sure, whose pastoral style, limited exposure to Roman politics, and warm personality combined to make him an appealing alternative to the cerebral Bavarian who had, with uncharacteristic dramatic bravura, opted for retirement.

O'Connell describes the scene following the sixth ballot when Bergoglio secured eighty-five votes, while his runners-up secured twenty (Scola of Milan), eight (Ouellet of the papal Curia), and two (Vallini, a senior Vatican prelate):

Once the counting was finished, there was no doubt: Cardinal Bergoglio had been elected pope. The first pope from Latin America, the first Jesuit pope … Then, immediately after the applause ended, Cardinal Bergoglio got up and went to Cardinal Scola, who was some seats down from him on the same row, and embraced him … Cardinal Re, who was presiding over the conclave, went to Bergoglio and standing in front of him, asked in the name of the whole college of electors: "*Do you accept your canonical election as Supreme Pontiff?*" Cardinal Bergoglio responded in Latin, with words that translated into

English mean: "*I am a great sinner, trusting in the mercy and patience of God, in suffering, I accept.*" ... As soon as Cardinal Bergoglio gave his consent, Cardinal Re asked him a second question: *By what name do you be wish to be called?* The new pope responded: Francesco.[15]

Bergoglio would have known that by choosing a name foreign to the annals of papal names, he was breaking with convention, just as Karol Wojtyla had done when he chose the double-barrelled John Paul II following upon the unexpected demise of the short-lived (barely a month) papacy of John Paul I. Bergoglio needed to explain *why Francis*, and he did so at a large gathering of journalists three days after the conclave. There he demonstrated his own comfort level with the media, his preference for transparency over speculation, and his resolve to embrace the legacy, and not only the name, of the poor one of Assisi:

During the election, I was seated next to the Archbishop Emeritus of São Paulo and Prefect Emeritus of the Congregation of Clergy, Cardinal Claudio Hummes [himself a Franciscan]: a good friend, a good friend! When things were looking dangerous, he encouraged me. And when the votes reached two thirds, there was the usual applause, because the Pope had been elected. And he gave me a hug and a kiss and said: "Don't forget the poor!" And those words came to me: the poor, the poor. Then, right away, thinking of the poor, I thought of Francis of Assisi. Then I thought of all the wars, as the votes were still being counted, till the end. Francis is also the man of peace. That is how the name came into my heart: Francis of Assisi. For me, he is the man of poverty, the man of peace, the man who loves and protects creation; these days we do not have a very good relationship with creation, do we? He is the man who gives us this spirit of peace, the poor man. How I would like a Church which is poor and for the poor.[16]

The name is a signifier of the intentions and directions of the pontiff. Ratzinger chose the name Benedict because of his admiration for the founder of Western monasticism, a man who shone the light of scholarship and faith in the encroaching darkness of imperial Rome's decline into chaos and invasions: Saint Benedict. But he also had in mind Benedict XV, the peace pope of the First World War whose valiant efforts to stave off, if not end, violence among the European powers resulted in failure. Earlier, Albino Luciani chose John Paul out of respect for the two popes of the Second Vatican Council, John XXIII and Paul VI, and Karol Wojtyla chose his name out of respect for all three of his predecessors.

And so it was that Cardinal Jean-Louis Tauran announced from the apostolic loggia the news: "*Annuntio vobis gaudium magnum, habemus Papam*" ("I announce a great joy to you. We have a pope!"). He added, after a lengthy and robust wave of applause from the large crowd gathered in St. Peter's Square: "*Eminentissimum ac Reverendissimum Dominum, Dominum Georgium Marium Sanctae Romanae Ecclesiae Cardinalem Bergoglio, qui sibi nomen imposuit Franciscum*" ("The most eminent and most reverend Lord, Lord Jorge Mario Bergoglio, cardinal of the Holy Roman Church, who has taken the name Francis").

Habemus Papam. Many of the electors and much of the Catholic world would soon discover what Rabbi Skorka presciently observed: "They don't know my Jorge."

But they most certainly will come to. For some it will be a breath of fresh air and for others, a disaster.

THE MAKINGS OF FRANCIS

There's a New Peter in Town

IT ISN'T EASY BEING pope. You carry the weight of a tradition two millennia in the making, you trace your roots back to the apostle Peter, you have an institution that claims divine origin but is essentially human in its lived reality, you have a storied record of genius and sanctity admixed with a sordid record of venality and power lust. Thomas Hobbes once called the papacy "the ghost of the deceased Roman Empire, sitting crowned upon the grave thereof." Not a great career choice.

So, when Jorge Mario Bergoglio became Francis, he became Peter. Or rather, when he became Peter, he took the name Francis. And what's in a name? Everything.

Peter first. He is the Bishop of Rome; all the other titles and dignities that have accrued over the centuries—Supreme Pontiff, Patriarch of the West, Primate of Italy, Head of the Vatican City State, Vicar of Christ, Successor of Peter, et cetera—are secondary to that designation. Pope John Paul II said as much in an address to the Seminary of Rome:

It is said—and this is true—that the Pope is Vicar of Christ. It is true and I accept it with all humility ... The attribution, the phrase in question, is undoubtedly a strong one that arouses trepidation. I must tell you that I prefer not to abuse this phrase, and so use it only rarely. I prefer indeed to say "Successor of Peter"; but I prefer even more to say "Bishop of Rome."[1]

Peter's claim for primacy—a source of biblical contestation, schisms, squabbles, and religious wars—is a claim his successors are not unaware of. Since the Second Vatican Council, they have sought to address it with ecumenical sensitivity. Dominican theologian J. M. R. Tillard makes the case for papal primacy in his seminal work *The Bishop of Rome*, a case that respects the historical and traditional perspectives but allows for important checks on the papal office and its exercise of power. Peter is *first among equals*, not a sacerdotal Caesar:

First (*protos*) but not unique! The other apostles are similar to him in everything except in holding the first place. If he is the rock, they too are the foundation ... if he declares the kerygma, they too must preach the gospel which makes disciples ... if he heals, they work signs and wonders too ... if he seals his witness in martyrdom, so do they. And the faith which he confesses is not different from that of his brother apostles. His primacy is that of a true *primus inter pares* (first among equals), a *primus* who is genuinely, and not merely in point of honour, first, while the *pares* are genuinely equal and do not derive their power or their mission from him. Only the Spirit of God can give these. The first does not absorb the others.[2]

The tension between the bishops—successors of the apostles—and the pope—the successor of Peter—has been a defining feature of Catholic history from the outset. Popes have struggled to assert their special powers and prerogatives often at the expense of the bishops, resulting in a dangerous imbalance in church leadership. Countertendencies with clear political colorations—Gallicanism, Josephinism—have been self-defeating, but conciliarism is a different matter. Righting Peter's rule is a matter of privileging the wisdom and authority of a council, recognizing papal rights and dignities but not subordinating the legitimate pastoral prerogatives of local bishops and their national conferences to papal adjudication.

But that careful ecclesial equipoise is not easily, if ever, achieved. And the struggle to achieve it is fraught with hostility, subterfuge, political gamesmanship, and personal opportunism. John Paul II's encyclical *Ut unum sint* (That they may be one) boldly called for ways to alter the exercise of the pope's office to make it less antagonistic to other faith communities, building on the positive dimension of the Petrine ministry: the nurturing of unity. John Paul II encouraged responses to his encyclical, and one brave soul produced a book of his own, taking up the boss's offer. John R. Quinn, archbishop of San Francisco, added his voice to the invited dialogue with *The Reform of the Papacy: The Costly Call to Christian Unity*, in which he argued that effective decentralization of the papal office will involve substantial reform of the administration that works to implement the pope's intentions, the Roman Curia, and that if the Curia resists change, failing to adapt to current global challenges, choosing to retain its hegemonic power to the detriment of devolution, refusing to share power with national hierarchies, it will find itself eventually emptied of all credible control.[3]

Poor Quinn. He took the papal invitation to make a contribution to the reform of the papacy at face value only to discover that, really, John Paul II had spoken on the issue, curial decentralization was not one of the pope's pastoral priorities, and several key players entrenched in the settled ways of a millennial ecclesiastical structure were not that keen on disestablishing themselves. Quinn never made cardinal. Nor did he leave San Francisco for a larger or more influential See. It was his last book on the subject.

The twentieth century was a turbulent one for an institution that prides itself on stability and constancy. There was the period of the dictators—Mussolini, Hitler, Stalin, Franco—that variously challenged the Holy See, and in many instances the response of the papacy to these autocratic threats was light years away from an enlightened democratic perspective; and there was the intellectual turbulence associated with a movement broadly labelled Modernism that Rome rigorously suppressed. By the 1950s, the papacy as an absolute monarchy—isolated in its quaint redoubt, a survivor of the Second World War's catastrophic civilization bust-up, its authority seemingly unassailable as embodied in that most august of pontiffs, Pius XII—was tottering from within. The status quo no longer worked. It no longer made sense.

Enter the Patriarch of Venice, one Angelo Giuseppe Roncalli: church historian, Vatican diplomat, a spiritual figure who dominated his time with his warmth, self-deprecating humour, and ecclesial vision. The 1958 conclave that resulted in his election as John XXIII would change the direction of Peter's barque. It would now sail in different seas.

When John XXIII summoned his ecumenical council, his announcement stunned his administration, and the world, Catholic and otherwise, was perplexed. Everything seemed to be working. Catholic institutions were flourishing—growth was apparent in many areas in the global community—and Catholicism exuded a much-admired corporate confidence.

But Roncalli knew otherwise. Time to open the windows; time to enter into dialogue with the world, with other faiths; time to recover the best of the tradition, to return to the roots of the church. Essentially, time for renewal.

But you don't hold a council of such range and magnitude without unleashing expectations. John died after the first session of the council; it would be his successor, Paul VI, Giovanni Battista Montini, a theologian and career Vatican apparatchik, who would be left with the task of continuing the work of the council, of bringing it to successful closure. And he did so in 1965, earning the respectful moniker "Pope of the Council."

But the pontificate of this pope—although distinguished by many fine documents, ecumenical initiatives, dramatic gestures (his attendance at the United Nations, making an impassioned plea for peace, was without precedent), and sterling defence of political and economic justice—paled by comparison to his reaffirmation of the traditional ban on all forms of artificial birth regulation: *Humanae vitae* (1968).

This encyclical was unsuccessful in persuading the majority of Catholics that the birth control pill and other prophylactics were inherently evil, that they were *contra naturam*, and that the constant and universal teaching of the church could not be subject to change. Determined to uphold papal authority, Paul actually undermined it; he created an ecclesiastical storm, pitting Catholics against each other and prompting many Catholic priests, as I mentioned in relation to Father Brocard Sewell in chapter 1, to dissent—inviting, in the process, censure, silencing, and suspension. Bit of a mess.

Subsequent popes felt obligated to defend Paul VI's position, although he never invoked the authority of infallibility in relation to this teaching; the short-termed John Paul I indicated some hesitation, while *his* successor, John Paul II, was an enthusiastic endorser of *Humanae vitae* and contributed a hefty literature in its defence. John Paul II used it as a foundation to build an architecture of teaching on human sexuality, personhood, gender complementarity, the gift of marriage, and the even greater gift of celibacy in the priestly and consecrated life; in doing so, he set the face of the institutional church firmly against all those practices that contradict the biblical anthropology he deemed essential to human meaning and salvation.

John Paul II embodied the *Ecclesia docens* (the church teaching), whereas Francis embodies the *Ecclesia discens* (the church listening). There's a big difference.

The difference that *is* Francis is the heart of my exploration, an exploration that is both academic and personal. Partly because one cannot respond to the Bergoglio mystique disengaged. Why his charismatic and magnetic appeal for many coexisting with his seemingly bottomless capacity to arouse resistance among others? Is he presiding over the end of the papacy as we know it, or is he reconfiguring it for a new age?

He is the Jesuit disruptor, after all, and in that we have our answer. Even the name he took as pope is a disruptor and not a name associated with Ignatius of Loyola and his Company of Jesus. The new pope confounded expectations from the outset. For sure, the appeal of Giovanni di Pietro di Bernardone—known to history as Francesco Bernardone (1182–1226) or Francis of Assisi—would be native for him. His Italian ancestry would dispose him devotionally to the commanding hold Saint Francis has on the Italian cultural and religious imagination.

The role of the Franciscan orders—Friars Minor, Conventuale, Capuchini, and countless further variations, along with the religious sisters and pious lay associations—combine to make the sons and daughters of Saint Francis the largest of the church's religious orders.

But Francis, the mendicant, the Poor One, the radical disciple of the disruptive genius of Jesus of Nazareth, is a natural for the Jesuit of Buenos Aires. For certain, there are qualities that we now ascribe to the merchant's son of Assisi, as well as qualities that have endured over the centuries, to make him, along with Joan of Arc, the saint of the Protestants—and that is some historical feat, given that both predate the Reformation. The matchless affection for Francis over the centuries, his appeal for those outside traditional religious boundaries, his iconic and cultic status among the romantic and conventional alike, his contemporary currency as the proto-saint of ecology and the environment, his skill as a poet of ordinary mysticism, and his reputation as a man who loved generously and freely (a troubadour of the soul) make Francis in many ways a very different kind of saint: a Gospel rebel rather than a confessor, or martyr, or holy virgin. In other words, a disruptor. The Francis of Italian filmmaker Franco Zeffirelli's art—*Brother Sun, Sister Moon*—is the Francis of mass appeal: handsome, lithe, charismatic, a natural lover (his relationship with Saint Clare, although chaste, is charged with passion), and a spiritual pathfinder of breathtaking originality.

Bergoglio is not quite the romantic figure of Franciscan legend, but he is a spiritual, ecclesial pathfinder of breathtaking originality.[4] Similarities between the two Francises bear inspection. G. K. Chesterton's biography, *Saint Francis of Assisi*, made much of the paradoxical qualities to be found in the

First Franciscan. Not surprising, given Chesterton's fondness for paradox as a concept and as a conceit, but rightly applied, it makes sense of the peculiar capacity of the Bergoglian mind and spirituality to hold in balance the contradictions that define Christian existence: the juxtaposition of agony with ecstasy, doubt with certitude, the mundane with the sublime, a life of service with a life of solitary prayer, leadership from below with leadership from above. Like the troubadours of medieval times, Francis the Italian mendicant and Francis the Argentine pope are *jongleurs de Dieu*, God's tumblers or jugglers, special performers for the divinity, poetic, beatific, subversive. Just the way God likes them.

But it would be foolishly reductive to think that facile comparisons can transcend scrutiny. Still, the radicality we find in the Poor Man of Assisi is not missing in the Poor Pope on the Tiber. The French scholar André Vauchez argues that the Francis of history, the Francis of pious legend, and the Francis of the contesting schools of Franciscanism that followed in his wake give us only an incomplete picture. Francis made a decision about the kind of Christ he would serve:

> Rereading the Gospel in the light of his own personal experience and that of civic and knightly culture, Francis chose to follow a poor and begging Christ, always on the road and sharing with the marginalized the precariousness of their conditions of life, and to worship a God full of mercy who made the sun shine and the rain fall on the good and the bad alike. In doing this, he was not replicating a model: he was creating one by virtue of his own personal sensibility, which was keen and which made for its originality.[5]

Like the Poor Man of Assisi, Jorge Bergoglio is on the road, consoling the marginalized, listening to the abandoned, serving the God of mercy over all else, creating "by virtue of his own personal sensibility" a new model of being Peter.

But he is *also* a Jesuit, and the greatest missionary of the first generation of Jesuits was also called Francis: in this case, Francis Xavier of noble Basque blood. This Companion of Jesus was prepared to go anywhere to bring the good news that is the Gospel, irrespective of distance, danger, and death. His zeal brought him to India, Ceylon (now Sri Lanka), the Malay peninsula, the Molucca Islands, and Japan. He died before he could arrive on Chinese soil—one of the deepest of his many evangelizing passions—and he is buried in Goa. Jorge Bergoglio was attracted to Xavier's concept of the bold and brave missionary and was influenced by that other great Basque, Pedro Arrupe, the superior general of the Society of Jesus during the turbulent post-conciliar period. Arrupe was trained in medicine, stationed in Hiroshima at the time of the perfidious nuclear detonation in 1945, and a model for respectful dialogue, witness, and enculturation—in sharp contrast to the predominant missiological thinking propelled for centuries by the belief that *Extra ecclesiam nulla salus* ("outside the church there is no salvation").

When commentators speculated on the reason for "Francis" as the new name to be added to the papal annals, it was not unreasonable to think of the second most famous of the original Jesuits after whom numberless churches, schools, universities, and institutes have been dedicated. So, it was a surprise—one of the first of many—that it was the other Francis he had in mind. But *both* actually work as they shared evangelizing zeal; a capacity to think outside the geographical and cultural boundaries of the Christendom that shaped them; a radical commitment to the barest economy of means; a willingness to take daring personal risks. They were also embedded in the origins of their new religious orders and canonized shortly after their deaths.

But in the end, Pope Francis is not a Franciscan; he is a Jesuit, and it is that tradition that comprehensively, integrally, existentially shapes him. The training to be a Jesuit is notoriously long. Their mystique as educators, scientists, poets, communicators, et cetera, is still very much intact, their influence in the Catholic world unparalleled, and their influence outside Catholicism sturdy, controversial, and long-lasting. But if we know them for their universities and their scholarship only, we miss what is at the heart of the Jesuit vocation: their spirituality. And that spirituality has been sifted through the rich, exquisitely complex, profoundly personal spiritual and psychological traumas—and trauma is the right word, and in the plural—that defined the early life of Ignatius of Loyola: soldier, courtier, ambitious young man on the make drawn from Spain's lower nobility, refined in a military and worldly way. The consummate careerist.

And then a cannonball got him!

All changed forever.

Forced into a prolonged convalescence by his injuries, with numerous failed surgeries, Ignatius was confined to his bed and forced to reconsider at the most foundational level his ambitions, his values, the very meaning of his life.

Out of the depths of his personal anguish would come arresting insights into his emotional makeup, a deep appropriation of the faith that hitherto was a superficial cultural accretion, an understanding of the psychological dynamics involved in a personal relationship with Christ. And this would all be distilled into a small handbook that has shaped the lives of millions—those who have read it and, more importantly, those who have lived it: *The Spiritual Exercises*.

Jack Costello, educator, philosopher, and past president of Regis College at the University of Toronto, nicely encapsulates the innovative and distinctive genius of the *Exercises*:

> The *Spiritual Exercises* is at the heart of Jesuit spirituality because it deals with life as a journey, as a journey of transformation in relation to the movement of history. It is not simply an internal conversion, but an internal conversion in relation to what God is doing in the world. Essentially, it raises the question "Can you dig it?" Can you put yourself on the side of this great thing that is happening in the world despite the horrors, despite the obvious sign that there is as much shadow as there is light? Can you be on the side of light and yet share in the experience of the shadow? There is a big difference between the Enlightenment maxim that says that if we don't do it it won't get done—and there is a great deal of Jesuit energy that goes into that kind of endeavour—and the more radical view of God, the view one finds in the *Exercises*, which argues that God is already doing it, that our first job is to be at God's side helping to realize the divine intention with everything we have by way of tools, intelligence, and human spirit.[6]

There is a strong pragmatic streak to Jesuit spirituality that emanates from its Christological core: what matters is engagement with the world, electing the light over the shadow, serving as God's accomplice, not usurper, adopting a world-friendly rather than world-condemning approach, being part of a journey into the recesses of Creation, of matter, and not a flight into cloistered denial, for all that lives is holy, as the English poet and artist William Blake was wont to say.

This pragmatic strain in Jesuit spirituality speaks to the pragmatic strain in the pastor Jorge Bergoglio. The God of the *Exercises* is a God to be experienced, not conceptualized; a God to be touched, not etherealized. Finding God in every event, in all things, requires the operating conviction that God is willfully inserted into human history, that this vital, energetic, engaging God is not indifferent to struggling humanity. The God of Ignatius, the God who can be found in all things,

is at once the God of our hearts and our intimacies as well as the God of our history and the histories of other peoples ... finding God in all things means caring for justice, and acting on behalf of those who are not being permitted to flourish as personal images and likenesses of God ... finding God in all things sees that every effort to behave truly is cutting a new path: it is a walking on water, a giving over of ourselves in faith and a discovering of the implications only much later.[7]

The God of Ignatius is, as the British Jesuit Gerard W. Hughes observed, the "God of Surprises," and that is precisely the kind of God that the Pope of Surprises can understand. One of the necessary surprises is the uncovering and remaking of self that occurs as the result of an existential conversion. Ignatius's own conversion provides the rudiments of the *Exercises*, allowing for the creation of a personal template with universal application. The formative moment occurred in Manresa, Spain, from March 1522 until February 1523, where he divided his time between a solitary cell attached to a Dominican priory and a cave overlooking the Cardoner River. It was here on the banks of the Cardoner that he experienced an overpowering illumination, an experience he describes in the autobiography he dictated near the end of his life:

> He was once on his way, out of devotion, to a church a little more than a mile from Manresa, which I think was called Saint Paul. The road followed the path of the river and he was taken up with his devotions; he sat down for a while facing the river flowing far below him. As he sat there the eyes of his understanding were opened and though he saw no vision he understood and perceived many things, numerous spiritual things as well as matters touching on faith and learning, and this was with an elucidation so bright that all these things seemed new to him. He cannot expound in detail what he then understood, for they were many things, but he can state that he received such a lucidity in understanding that during the course of his entire life—now having passed his sixty-second year—if he were to gather all the helps he received from God and everything he knew, and add them together, he does not think that they would add up to all that he received on that one occasion.[8]

What is critical in the Manresa experience—the absolute uprooting of identity and the subsequent reconstitution of the self—was to prove fundamental in shaping Ignatius's perception of the radical nature of authentic conversion and the reorientation or new life commitment necessitated by such a conversion.[9] The Jesuit psychiatrist, Harvard professor, and Ignatius biographer W. W. Meissner writes of this core experience from his own distinctly Freudian perspective:

The reshaping of identity that the pilgrim [Ignatius identified himself regularly as "the pilgrim"] sought in the cave of Manresa was distilled into the practices of the *Spiritual Exercises*. He proposed to his followers and to those whom he directed in the *Exercises* the same end—a restructuring of the self, of one's sense of self, one's identity, in terms of total commitment to God's will and to unstinting enlisting in His service. The entire corpus of the *Exercises* is organized and directed to this end. It proposes nothing less than the restructuring of one's life, one's ideals and values, one's goals and hopes, and the commitment of that life to the service of the King of Kings.[10]

The *Spiritual Exercises* define Jesuit identity. They bear the distinct stamp of Ignatius's own personality: his acute intro-spectiveness; his preference for an orderly and programmed way of experiencing and understanding God (in that order); his creative and unrestricted use of all that is material, of all that is human, in his relentless pursuit of the Divine Majesty. This is Bergoglio's tradition, his spiritual framework: Ignatius and his spiritual manual, the *Exercises*—formidable forces that shape and direct the life and ministry of the first Jesuit pope. The *Spiritual Exercises* is "a slim book, with its hobbling syntax and almost total absence of literary grace,"[11] yet it manages somehow to generate a transformative change in the life of those who are carefully guided to integrate its methodology into their own spiritual pilgrimage. You don't just read the *Exercises*; you *do* them, or they do you, working their wisdom into the pores, sinews, nerves, and viscera of the total human person—the imagination, the heart, the mind, the body: "For, just as taking a walk, travelling on foot, and running are physical exercises, so is the name of spiritual exercises given to any means of preparing and disposing our soul to rid itself of all its disordered affections and then, after their removal, of seeking and finding God's will in the ordering of our life for the salvation of our soul."[12]

The *Exercises* are flexible and versatile. They were conceived as a malleable framework that allows for the one directing the Exercises—the director—and the one doing the Exercises—the exercitant—to find the best way of moving forward. It is a dialogue, a momentum built on mature self-knowledge, deep interiority, refined discernment, lacerating self-honesty. It is not for those seeking easy spiritual nostrums, a spiritual therapy that is more chicken soup than a healthy broth with a pungent aftertaste. As the Jesuit spiritual master John English observed, the *Exercises* is not a compendium of ethereal maxims, a handbook for the gnostic or spiritually elite, but a rustic and unpolished product of "a simple lay person with very little education who had this great experience at Manresa." English writes of the Exercises dynamic: "It brings me from my foundational experience of creaturehood, to that of my brokenness or sinfulness, to my transforming experience of forgiveness, of being forgiven unconditionally. Out of this triadic experience comes a sense of call: 'I have to do something.'"[13]

When the young Bergoglio did the Exercises for the first time—the Jesuits make the Exercises a minimum of two times in the course of their lives as Jesuits—he would have understood that the call he faced demanded nothing less than action on *his* part. To better understand what that call consists of, it is essential to know something of the psycho-spiritual dynamic involved in doing the Exercises. John English explains it this way:

The way I tend to go is to follow Ignatius's own dynamic. I start with our creaturehood, like he does with the Principle and Foundation, and talk about how I am sustained by God and need to become free of everything that is not God. That helps me to get a sense of a benevolent God who brought me into being and sustains me, a creature, in love. Then, and only then, I move to sin and discover something else about myself and the world. I look at myself, my own disorder, and I reflect on the destructive forces in humanity, in which I participate. And then I discover what forgiveness is, and I get a whole new awareness of God.[14]

Fully cognizant, then, of his own disorders—and yet fully aware that he has been loved into existence by God—Bergoglio's "whole new awareness of God" propels him to engage in the world in a new and revolutionary way. There is a strong evangelistic streak in Bergoglio's personality and spirituality, and it is directly attributable to his Jesuit formation. And an especially significant consideration in this regard is the Ignatian notion of the *magis*. For Ignatius, the *magis* or "more" is the invitation to move beyond the sufficient or *satis*. The call of the Gospel is the call to do more, and that call is an invitation to serve Christ beyond the adequate. It is an invitation that is a summons to spiritual heroism, proposing a response that is grounded in the energy of a rejuvenating awakening, a coming to terms with the adventures—unknown, ennobling, and terrifying—that await the pilgrim of the spirit. As André Brouillette defines it:

it is not about doing enough or not doing enough or doing more. It's not a question of quantifying anything. It's about entering into the logic of an incarnate love—through deeds more than through words—that will grow deeper. The lover wants to share everything with the beloved and vice versa. This mutual self-giving is dynamic, always wanting to give more; the relationship deepens, love becomes more unitive, purer, truer, greater. Love always keeps us moving, growing. This is the heart of the experience of the Ignatian *magis*—a love that continuously opens us to the possibility of renewed incarnation.[15]

Bergoglio's Ignatian spirituality is a spirituality in endless formation because the human person, the human project, is forever in formation. It is not enough to be grounded in the principles and exhortations of the text; one must be grounded in the now, attentive to the Spirit's disclosure in the present lived experience. In Bergoglio's mind, the Jesuit must be a romantic realist, juggling knowledge of the luminous with the shadow. In a series of interviews with Jesuits, the Jesuit pope made clear his conviction, articulated by the Jesuit theologian Hugo Rahner, that "the Jesuit should be a man of supernatural flair, that is to say that he should be endowed with a sense of the divine and the diabolical in the face of the events of human life and history. The Jesuit must, therefore, be capable of discernment in the field of God and in the field of the Devil."[16]

That "supernatural flair" involves an anxious heart and unquiet structures. For Francis, pope and Jesuit, we are in an open sea, and we must not be afraid. The dynamic of the Spirit cannot be contained by rules, regulations, dogmas even, and the securities and certitudes inherent in ways of doing things that calm the questing spirit, our nervous yearning for God, can quickly turn into instruments of the Devil, distancing us from the Love that calls us forth into the turbulence of living deeply and authentically. Jesuits need to "go and walk together and don't stay locked in rigid perspectives because in them there is no possibility of reform."[17]

If *The Spiritual Exercises* freed Bergoglio from the "rigid perspectives" he laments, it didn't happen early in his life as a Jesuit. His conflicted and often controversial tenure as provincial in Argentina and his occasional bouts of stubbornness when encountering facts he found disagreeable and untenable—his resolute resistance to an episcopal appointment in Chile against the wishes of the people comes to mind as but one instance—his constancy on the matter of being liberated by the spirituality of Ignatius remains a fixed element in the Francis firmament.

He regularly denounces the predilection many prelates have for stability and continuity precisely because such devout adherence to the past forecloses the imagination, restricts the operations of the Spirit, and confines and delimits the church in her ministry to humanity. The Spirit must breathe; the heart must soar; the imagination must be unshackled. But these are not the ecclesiastical equivalents of politically correct views; they are rooted in serious thinking. One of those serious thinkers who was in the Jesuit airspace for decades, profoundly influential in both Jesuit and non-Jesuit circles, is Francis's fellow Jesuit, Canadian philosophical theologian Bernard Lonergan. Although Lonergan died in 1984—in the same year, as it happens, as his equally influential fellow Jesuit Karl Rahner—his influence has grown courtesy the publication of all his work by the University of Toronto Press, the rising number of doctoral students doing work on Lonergan, and the wide appeal of his interdisciplinarity. Lonergan's view of the Catholic world after the Second Vatican Council is a prescient summary of the reality-on-the-ground philosophy of Francis and is perfectly consonant with his ecclesiological and pastoral thinking:

> There is bound to be formed a solid right that is determined
> to live in a world that no longer exists. There is bound to be
> formed a scattered left, captivated by now this, now that new
> development, exploring now this and now that new possibility.
> But what will count is a perhaps not numerous center, big
> enough to be at home in both the old and the new, pains-
> taking enough to work out one by one the transitions to be
> made, strong enough to refuse half-measures and insist on
> complete solutions even though it has to wait.[18]

Jesuit theologian Gordon A. Rixon identifies several points of connection between Francis and Lonergan, especially in light of their shared appreciation of multivalent dimensions of culture and truth-seeking:

> social groups develop distinct ways of living together shaped
> by different, evolving meanings and values. Lonergan recog-
> nizes this cultural dynamism as a truth of human existence.
> Francis affirms and celebrates this cultural diversity as a creative
> expression of human and divine artistry. As persons of critical
> reason and religious faith, both recognize the continuity of
> diverse cultural solutions with the evolutionary dynamism of
> cosmological process and anticipate that every path of cultural
> development is founded upon the gifts of creation and is finally
> sublated in a self-and-species-transcending religious fulfilment.[19]

Francis's intellectual horizon is similar to Lonergan's, although the colouration of temperament, philosophical disposition, and manner of approach—the way they approach the apprehension of truth—vary. For Francis, methodology takes a second seat to pastoral intuition, and he lacks the systematician's love of order and category that defined Lonergan's approach, but at the deepest level, they share a number of working convictions.

One of those convictions that continues to animate the Bergoglio leadership is their mutual appreciation of the post–Second Vatican Council world, the foundational shift in consciousness that defines a meaningful relationship with a modern, indeed postmodern, world. Francis would give a mighty amen to Lonergan's assessment that we have moved from a classicist to a historicist paradigm and that this paradigm, in all its contours and configurations, is still unfolding:

> What breathed life and form into the civilization of Greece and Rome, what was born again in a European Renaissance, what provided the chrysalis whence issued modern languages and literatures, modern mathematics and science, modern philosophy and history, held its own right into the twentieth century; but today, nearly everywhere, it is dead and almost forgotten. Classical culture has given way to a modern culture, and, I would submit, the crisis of our age is in no small measure the fact that modern culture has not yet reached its maturity. The classical mediation of meaning has broken down; the breakdown has been effected by a whole array of new and more effective techniques; but their very multiplicity and complexity leave us bewildered, disorientated, confused, preyed upon by anxiety, dreading lest we fall victims to the up-to-date myth of ideology and the hypnotic, highly effective magic of thought control.[20]

Given the geopolitical realities that have emerged in the decades following Lonergan's death, his anxieties around current ideologies and their corrosive hypnotism, compounded by unchecked social media competition for suzerainty among Facebook, Twitter, Instagram, and their proliferating wannabes, seem more than validated. The shift in an epistemological culture—with all the accompanying upheaval—and a more fluid, less static grasp of what we understand truth, human meaning, and divine purpose to be confirms Lonergan's vision and Francis's reality.

The philosophical architect—Lonergan—and the shepherd—Francis—approached their respective Jesuit vocations deploying their personal gifts and talents, and therein lie distinct differences. But they are aligned in their preference for empirical rather than an *a priori* argumentation, for their determination to rid their own thinking of any conceptualist rigidity, and in their openness to a seismic overturning of the way we have been acclimated to think, moving into that messy terrain called life with a freedom of the spirit that has liberated both from the clerical parochialism, the constrictive Thomism, of their early training.

If there was a cognitional and pastoral attunement between these two lofty Jesuits, there was even more of a cosympathy between the pope and the Trappist. Thomas Merton, the monk-poet, contemplative, and socio-political essayist—he died in 1968 somewhat mysteriously by electrocution outside of Bangkok, having just delivered a provocative address on "Monasticism and Marxist Perspectives"—was one of those towering Catholic figures who dominated mid-twentieth-century Catholic life. Intellectuals, literary specialists, religious leaders—Catholic, ecumenical, and interfaith—were familiar with his work and often champions of his numerous causes: civil liberties for Black Americans, nuclear deterrence, the recovery of the "archaic wisdom" of Indigenous cultures extirpated by Western imperial powers, the importance of contemplation as a key component of human freedom, the debilitating effects of a practical philosophy of technologism, and the liberating dimensions of silence.

Merton's autobiography, *The Seven Storey Mountain*, stunned the world with its popularity and timing. Published three years after the Second World War ended, it proffered a romantic antidote to the existential despair and rootlessness that beset a shattered world. His subsequent journals that continued his autobiographical forays up to his untimely death at the age of fifty-three—*The Sign of Jonas, Conjectures of a Guilty Bystander, A Vow of Conversation,* and *The Asian Journal*—enjoyed immense success in both the Catholic and non-Catholic worlds.

In addition, Merton's fluency in Spanish and his translations of many Central and South American poets, designed to introduce them to a culturally and spiritually myopic United States, established him as a key figure among both Hispanic and Portuguese literary figures, including the Peruvian César Vallejo, the Nicaraguans Alfonso Cortés and Azarías H. Pallais, and the Chilean Nicanor Parra. There were others, too, including Brazilian poets with "their Franciscan love of life,"[21] as well as a prolific and wide-ranging panorama of correspondence with Latin American intellectuals and religious figures, all of which marked Merton as a known and esteemed entity in the Ibero-American universe.

At one point, Merton thought seriously of moving from his monastery in Kentucky to Nicaragua to join the spiritual community founded on the Solentiname islands by his former Trappist novice and fellow poet Ernesto Cardenal. Like all his previous efforts to secure abbatial and Roman approval for moving outside his cloister, it came to naught. But his friendship with Cardenal was long-enduring. The friendship of these two priest-poets was rooted in a shared spirituality and commitment to social justice. They both wrestled with ecclesiastical authorities—censored, delated, and ordered to obey on matters of both church and political polity—but in Cardenal's case, Roman wrath was not deflected. In 1983, on the occasion of a papal visit to Nicaragua, Pope John Paul II publicly rebuked a kneeling Cardenal in full view of the international media covering the trip, with a suspension of Cardenal's priestly duties enacted the following year. Merton, too, had been silenced by his superiors on the issue of peace in a nuclear age, but Cardenal was more severely disciplined by being deprived of his right to exercise priestly ministry; no such sanction was ever imposed on Merton.

There is a sweet irony in this, in that thirty years after John Paul's canonical censure, another pope, Francis, reinstated Cardenal to the priesthood. Merton would have rejoiced that an unjust act was righted.

Francis wrote of Merton in glowing terms when he gave his address to a joint session of the US Congress on September 24, 2015, listing him among the moral prophets of American history: Abraham Lincoln, Martin Luther King, Dorothy Day, and Merton. These people, in the pope's phrasing, "offer us a way of seeing and interpreting reality. In honouring their memory, we are inspired, even amid conflicts, and in the here and now of each day, to draw upon our deepest cultural reserves."

Merton's expansive and inclusive spirituality, his peace activism, his creative integration of prayer and witness, appealed to

Francis long before he made his storied trip to the Potomac. Francis sees in Merton something of himself, warring against a suffocating legalism that ensnares faith, paralyzes the human will, and reduces the radicality of Christian morality to a series of static nostrums:

> Merton, some 50 years ago, saw that the attempt to imprison faith in the realm of moral precepts is to "condemn it to sterility, and rob it of its real reason for existing, which is love" ... Bergoglio made exactly this point in a 2004 talk [obviously pre-papal in its genesis and delivery] on the anniversary of *Veritatis Splendor*, John Paul II's defense of objective truth against the threat of relativism ... if morality is no more than a kind of judicial code, imposed from the outside rather than a free response of the heart to the experience of God's mercy, relativism becomes an assertion of freedom, an affirmation of divinely ingrained autonomy against an iron cage.[22]

Merton's thought and spirituality are built on his understanding of the Creative Contraries of William Blake, the notion that the elimination or erasure of the opposites, the polarities, that define existence is an uprooting of all that is, and "Everything that lives is holy." As Blake says in his poem *The Marriage of Heaven and Hell*: "Attraction and Repulsion, Reason and Energy, / Love and Hate, are necessary to Human Existence."

Merton's effort to achieve unity, balancing the Contraries in his own life and faith, was an effort that spanned his monastic tenure in the Abbey of Gethsemani. He struggled to unite in himself the disparate strains of feeling, culture, history, and religion that constituted his extraterritorial existence: he was the organic conservative at the same time as he was the intellectual mongrel; a traditionalist with the heart and imagination of a bohemian; rooted in one religious culture but eager to incorporate the "truth" of all; the perfect wandering monk or gyrovague hell-bent on tasting the eclectic, the novel, the forbidden, yet at the same time grounded in a tradition centuries-old lumbering through time sustained by bursts of divine energy or grace.

This very much sounds like the kind of church Francis is most comfortable with, a church that is not enamoured of absolutes, nor hidebound by convention, rubric, and canon, and that is not theologically narrow but expansive in its horizon. Merton was a progressive thinker, but his maturation was a sometimes long and painful one. He needed to be grounded at the same time as he needed to explore; he rebelled against the strictures of authority at the same time as he understood their value. In this, his experience of religious formation was akin to Bergoglio's, moving from a highly conservative and institutional approach to a more flexible and personalist one.

Critical to Merton's intellectual evolution was precisely the balancing of the opposites, the complementarity of the antinomies that make up human life. Merton rejected a simplistic model of unity and harmony that collapsed the creative tensions that define us. In one famous passage from his 1960s journal, *Conjectures of a Guilty Bystander*, he underscored what it means to unite all things in himself:

> If I can unite *in myself* the thought and devotion of Eastern and Western Christendom, the Greek and the Latin Fathers, the Russians with the Spanish mystics, I can prepare in myself the reunion of divided Christians. From that secret and unspoken unity in myself can eventually come a visible and manifest

unity of all Christians. If we want to bring together what is divided, we cannot do so by imposing one division upon the other or absorbing one division into the other. But if we do this, the union is not Christian. It is political, and doomed to further conflict. We must contain all divided worlds in ourselves and transcend them in Christ.[23]

This is pure Bergoglio: eager to balance the polarities not by erasure but with spiritual equipoise. One moves forward as an individual, as a church, and as a society when one moves from parochialism to universalism, recognizing the integrity of traditions that can be in legitimate conflict but without descending into hostility and incomprehension, triumphalism and self-righteousness. It is that openness of Merton to the "other," that desire of Merton's to embody in himself the plenitude of other faiths without obliterating the uniqueness of his own christocentrism and Catholic contemplative vocation, that appealed increasingly to the post-Córdoba Bergoglio.

Merton scholar Christopher Pramuk insightfully comments on the shared spirituality of Merton and Francis:

Much like Merton, Francis's root spirituality is profoundly incarnational; true to his Jesuit and Franciscan sensibilities, it is also profoundly cosmic and creational, trusting that the whole of human life, inclusive of our bodies, is part of a greater mystery about which we are still profoundly ignorant, still wondering, still learning. This yields in both Merton and Francis a deep-seated pilgrim spirituality. Like the disciples on the road to Emmaus, a favourite text of Merton's, both call us to a way of proceeding that is "ever on the move," marked by openness and intellectual humility more than dogmatic certainty, induction from broad human experience more than deduction from abstract principles, and a positive expectation that new understanding and wisdom will emerge at the axis of encounter with others in freedom and grace.[24]

Merton entertained no illusions about the mentality of entombment characteristic of institutions fearful of change, a mentality that is resistant to the proddings of the Holy Spirit— the source of endless renewal and vivification in the church. In a letter to his friend and fellow monk the Benedictine scholar Jean Leclercq, Merton lamented the setting in of spiritual rot in American society at large, as well as in the Catholic Church and most especially in his own community of Trappist monks: "there is a stink of decay, not the decay of oldness, the enfeeblement of something past its prime: but rather a splendid cancerous fullness that shines with a kind of health, a richness and a flowering of something overgrown, overdeveloped, and lacking in basic intelligence, above all in living wisdom."[25]

This kind of sharp language, a full-out assault on institutional rigidity and spiritual complacency, presages Bergoglio's unapologetic broadsides against those curial cardinals who prefer privilege and stability—the comforts and consolations of a static reality—to the unsettling and challenging imperatives of Christian leadership. Bergoglio also has stern things to say about clergy whose lifeless liturgies betray a corrosive psychological and spiritual narcissism, who serve as "inadequate models," distorting the beauty of public prayer with

rigid austerity or an exasperating creativity, a spiritualizing mysticism or a practical functionalism, a rushed briskness or an overemphasized slowness, a sloppy carelessness or an excessive finickiness, a superabundant friendliness or priestly impassibility … I think that the inadequacy of these models of presiding [at the liturgy] have a common root: a heightened personalism of the celebrating style which at times expresses a poorly concealed mania to be the centre of attention.[26]

But it is not just, or primarily, the tone of reproach that unites the voices respectively of the monk and the pontiff, but their shared commitment to the deeper truth of contemplation and dialogue as the way forward to a more prayerful and healing church. Francis would agree with Merton, who wrote initially, at the behest of an earlier pope, Paul VI, that "the contemplative life is … search for peace not in an abstract exclusion of all outside reality, not in a barren negative closing of the senses upon the world, but in the openness of love."[27]

The struggles of Francis to balance the contraries, to weigh the arguments of opposition with equanimity and prudence, to attend to the competing priorities of seemingly irreconcilable positions, are framed within the epistemology of naturalized German thinker Romano Guardini, one of the persistent theological and philosophical influences of his life. For Guardini, a key forerunner of the Second Vatican Council, polar opposition is not

a "synthesis" of two moments into a third. Nor is it a whole, of which the two moments constitute "parts." Still less is it a mixture, in some sort of compromise. It is, rather, an entirely distinct, original relationship of an original phenomenon. Neither pole can be deduced from the other, nor rediscovered starting from the other … Rather, both parts are contemporaneous, thinkable, and possible only thanks to each other. This is opposition: two moments are each in themselves without being able to be deduced, transposed, confused, and yet are inextricably linked to each other; on the contrary, they can be thought of only one in the other and one thanks to the other.[28]

If Guardini was a direct shaper of the thought and sensibility of Francis, Merton's structural frame of integrating the Contraries, as poet and visionary William Blake calls them, has been his abiding pastoral and spiritual strategy.

Francis's indebtedness to Merton is not, of course, grounded in his familiarity with Merton's literary and spiritual antecedents, but rather in his contemplative witness, in the monk's constitutional openness to dialogue. Merton understood that dialogue is minimally a courteous exchange of opinions; it is a process of unfolding that elicits substantive change. Merton

was open to the fact that his own *understanding* sometimes needed tacit correction, added depth and breadth, and would continue to open up through a mutually beneficial dialogical process. He discovered through that process that "we are already one" in the "mystery of unity" but believed that continuing the process could create a more robust community of *explicitly* shared meanings and values, a catholic unity in which "all men and women share, though differently, in that same mystery of salvation through Jesus Christ in the Spirit."[29]

In his address to the United States Congress in 2015, while speaking of Merton's "perspective of dialogue," Pope Francis gave ample endorsement to all those political efforts that seek to overcome historic differences and, in the strongest terms, asserted his commitment as *pontifex maximus* (bridge builder) to do likewise. He sees it as his duty to help all those seeking resolution of their political conflicts: "When countries which have been at odds resume the path of dialogue—a dialogue that may have been interrupted for the most legitimate of reasons—new opportunities open up for all. This has required, and requires, courage and daring, which is not the same as irresponsibility. A good political leader is one who, with the interests of all in mind, seizes the moment in a spirit of openness and pragmatism."[30]

For sure, as a general statement on how to operate in a world of combative ideologies, Francis's underscoring for dialogue as embodied in the life and ministry of Merton makes attractive good sense. But when he translates his philosophy of dialogue into the political sphere, things become messy. As he must have known they would. His insistence on dialogue—constructive conversation built on patience and mutual respect, even when strained—has generated great unhappiness among many of his hitherto devoted supporters. The Vatican's determination to build a relationship with the totalizing Chinese regime of President Xi Jinping in an effort to ensure control over the appointment of bishops that are acceptable to Beijing *and* the Vatican has outraged Catholics who have suffered under the Communist government of mainland China and who watch with trepidation the monolithic totalitarianism of an increasingly pugilistic, jingoistic, and bellicose China. The last British governor of Hong Kong, Lord Christopher Patten, the chancellor of Oxford University, esteemed diplomat, author, and avowedly Catholic public intellectual, has been uncommonly critical of what he sees as Francis's political myopia in negotiating with a power that has an empirical and sordid record of deception. After all, it was Patten who skillfully arranged for the cessation of Hong Kong from Britain with the firm guarantee that the island power would be able to maintain its current political and economic status as separate from a greater mainland China for fifty years. That was not to be.

Francis's commitment to dialogue, to listening as an *act*—the premier act of effective engagement—has been tested to the extreme by the political realities of a globally aggressive China and a fiercely territorial Russia. The resurgence of "holy Russia" under "Tsar" Vladimir Putin has posed an especially pointed challenge to the Bishop of Rome. His determination to build bridges with the Orthodox Church of Russia has been a theological and pastoral priority for Francis from the onset of this papacy. The long and tortured history of Rome and Moscow, competing Sees that have come to define what it is to be a Christian of the West as opposed to a Christian of the East—although such claims are rightly contested by other seats of Christian power and influence, including Canterbury, Geneva, and Constantinople (Istanbul)—nonetheless provides ample ground for true ecumenical rapprochement. The Vatican has made many overtures to Bishop Kirill, Patriarch of Moscow and all Rus' and Primate of the Russian Orthodox Church, to seek common ground by first establishing an in-person meeting. A meeting on Russian soil, ideally.

Putin's invasion of Ukraine in February 2022 undermined Francis's efforts to engage with Kirill and soured his relations with many of the Greek Catholic or Byzantine churches that comprise over twenty long-established and independent churches that are in communion with the Latin Rite church headed by Francis but retain their own unique liturgies, spiritual and theological traditions, and codes of canon law. By not forthrightly denouncing President Putin's unlawful invasion, the consequent loss of life, mass migration of peoples, and profound unsettling of the world order, Francis was seen as too soft, an ardent follower of the Vatican's own policy of *Ostpolitik* largely formulated under the papacy of Paul VI and his able secretary of state, Agostino Casaroli. In this regard, Francis can be seen in agreement with theologian Paul J. Griffiths's sober assessment of political pathology:

> [All political entities] want what they want, and kill for it, combatants and non-combatants both; we want what we want, and kill for it, combatants and non-combatants both. That is what all sovereign states do when they can; it is the burden and overflow of the *libido dominandi* under which all of them, including the United States, struggle and sink. It would be better to look this in the eye than to rick it out with moral glosses it cannot bear.[31]

Although Francis views such a political pathology through the lens of Original Sin, he does not subscribe to such a Hobbesian perspective; he doesn't embrace the Clausewitzian theory that "war is the continuation of policy with other means" or the Kissingerian pragmatism that presents itself as rational accommodation. He is a stalwart believer in a redeemed humanity. No misanthropic philosophy for him. Balancing his Christian humanism, Ignatian spirituality, and the political necessities that are unrelenting is often a bit of a papal mug's game. But for some of his strong admirers, this balancing act has gone too far. Greek Catholic and Ukrainian priest-theologian Myroslaw Tataryn, in his entry "Vatican Diplomacy or Gospel Solidarity?" for the ecclesial reform blog *Go, Rebuild My House*, did not pull any punches:

The breath of fresh air ushered in by Pope Francis is due, to an extent, to his enunciation of the Church's need to attend to the marginalized, not through charity, but through solidarity. But can diplomacy and solidarity walk hand in hand? ... In 1863 an official document of the Imperial Russian state declared: "the Ukrainian language never existed, does not exist, and shall never exist." Prior to the 2022 invasion President Putin openly denied Ukraine's right to exist and laid claim to it as "historically Russian land." In the weeks before the Russian invasion Putin used a Russian phrase referring to a rape, but applied it to Ukraine: "Like it or not, my beauty, you have to put up with it." It's time for the Vatican to realize that Christ calls us to solidarity with the victim of rape, not a deal with the rapist.[32]

Francis is not unaware of the tightrope he is walking. After all, his predecessor Pius XII continues to be the subject of fiery debate around his elected silence on the matter of condemning Nazi atrocities against the Jews. A long history of Vatican neutrality—maintaining detachment from competing ideological battles in the interests of credible impartiality—has redounded to its discredit. Still, in keeping with his commitment to listening and not judging, Francis prefers the platitudinous to the denunciatory, fully aware that general laments and broad exhortations, essentially impotent though they be, are a necessary prelude to winning the minimum trust required for dialogue.

In essence, without diluting institutional integrity or doctrinal purity, the church works out a *modus vivendi* that respects the political realities as they are, not as one would want them to be. You build *toward* a culture of tolerance by working diligently and with patience, erecting structures of agreement rather than multiplying fissures of division: that means dialogue with the unsavoury, the autocratic, expansionist egomaniacs, and the hopelessly benighted. No adversary must be excluded; dialogue alone constructs a world of harmony, no matter how elusive.

Francis's realization that dialogue has many layers—political, theological, ecclesiological, spiritual, and cultural—allows him to structure his leadership in such a way that it is built on the multifaceted dimensions of a dialogue that privileges listening. The alternatives are endless strife, human diminishment, and possibly global catastrophe. But his steadfast commitment to the way of dialogue has countless drawbacks, including the moral consequences that derive from the *via compromissum*. There will be sacrifices made, principles diluted, agreements secured with ideologically hostile forces, but with the arc of history working in favour of dialogue as the preferred political mode.

Francis as an ecclesiastical pragmatist steeped in *realpolitik* may be unsettling for his progressive followers and red meat for his critics, but it is not that much of a departure from many of his pontifical predecessors. The Vatican City State knows something about political alliances, the art of survival in a shifting political universe, the deals that need to be made. And although it is Pietro Parolin who is secretary of state, and the equally able secretary for relations with states, Paul Gallagher, the foreign affairs equivalent, who manage the day-to-day politics of the Vatican, policy is a papal prerogative, and Francis is at the heart of it all.

His insistence on dialogue—regardless of the conflict— highlights the Vatican's commitment to neutrality and for many, including British Italophile, novelist, and translator Tim Parks, doesn't work. In an essay reviewing two starkly different books assessing the pontificate of Pius XII—*The Pope at War: The Secret History of Pius XII, Mussolini and Hitler* by David I. Kertzer and *The Pope and the Holocaust: Pius XII and the Vatican Secret Archives* by Michael Hesemann—Parks pointedly notes: "No doubt the fight over the pope's record and the church's involvement in the war will go on, especially in light of the present pope's response to Russian aggression in Ukraine, his insistence that NATO largely provoked the conflict, and his remark that 'there are no metaphysical good guys and bad guys, in the abstract.'"[33]

Parks is not entirely fair as he selects from Francis's many comments to the media and in public addresses those passages, mostly early in the conflict, that favour a moral equivalence. Subsequent commentary by the pope is more directly anti-Putin, although he religiously avoids mentioning his name.

Francis the politician was in great part shaped by the crucible of the Argentine Dirty War, its festering aftermath, and its ruinous legacy of national polarization, so he sees in the larger global conflict of the West with an aggressive Russia and roguish China the recurrence of a scarring memory.

The "makings" then, and I intend the plural, of Pope Francis—the intellectual and spiritual influences, the dominant religious personalities, the political horizons that shape him—are best distilled in his 2020 encyclical *Fratelli tutti* (All Brothers: On Fraternity and Social Friendship). It is this work, with its broad embrace of humanity, that has become his magna carta for a new Christian humanism. Other works speak to his dream of a harmonized humanity, of his passion for our common home, for expanded global understanding, and for Catholic tolerance—*ad intra* and *ad extra*—but *Fratelli tutti* has priority in the Bergoglio orbit.

The encyclical's thesis is reducible to the witness and radical Christian vision embodied in Francis of Assisi. This papal letter is the pope's most public declaration of indebtedness to the Umbrian mendicant who reshaped Christendom. Francis knows *his* Francis and roots his papacy in his namesake's holy and literal simplicity. The twelfth-century Italian revolutionary is a living template for the twenty-first-century Argentine pontiff. Saint Francis was neither intellectually shackled nor spiritually encumbered by doctrine or ideology:

> Francis did not wage a war of words aimed at imposing doctrines; he simply spread the love of God. He understood that "'God is love and those who abide in love abide in God'" (*1 Jn* 4:16). In this way, he became father to all and inspired the vision of a fraternal society[34] ... In the world of [Saint Francis's] time, bristling with watchtowers and defensive walls, cities were a theatre of brutal wars between powerful families, even as poverty was spreading through the countryside. Yet there Francis was able to welcome true peace into his heart and free himself of the desire to wield power over others ... He became one of the poor and sought to live in harmony with all. Francis has inspired these pages. (*Fratelli tutti*, section 4)

And not just in terms of a general sweep. The particulars of the pope's time call out for the proto-Francis's spiritual remedies. The bold and dangerous initiative of Francis of Assisi in crossing the borders of Crusaders and Saracens to speak directly with the Sultan al-Malik al-Kamil at Damietta, Egypt, in 1219 serves as a model for dialogue over mutual destruction. Although various hagiographers, biographers, historians, and interreligious specialists debate the specifics of the meeting between sultan and friar, the content of their conversations, the motivations of the players, and the immediate effect of the encounter, the authoritative sources all confirm that such a meeting did take place, and it has been fully integrated into the perduring legend that is Francis.

The witness of the poor man of Umbria then runs through this encyclical with his abiding belief in the common humanity of all, a humanity imperilled by several of our contemporary Thrones and Dominions—and not those of the benign angelic persuasion. His twenty-first-century disciple then is committed to a "new vision of fraternity and social friendship that will not remain at the level of words." Like Francis of Assisi, who is alleged to have said "preach the Gospel always and, if necessary, use words," Pope Francis is emboldened to do likewise. But first, the words. Lots of words.

Fratelli tutti denounces all instances of "myopic, extremist, resentful and aggressive nationalism," of a "massified world that promotes individual interests and weakens the communitarian dimension of life," of a politics that promotes "slick marketing techniques primarily aimed at discrediting others," of a cultural mindset that builds walls consigning those who erect them to "end up as slaves ... left without horizons [and lacking] interchange with others," and of a Catholic media where "limits can be overstepped, defamation and slander can become commonplace, and all ethical standards and respect for the good name of others can be abandoned."

Certainly, on this latter point Francis is being personal. Yet, the thrust of his letter is not a private apologia or even a fiercely expressed polemic against the dark forces of the world but an impassioned plea to listen to the other and to enter into solidarity without bracketing and reservation because "Service is never ideological, for we do not serve ideas, we serve people." When people become abstractions, theories supplant visceral connectedness, and tyrannies take root.

A central leitmotif that runs through *Fratelli tutti* and is found in the early Bergoglio as well is his commitment to dialogue at any price: as he says in an earlier publication in 2020, *Querida Amazonia* (Beloved Amazonia), which he quotes in *Fratelli tutti*: "our own cultural identity is strengthened and enriched as a result of dialogue with those unlike ourselves. Nor is our authentic identity preserved by an impoverished isolation."

Much of this is, of course, papal boilerplate. His immediate predecessors have made similar arguments—without the folksy style and pockets of informality. What makes *Fratelli tutti* original is the pope's direct assault on the purveyors of a false notion of what we mean by the people, those populists who have suborned the true meaning of "popular."

For sure, many political leaders at the time of the encyclical's appearance would fall under Francis's judgment, such as Rodrigo Duterte (Philippines), Nicolás Maduro (Venezuela), and Viktor Orbán (Hungary)—but only the US president of the time manages to be at the very top of Francis's lament of morally impoverished leaders. Donald Trump's philosophy of personal and political success is unabashedly Manichaean: there are, as his father, Fred, drilled into him, only killers and zeros, winners and losers. But when the pope speaks of what he calls "political love," by which he means "a lofty form of charity that ennobles [one's] political activity," it is impossible to see the Trumpian *modus operandi*.[35]

The encyclical, then, is a substantive examination of humanity's desperate need for meaningful connection, for a human communion built on a notion of what it is to be a people that is not reducible to either a logical or mystical category but a lived reality grounded in a "shared identity arising from social and cultural bonds. And that is not something automatic, but rather a slow, difficult process," a long-term process of humanization, as a fellow Jesuit, the scientist Pierre Teilhard de Chardin, might describe it.

But Francis does not simply call out the failings of political leaders and the inadequacies of political systems, no matter how glaring and egregious. He also calls on his own church to do more than issue words; he calls on the church to act boldly. When speaking of the various economic and military means by which we eliminate others, he identifies one way that is not aimed at nations but at individual citizens: "It is the death penalty. Saint John Paul II stated clearly and firmly that the death penalty is inadequate from a moral standpoint and no longer necessary from that of penal justice. There can be no stepping back from this position. Today we state clearly that 'the death penalty is inadmissible' and the Church is firmly committed to calling for its abolition worldwide" (*Fratelli tutti*, section 263).

Although teaching had evolved on the use of the death penalty from John Paul II's provisional condemnation to the changes made to the official *Catechism of the Catholic Church* in 2018 adumbrating the position now vigorously declared by Francis, the pope spends several pages outlining the history of the church's teaching, the false reasoning of governments that maintain the death penalty, and the need for its abolition. In fact, he goes further and identifies a life sentence as a "secret death penalty."

Bergoglio is not intimidated by tradition; he is in dialogue with it. In his mind, that is why tradition lives: because it refuses to be entombed by custom, archaic habits of thought, and the insulating power of fear.

The personalities, intellectual forces, and historical exigencies of his time, the "makers of Pope Francis," whether historical models, icons of holiness, or thinkers, prepare him to attend on the Spirit, to unearth the deep sources of renewal at the heart of the Second Vatican Council, and to make them guideposts for a future *ecclesia* birthed in the heart of God and quickened in our time for a humanity aching for harmony and joy.

"WHO AM I TO JUDGE?"

Francis and the Sex Wars

"TICKING PEOPLE OFF WON'T achieve anything and neither will prohibitions or regulations. Our Church must become humbler, more modest, more honest and more transparent ... We must understand and share people's worries and not just recite Church teaching and the Catechism from the balcony." These words sound perfectly Bergoglian in their tone and disposition. But it was not Francis who uttered them, although without Francis they would not have been possible. It was no less a figure than the new Bishop of Chur, Switzerland, Joseph Maria Bonnemain, a physician and canon lawyer, who spoke of his new diocese needing therapy. At his installation as bishop on March 19, 2021, the readings and blessings were proclaimed and spoken by women, other Christian denominations were represented, and a number of male and female prostitutes from Zürich were in attendance. Talk about ticking people off. Nothing gets the Roman Catholic Church's knickers in a knot faster than sexual matters, specifically same-sex matters.

Official Roman Catholic teaching on homosexuality, homo-sexual relations, the very nature of homosexuality itself, is not exactly a subtle matter. Until recently, that is.

Vatican decrees on homosexual behaviour have been consistently clear and categorical. Documents such as the Congregation for the Doctrine of the Faith's *Declaration on Certain Questions Concerning Sexual Ethics* (December 29, 1975) and the same Congregation's later decree *Letter to the Bishops of the Catholic Church on the Pastoral Care of Homosexual Persons* (October 1, 1986) speak of individual homosexual actions as "deprived of their essential and indispensable finality" and state that although "the particular inclination of the homosexual person is not a sin, it is more or less a strong tendency ordered toward an intrinsic moral evil; and thus the inclination itself must be seen as an objective disorder."

Although the *Catechism of the Catholic Church* and several pastoral documents issued by various Catholic hierarchies throughout the world sought to mitigate the harsh language of these official decrees with their clinical, cold, canonical tone by adopting a more directly pastoral and sympathetic approach, no one was left in any doubt about the absolutist judgment contained in the Vatican documents.

There was a chasm between the LGBTQ+ community and Catholicism that seemed unbridgeable. As Jesuit writer and justice activist James Martin has noted in his groundbreaking book, *Building a Bridge: How the Catholic Church and the LGBT Community Can Enter into a Relationship of Respect, Compassion, and Sensitivity*, the tensions that often arise between the church and its LGBTQ+ members are the result of poor communication, if any at all, and of a history of mistrust specifically with the hierarchy. A bridge needs to be erected.[1]

That bridge would prove to be the *pontifex maximus* himself, Francis, the Great Bridge-Builder.[2] On a plane trip returning from a World Youth Day extravaganza in Brazil in July 2013, when asked by a reporter about gay priests, the pope responded: "If a person is gay and seeks God and has good will, who am I to judge?" It was one of his first press scrums; his very use of the word "gay" itself was a first for popes. It was clear to the world only a few months into this pontificate that this pope was cut from a different cloth.

And more was to come.

In an interview with fellow Jesuit Antonio Spadaro the following August, Francis expanded on the comments he'd made earlier, fully aware that they had created a whirlwind of media commentary, prelatical befuddlement, and wild expectations of papal reversals. He makes clear his notion of the church as a "field hospital," an ecclesial trope that runs through all his preaching and spirituality, and in that context situates the healing ministry of the church:

> In Buenos Aires I used to receive letters from homosexual persons who are "socially wounded" because they tell me that they feel like the church has always condemned them. But the church does not want to do this ... Religion has the right to express its opinion in the service of the people, but God has set us free: it is *not* possible to interfere spiritually in the life of a person ... I was once asked, in a provocative manner, if I approved of homosexuality. I replied with another question: "Tell me, when God looks at a gay person, does he endorse

the existence of this person with love or reject and condemn this person?" In life, God accompanies persons, and we must accompany them, starting from their situation and it is necessary to accompany them with mercy.[3]

How the church deals with gays is determined in great measure by the cultural and political context in which it finds itself securely implanted, or in some cases not so securely implanted. For instance, the church in Italy, the pope's own home base, provides a dramatic case of colliding priorities. The church has always been a powerful player in Italian culture, shaping political policies, working behind the scenes to ensure its institutional goals, nicely poised at the nexus of the country's history. And all of this in spite of the country's notoriously endemic anti-clericalism, the residual hostilities by a political left cognizant of the church's past alliance with Fascism, even if only temporary, and an intelligentsia and artist community resistant to the old order. The church in Italy as well as the Vatican—and they remain discrete entities although enjoying a unique historical connection—have to continually negotiate between the conflicting struggles of the civil rights movements and long-established religious norms.

As religion scholar Giulia Evolvi wryly comments:

Pope Francis does not want to judge homosexuals, but the debate around LGBTQ rights in Italy often includes such judgments. Atheist groups judge homosexuals as marginalized because of their lack of civil rights. Certain Catholic groups judge them to be unhappy because they cannot conform to the principles of the traditional family. The LGBTQ debate in Italy is often intertwined with the rejection or endorsement of Catholic values, which inevitably leads to people passing judgment.[4]

Getting people not to judge is a Sisyphean task even for a pope. Maybe especially for a pope, given the wide perception in most quarters that that is precisely what popes do: *judge*!

Although societal, medical, and cultural attitudes toward homosexuality have changed in many political jurisdictions, these shifts are a recent development. Controversies rage ferocious and uncontained in many African and Asian countries, with severe penalties for any gay activity or advocacy; legislation ensuring gay civil rights is vigorously contested in some Western democracies; mainstream established religions wrestle with sanctions against gays found in their traditions, doctrines, and pastoral practices; and many spiritual leaders are agog and aflutter when institutional hypocrisies around covert gay behaviour are publicly revealed. Not a few US televangelists, Episcopal bishops, and members of Catholic religious orders have been dramatically outed.

It is not surprising, then, that the Roman Catholic Church would find itself at the centre of a great deal of media attention concerning its authoritative positions around gay genital activity, gay orientation, gay marriage, and queer theology. The papacy of John Paul II was mostly about doctrinal orthodoxy in an age of moral relativism, prompting the pope to issue *monita* or warnings, apostolic exhortations, and encyclicals trying to steady the church's moral teaching in an organic and traditional way in a sea of theological and ethical turbulence. John Paul II's teaching on gender, sexual complementarity, and the specific roles accorded women by nature and Christian tradition, calling for a "culture of life" to challenge the growing prevalence of a "culture of death," found focused expression in both his encyclical *Evangelium vitae* (The Gospel of Life: On the Value and Inviolability of Human Life) and his *Theology of the Body*, a composite of over a hundred lectures on human sexuality.

Benedict XVI, John Paul's successor, was of like mind when it came to the biblical anthropology that undergirds the church's teaching on sexuality, a teaching that was firmly rooted in its centuries-shaped understanding of natural law. But it never became a high priority for the cerebral Benedict. He had other philosophical and theological fish to fry: nothing less than reclaiming Europe for Christianity and tackling head-on the post-Enlightenment philosophies that he viewed from his perch on the Tiber as ultimately anti-human in their thrust to celebrate the human divorced from the Transcendent. He rejected the facile opposition of faith and reason, and he articulated Catholic truth with a certainty that was unflappable and titanic in its intellectual self-assurance. David Gibson presciently outlined the need for a pope who would redress the rigidities of the Benedictine era before the opportunity for a new pope became necessary. That happened, as noted earlier, on February 28, 2013, when the 266th pope shocked the world by tendering his resignation.

Gibson had written of the Benedictine papacy with a great deal of sympathy and understanding but with strong reservations over the direction Benedict was taking the church. It was drifting too far from the spirit of *ressourcement* and *aggiornamento*, the dual legacy of the Second Vatican Council, and it was time to reclaim the momentum and genius of that council. To that end, an evangelical Catholicism was required and, as Gibson writes in *The Rule of Benedict: Pope Benedict XVI and His Battle with the Modern World*, an evangelical Catholicism is dependent on there being an evangelical pope as they are inextricably linked, a shared witness to the Good News proclaimed by the carpenter's son.[5]

Some six years after writing this, Gibson would have his evangelical pope. And no one would see this coming.

Benedict's pontificate was short-lived—seven years, ten months, and nine days—in sharp contrast with his immediate predecessor, John Paul II, whose reign of twenty-six years, five months, and fifteen days was one of the longest in history. There was no reason to think that Benedict would not be in it for the long haul. Of delicate health, but far from fragile, Benedict was made of sturdy stuff—intellectually formidable, strong-willed, aesthetically cultivated, and much accustomed to how things worked. He had, after all, been the Grand Inquisitor for the majority of John Paul's papacy. He could be hard nosed, but he was not thick skinned. He bristled under criticism.

His pontificate was not a smooth one. Controversies roiled the church he governed; he was personally pained by what he saw as episcopal disloyalty, and he was a leader who attached high importance to personal loyalty. He frequently rewarded his allies with promotions. He wrote a public letter to his brother bishops lamenting the harsh judgment levelled at him because he chose to lift the excommunications imposed on the apostate bishops of the Society of Saint Pius X—a divisive and schismatic group opposed to the teachings of the Second Vatican Council that Benedict laboured to bring into Roman communion—but the communication of this development failed to take into account that one of these bishops, the Cambridge-educated Richard Williamson, was an ardent anti-Semite. The fallout was immediate and devastating for Benedict. He was caught unawares; his own team failed him by failing to do due diligence.

He anticipated criticism from secular quarters during his papacy, but he did not expect it from those in the episcopacy. He found that hard to bear, and it grew increasingly vocal. And then, during the penultimate year of his pontificate, his own *annus horribilis*, he had to face the massive damage created to the reputation of the church because of Vatileaks, the in-house revelations of sexual and fiscal impropriety of near–Reformation era proportions. All this compounded by the fact, as noted earlier, that these disclosures were the result of the personal betrayal of his butler, Paulo Gabriele, who admitted to stealing private Vatican documents ostensibly on the grounds that their exposure of deep corruption in the Holy See needed airing *precisely* to protect the pope, as he was unaware of the rot around him. Regardless of the credibility of this argument, Gabriele's theft triggered the pope's end days.

Dispirited, Benedict, unlike John Paul, was not disposed by temperament or physical constitution for robust confrontation. He was not energized by the large crowds and inhuman schedules that fuelled the Polish goliath. He preferred to monitor the faith's integrity and vitality from the quiet corridors of the Holy Office rather than from the majesty of the Apostolic Palace.

Leaving the role of Peter was a relief, a mercy, for Benedict. For the Catholic world, it was a seismic turn of events, tried only once before by Celestine V in the Middle Ages.

What now?

In no small part, it was the turmoil created by the charges of gay sex among Vatican prelates and their subordinates that persuaded Benedict to think of an option to exercising the primacy of Peter. The rumours and realities of cupidity in the Vatican are not new; there is a well-documented history going back for centuries. It is a feature of Vatican life for some—a closeted existence for the saintly as well as a covering for the ambitious—but far from the reality on the ground for most who live and work within the confines of the Vatican. Still, scandal saps credibility.

As one priest from South Carolina, trained at the storied North American College in Rome, and now resigned from active ministry, wrote of his own experience:

> I know the machinations of the Vatican better than most gay men. I lived there for four years in preparation for ordination to the priesthood. In my experience, there is a toxic kind of homosexuality that runs through the Vatican: it is closeted, bitter and hate-filled. Men struggling with their true nature end up either repressing their authentic selves or living double lives. This toxic dysfunction becomes a prism through which many Vatican officials understand gay relationships. I get it. I know what self-hate feels like. It is both tragic and dangerous because that hatred has to go somewhere: it will be either projected outward or it will be turned inward in self-destructive ways. Suicide among priests for this reason is not unknown. When your own church tells you that a fundamental part of your being is intrinsically disordered, why should we be surprised that some people decide that life is not worth living?[6]

Personal confessions of this order are now ubiquitous in Catholic literature on the subject. It is the magnitude of institutional hypocrisy that is the problem. Denunciations of a gay lobby in the Vatican have become a trope deployed by both conservative and progressive Catholics, and although Francis joked that he has never encountered a card-carrying member of such a lobby, he doesn't make light of the personal damage inflicted on those clerics who are at war with their sexuality and are forced to live inauthentically as ministers of sacrament and word.

Benedict had enough of such scandals; his efforts at purifying the Vatican bureaucracy of corruption—venal and venereal—were limited in their effect.

And so along comes Francis.

From the outset of his own ministry, Francis moves to situate the ferociously conflictive issue of gay sexuality, the history of Vatican censure, the constant teaching of the church, clerical double lives, and the damage to the church's own credibility as witness to the mercy of Christ by neither diminishing its seriousness nor framing it as *the* highest priority of the church.

Francis understands the power of symbolism, the substantive gesture that speaks loudly but not provocatively. A perfect example of this Bergoglian way of operating can be seen in how he dealt with New Ways Ministry. Founded in 1977 by Jeannine Gramick, a nun, and Robert Nugent, a priest, it was designed as a pastoral outreach to gay Catholics—non-judgmental, supportive, nurturing—but generated Vatican concern about its moral orthodoxy and non-conformist style. The Vatican conducted an investigation of Gramick's ministry, and she was instructed to cease her work. She switched religious congregations, moving from the School Sisters of Notre Dame to the Loretto Sisters, skillfully dodged the inquisitor's bullet again and again in spite of pressure to bring her LGBTQ+ ministry to an end, and was honoured by the Association of US Catholic Priests for her bravery and bold witness. Then Francis wrote personally to New Ways Ministry, bringing an end to the Vatican's investigations, praising Gramick's work and describing her as a "valiant woman."[7]

Although Francis's approach is not to repudiate official teaching but to open it to the light of deeper inspection, doing what Vatican correspondent Christopher Lamb identifies as an opening, an aperture to an understanding grounded in humility: "Time, as Francis says, is greater than space, and reality is more important than ideas. The critical test for a doctrine is how it is received by the Church's community, and the Pope's response opens up for us a space for the conversation to continue."[8]

To his critics, such thinking is woolly and weaselly, averse as it is to clear and organic teaching, a false irenicism, building on a plank that cannot withstand close scrutiny. The teaching for these critics is firm, intelligible, unfaltering. Francis doesn't contest the truth of traditional teaching; what he does is refuse to encase it in categories resistant to the changing reality of human life. Simply put, he prefers an existential as opposed to a metaphysical ethics, and that is why he will not foreclose discussion. To be fully human is to be open to the risks and demands of evolving circumstances. Retreat from the world, from its joys and sorrows, isn't a pastoral strategy that speaks to him.

He hears in his heart the ardent cry of those struggling sexually to live their lives of faith in a religious milieu that is unwelcoming at best, imposing a code of silence, a tacit understating that what is irreconcilable is best kept mute and secluded. An ecclesiastical variant of US president Bill Clinton's "Don't ask, don't tell." That kind of morally duplicitous accommodation may once have worked but increasingly has little remaining political capital. Catholic same-sex counsellor, chaplain, high school administrator, and self-identified lesbian Joan Grundy has decades of experience to offer Catholic LGBTQ+

youth. She has done so in a public letter, showing that the Bergoglian pastoral approach has currency in many Catholic education circles:

> I have worked with a number of LGBTQ+ Catholic teens who have interpreted the church's teachings against same-sex relationships as God turning His/Her back on them. They equated their spirituality (personal relationship with God) with their religion (formalized expression of their spirituality) and therefore, when they felt rejected by their church, they felt rejected by their God ... So, if you only remember one thing you have read here, let it be this: You are precious in God's eyes. Celebrate the wonderfully created human being that you are. Never ever apologize for who you are, and how you love.[9]

It is the matter of "how you love" that is the nub of the moral quandary facing Rome. That all humans are loved into existence by God, and unconditionally so, is not a disputable theological maxim. The church recognizes and celebrates God's gratuitousness, God's unbounded generosity. But there are, nonetheless, human bounds that are dictated by the laws of nature and of divine revelation. Previous popes were satisfied to draw on these unvarying sources of truth and tradition, cognizant that a good number of believers would be reluctantly compliant, but still knowing that when deviating from God's path, the church would be there for them, reconciling and absolving. And the teachings and the rules would remain in place—of that, there would be no doubt.

Francis, however, recognizes that the church's rote response to the many moral issues facing contemporary persons in their lives as sexual beings is not only insufficient but a source of growing alienation. He called for a Synod on the Family in 2014—an Extraordinary synod falling outside the standard cycle of every four years—and he ushered in many major fundamental changes to the way a synod operates: he insisted that the bishop-delegates representing all the various jurisdictions of the global church speak their minds unhampered by fear and spiritual timidity. This in itself was a tall order, given the straitjacket approach of the previous popes—most especially John Paul II—who controlled the agenda, the process, and the results of each synod during his papacy.

The synod was spread over two years—a hitherto unprecedented decision. It tackled many of the neuralgic issues plaguing the church and in a way that was uncharacteristically open. Francis knew the risks he was taking so early in his pontificate but would not be thwarted; it was time to be daring:

> The Pope himself last year pointed out that a consultative body where everyone agreed served little purpose. He need not have worried because as we come down to the wire a second time round, it is very clear that not everyone is in agreement. In an April interview with the online Italian publication, *La Nuova Bussola*, Cardinal [Raymond] Burke raked over the old coals when he complained of "forces pushing a gay agenda" in relation to the Synod ... In the meantime what are we to read into a one-day study meeting in May at the Pontifical Gregorian University, hosted by the Presidents of the Bishops Conferences of Germany, Switzerland, and France, namely Cardinal Reinhard Marx, Bishop Markus Buchel and Archbishop Georges Pontier? Around fifty people ... took part in a meeting which appears to have considered "pastoral innovations" in relation to the upcoming Synod,

including how the Church might better welcome those in stable same-sex unions.[10]

Changes in church practice and thinking were not imminent, but what was happening—and this in itself Francis's critics understood fully—was that an opening was being created that would allow the church to move from an apodictic to an inquisitive posture, less dogmatic and more pastoral, a listening and not judging church.

To paraphrase an apposite image coined by journalist Tom Rachman when speaking of government regulatory bodies, the church inches toward updating like caterpillars watching trains pass.

And if this is so on matters of small consequence—rules that can be easily altered without threatening the larger architecture of dogma—changing the institution's thinking on sexual matters could have the caterpillars stationary for centuries.

In *Amoris laetitia*, the 2016 document issued by Francis following the conclusion of the synod after its two-phase deliberations in 2014 and 2015, the pope moved deftly between affirming the traditionalists at the same time that he left open the potential for change in the future.

In a masterful display of Jesuit-like subtlety, perhaps veering a bit too close to sophistry but skillfully navigating some dangerous shoals withal, the Irish Jesuit scholar Gerry O'Hanlon underscores the risks, the necessary risks, involved in addressing contentious issues that will not, cannot, go away:

> One must bear in mind [when considering] contraception, homosexuality, women priests—it is clearly the *teaching* and not just the *practice/discipline* that is in question … for the

issue of doctrinal change is clearly central: if homosexual relationships may be considered natural to those of a homosexual orientation, if women have innate leadership capacities and the findings of the Pontifical Biblical Commission on the non-determinative nature of the Scriptural evidence on the issue of female ordination are respected, then surely it is unjust, lacking in mercy, to burden *conscience* with the discernment of going against a Church teaching which itself seems to require revision.[11]

"Seems to require revision" is a clever theologian's way of phrasing what is self-evident to a Catholic progressive and feared by a Catholic traditionalist. O'Hanlon has read Francis's mind perfectly. Let's not confrontationally throw Catholic teaching into the dustbin of history *or* madly embrace current streams of thought. What is critical is an incremental or gradualist approach to change.

To further highlight the unfolding strategy of warm engagement that Francis sees as essential to building on the lively conversations initiated by the synod and captured in *Amoris laetitia*, he responded, in one of those unscripted news conferences he provides to media personnel travelling on the papal plane, to a question about the Orlando, Florida, gay nightclub shooting that claimed dozens of lives in June 2016. He was asked if the church should apologize or at least bear some responsibility historically for the hatred toward the LGBTQ+ community. He agreed that the church has much to apologize for and that it should apologize to any gay person offended by the behaviour of Catholics, but then proceeded to elaborate that this applies to all those who have been offended by the church: the poor, the exploited, women, et cetera. To some, this appears as a widening and meaningless conflation of the sufferings of the marginalized into one entity. But Francis prefers a different reading. By broadening the discussion to include all those offended, he decentralizes the issue as a gay matter, incorporating the legitimate complaints of gays along with others rather than having them considered as a special subset. In this way he strengthens his pastoral priority by making it inclusive, non-ideological, part of a plan of moral reparation that is not driven by special pleading or by aggressive ecclesiastical lobbyists.

This is very different in kind and tone from the approach of his two immediate predecessors, particularly Benedict XVI. On the occasion of the latter's death on December 31, 2022, John Montague, a Catholic gay activist, retired social worker, and pastoral animator for parents of gay children, wrote to me in a measured way amid the flurry of encomia, bromides, vitriol, and holy waffle that dominated social media outlets following Benedict's death:

> Joseph Ratzinger was no friend of LGBT Catholics. When asked if he ever met a gay person, he is quoted as saying that when Pope John Paul II travelled to Berlin, he took note that some gays were demonstrating. Surrounded as he was in the Vatican by gay clerics, his psychological awareness was myopic. His preoccupation with an abstract theology prevented him from understanding human sexual behaviour in its complexity. Upon hearing of his death, I realize now that this very failure to listen created the vacuum that not only permitted but propelled Francis to promote dialogue and synodality.[12]

Indeed, Francis was propelled to promote dialogue and did so on many occasions in his customary way: instantaneous, unprogrammed, personal, and originating in his conviction that condemnation and admonishment don't work, that we are all sinners, and that our capacity to choose judging over understanding runs counter to the Gospel. In May 2018, the pope met with a Chilean survivor of clerical sex abuse, Juan Carlos Cruz, and told him that "your being gay does not matter. God made you like this and loves you like this and I don't care. The pope loves you like this. You have to be happy with who you are." This is not the language of intrinsic disorder. It goes further than simply saying that the church loves gays but not their condition or orientation. It affirms the right of gay individuals to equal status in the orbit of God's love. It does not approve of gay genital relations, but by overtly claiming that gays are called by God to be happy with who they are, Francis moves the discussion forward. Throughout the synod and after, Francis is committed to moving the church to a new way of thinking about same-sex relations, keeping in mind the sinkhole of inconsistencies that plague many papal texts and at the same time skirting around explicit ruptures with past teaching. No easy feat.

Charles Reid situates Francis's dilemma in the context of the thirty-two years leading up to his election:

Section 2357 of the Catechism of the Catholic Church described homosexual acts … "as contrary to the natural law" and cannot "proceed from a genuine affective and sexual complementarity." On the other hand section 2358 counseled that men and women who experience same-sex attraction "must be accepted with respect, compassion and sensitivity. Every sign of unjust discrimination in their regard should be avoided." The inconsistencies are evident. What is meant by respect or compassion if the experiences of gay persons are denied (how else can one read the denial of "genuine affective and sexual complementarity")? Similarly, what is meant by "unjust discrimination," given that the *Catechism* was published around the same time the Congregation for the Doctrine of the Faith was hinting at the need to retain the old anti-sodomy laws?[13]

In 2020, Evgeny Afineevsky released his documentary *Francesco*. In the film, Francis says that "homosexuals have a right to be part of the family. They are children of God. Nobody should be thrown out or to be made miserable. We have to create a civil union law. I stood up for that." These comments on same-sex unions generated a new tranche of contested positions—Did he say what Afineevsky has him say? Were there selective edits? Is the argument around Vatican advocacy for civil laws legitimating same-sex unions a departure from its previous position on discouraging such state initiatives? Is Francis testing the waters for future Vatican adjustments?—all designed to muddy the waters of the Vatican's position. Is it shifting, but subtly, or is it wobbly and faltering? Or is it another sign of the Bergoglio strategy—opening up hitherto forbidden topics for intelligent, faith-inspired probings, neither junking tradition nor embracing the innovative?

Catholic author Paul Elie nicely encapsulates Francis's approach in his *New Yorker* article "Pope Francis Supports Same-Sex Civil Unions, but the Church Must Do More" when he argues that Francis appears to complicate the church's position rather than further elucidating and defending its continuing relevance by opting for a more incremental approach, what moral theologians conceive of as "gradualism"—that is, the slow adaptation to the call for moral and spiritual perfection, the refining of the virtues, the full engagement with the costs of discipleship. In short, we ache into holiness, our progress a life undertaking. What Francis does is take this model of moral living focused on the individual and their relationship with the church and apply it to the structure of the church itself. As Elie says, "there are good reasons for him to act incrementally, and offhandedly, rather than directly. For one thing, his efforts to advance bold objectives through the formal structures of the papacy—on climate change, immigration, or income inequality—have met with something less than acclamation from the Catholic populace. For another, the Church's understanding of LGBTQ people can't simply be changed by papal decree."[14]

Therein lies the Bergoglio quandary: how to move forward, indirectly advancing ideas that are overtly threatening to traditional teaching without formally abandoning such teaching. This leaves the pope open to the charge that his Jesuitical approach is hostile to orthodox teaching and that he is being duplicitous in his pastoral leadership.

In many ways, *Francesco* underscored the papal Scylla and Charybdis dilemma faced by the pope: alienate the marginalized Catholics he wants to bring home, or alienate traditionalist Catholics who adhere to a long-standing biblical anthropology and are not disposed to entertain any compromises. And the tensions tighten.

In 2010, my co-author, CBC producer and lawyer Peter Kavanagh, and I were attending an event sponsored by the International Federation of Catholic Universities at a pontifical university in Rome. We travelled separately. When Peter arrived, he told me of an incident that happened upon arrival at Frankfurt that illustrates the challenges faced by gay Catholics who struggle to reconcile the seemingly irreconcilable.

While waiting for his luggage, Peter overheard a conversation between a middle-aged Californian who was flirting with a Lufthansa pilot. In Peter's telling, she was quite importunate, prompting the increasingly uncomfortable pilot to disclose that he *both* was a practising Catholic and had a husband. Dumbfounded, she asked how that could be possible. He responded, "In the eyes of the state I am married; in the eyes of the church, I am not. But that is a conversation between my church and me."

Francis wants to be part of that conversation; he wants to keep it alive. Once again, the church as "field hospital" figures in his strategy of a living rapprochement with marginalized Catholics. The church is the messy place where the broken gather for solace, the maimed are healed, and the abandoned embraced.

This is the heart of the Bergoglio papacy, and gays are a critical constituency requiring special attention and advocacy. They are the subject of ruthless persecution in Russia and in various other post-Soviet satraps, like Belarus. They are increasingly under siege in several African jurisdictions, including Uganda, Nigeria, and Kenya, and even in that self-proclaimed beacon of liberal democracy, the United States. Homophobia is a hydra, most often egregious in expression, but also subtle and invidious. Catholic ecclesiastical authorities, as a universal collectivity, incline to be protectionist, supportive of government measures that suppress or limit what they perceive as a "gay agenda," and they use every social and political prop to maintain the moral status quo. Although the *Catechism of the Catholic Church* and numerous Vatican declarations make it abundantly clear that any form of intimidation, persecution, or restriction imposed on the gay community is to be vigorously and consistently denounced, the Catholic magisterium has yet to move beyond its fundamental opposition to a sexuality it considers *contra naturam*.

I recall an incident when I was on the executive of the Association of Catholic Colleges and Universities in Canada when my colleagues and I met with the papal nuncio, Luigi Ventura, and some of his senior clerical staff for dinner and conversation in his sumptuous residence. Courteous, inquiring, and engaging, Ventura welcomed us to an open evening of chat and his preferred beverage. Every inch the classic Roman-trained diplomat.

One of Ventura's staff, whom the presidents of the universities subsequently dubbed Monsignor Rottweiler, had a somewhat less cordial approach. He admonished us for presiding over institutions that were awash in homoerotic libertinism. For those of us at the table where the crazed monsignor fulminated, this was more than unsettling. It was an irrational eruption of bile.

Ironically, the monsignor's boss, Ventura, was subsequently sent from Ottawa to the apex of papal nunciatures, Paris, where he was ultimately recalled as a result of a charge of sexual moles-tation against a male city official. Shortly after the Vatican lifted his diplomatic immunity, the nunciature in Ottawa confirmed that it had received a complaint of sexual misconduct during his tenure in Canada as well. It would appear that the monsignor's moral tirade missed its target.

This world of presbyteral hypocrisy, a world in which profes-sional clerics live double lives, is frequently employed as an argument for the inefficacy of imposed celibacy but also the contradictions at the very core of Catholic morality. Francis knows this world—its moral imperfections, pharisaic flaws, institutional fissures—and is only too familiar with various disclosures, reports, publications, and investigations that have highlighted the persistence of a Vatican gay lobby. He refutes the existence of such—yet another conspiracy phantasm—but he does concede the existence of subcultures in clerical ranks that permit or even rationalize departures from chastity, just as there are groups of prelates keen on preserving their Renaissance-like dignities and privileges in defiance of his call for a witness of evangelical poverty. He is a stern critic of moral lapses—venereal and venal—by those who profess a self-righteous posture and quickly judge others. In other words, the very religious leaders Jesus himself berated for their judgmentalism.

Francis remarked to the British comedian Stephen Amos, who was in Rome for a BBC documentary, that discriminating against gays because of their sexuality was to misplace the emphasis, choosing the adjective "gay" over the noun or person: "there are people who prefer to select or discard people because of the adjective. These people don't have a human heart." So much for Monsignor Rottweiler.

The tightrope that Francis walks has very little in the nature of a safety net. He is disposed pastorally to the position of the self-confessed gay priest-theologian James Alison when he argues that we need to move on from "tantrum teaching," whereby he means the kind of moral absolutism we identify with petulant infants, to a "wisdom teaching" that opens us up to "the reality of what is ... Only a theological anthropology of learning that accompanies how we do, in fact, learn can help with this. Not one which demands a series of deductions from presumed first principles, and then discards the bits of reality which don't fit."[15]

But he is also obligated, by virtue of his position as Successor of Peter, to uphold and not weaken Catholic teaching and to that end be clear about what is and what is not allowable, reality be damned. Shifting the emphasis from doctrinal to pastoral involves a choreography of gesture and content that Francis hasn't quite perfected yet. But what he is doing, in the words of the Stanford-educated political scientist and Bishop of San Diego, California, Cardinal Robert McElroy, is to insert into Catholic moral decision making a much-needed equipoise wherein the "pastoral cannot be eclipsed by doctrine. For the pastoral ministry of Jesus Christ stands at the heart of any balanced understanding of the church that we are called to be. And pastoral authenticity is as important as philosophical authenticity or authenticity in law in contouring the life of the church to the charter our Lord himself has given to us."[16]

McElroy understands what Francis is labouring to achieve. One specific moment that highlighted that effort on the pope's part to contour "the life of the church to the charter of our Lord" could be found in his wading into the rough seas of same-sex blessings.

In an effort to address the worries of numerous bishops and canonists that blessing same-sex couples could be seen as analogous to nuptial blessings for straight couples and thereby compromise the sacrament of marriage itself, on March 15, 2021, the Congregation for the Doctrine of the Church issued a ruling that

> it is not licit to impart a blessing on relationships, or partnerships, even stable, that involve sexual activity outside of marriage (i.e., outside the indissoluble union of a man and a women open itself to the transmission of life), as is the case of the unions between persons of the same sex. The

presence in such relationships of positive elements, which are in themselves to be valued and appreciated, cannot justify these relationships and render them legitimate objects of an ecclesial blessing, since the positive elements exist within the context of a union not ordered to the Creator's plan.

Undoubtedly designed to calm the waters whipped up by the pope's "Who am I to judge?" his generous reception accorded gay Catholics and his frankness in the *Francesco* documentary by the openly gay Bergogliophile Evgeny Afineevsky, in which he said that "homosexuals have a right to be part of a family," the ruling created a frenzy of disappointed, puzzled, and hostile responses.

Theologian Paul Lakeland captured the mood and primary objection to the ruling—its inherent contradictoriness—when he wrote:

> it seems pretty clear that what makes sex sinful is not the absence of sacramental marriage but the absence of love. If the Church wishes to continue to insist that same-sex unions are not candidates for sacramental marriage, that is the Church's prerogative, though that does not make it in itself a correct judgement. But it is absolutely unacceptable that any loving relationship be declared beyond God's blessing. The Church evidently believes that God blesses all individuals, gay and straight alike, made in the divine image and likeness. But apparently not the former if they enter into a loving relationship. How crazy is that?[17]

Many episcopal jurisdictions have indeed thought it crazy. As a consequence, they have allowed for the continuance or commencement of priests blessing same-sex unions in various German and Flemish dioceses, hundreds of theologians signed a protest letter deploring the Congregation's lack of scientific insights, and the pope was left trying to reconcile his signing off on the ruling—presented to him by fellow Jesuit and Prefect Cardinal Luis Ladaria for his official approval—with his own pastoral predilections.

Journalists, gay Catholics, and the Francis-friendly faithful suddenly found themselves whiplashed by a seeming reversal of priorities. Love homosexuals but don't bless their love. Recognize their right to be a family but declare unequivocally that their union is not ordered according to God's plan of Creation. And so, scrambling for an explanation, for some kind of justification for the timing and the content of the ruling, many Vatican insiders—opting for anonymity—and many Vatican commentators desperate for a coherent narrative took solace in the Angelus address given by the pope just after the release of the ruling. Speaking to the multitudes gathered in St. Peter's Square for his weekly Wednesday blessing and homily, Francis underscored the centrality of "sowing seeds of love, not with fleeting words but through concrete, simple and courageous examples, not with theoretical condemnations, but with gestures of love. Then the Lord, with his grace, makes us bear fruit, even when the soil is dry due to misunderstandings, difficulty or persecution, or claims of legalism or clerical moralism."[18]

Was this Wednesday address designed in some way as a corrective to the legalism and clerical moralism exhibited by the ruling, as some have suggested, a subtle exercise in Jesuit-like reasoning for the sympathetic, or another instance of Jesuitical flummery in the eyes of the wary?

To date, it was Francis's trickiest tightrope challenge, and it was not managed with his customary frankness mingled with adroitness. It fed the disaffected with the fuel they needed to question the integrity and the future of this pope, and it created disquiet among his core admirers as they feared the proliferation of double messages around gays, their sexuality, and their full inclusion into sacramental life. But this casuistry would change, and the pastoral approach of Francis would become increasingly normative.[19]

Francis, however, has been less than progressive in his views regarding gay sexuality and seminaries. Given the flood of scandals occasioned by the publication of various writers and commentators chronicling the variety and volume of sexual improprieties in the Vatican—some of this literature is nothing short of paparazzi-driven drivel, some is conveniently speculative, but much is the result of empirically verifiable journalism—and given the continuing aftershocks of Vatileaks, Benedict's butler escapades, and the relentless criticism in conservative Catholic circles that the reason for the proliferation of clerical sex abuse is attributable directly to the "gayification" of the seminaries in the 1970s, it is not surprising that Francis would try to impose some consistent message of institutional correction.

But he didn't get it quite right.

In a book-length interview in his native Spanish with a Claretian editor published in Madrid in 2018,[20] which preceded the controversies around the 2020 documentary and the same-sex union blessings, Francis made clear his abomination of those who compromised their ministry by living double lives. He unequivocally upheld the discipline of mandatory celibacy for the priesthood, although subsequent interviews and addresses by him would allow for possible relaxation of the rules if regional episcopal conferences were to petition Rome for exceptions for the ordination of mature married men, the *viri probati*, in light of a severe dearth of available clergy to meet the sacramental needs of their respective churches.

The passage in the Claretian interview that provoked controversy was not around the legal requirement of celibacy but rather his opinion that those with an "ingrained tendency" toward homoerotic affection "should not be accepted into the ministry or consecrated life."

In the interview, Francis recounted anecdotal evidence drawn from bishops and heads of religious orders who were seemingly perplexed by the number of gays in their charge. He observed that "the issue of homosexuality is a very serious issue that must be adequately discerned from the beginning with the candidates" for both priestly and religious life. He urged homosexual clergy and men and women religious to be "impeccably responsible" and to try never to scandalize "their communities or the faithful holy people of God by living a double life." In addition, he exhorted those in charge of formation to recognize the limits of what can be tolerated and to ensure that when there are applicants "with neurosis, [who have] marked imbalances [that are] difficult to channel not even with therapeutic help, they shouldn't be accepted to either the priesthood or the religious life."

Francis's approach, although desperately remedial in light of the deluge of abuse scandals, is entrenched in traditional clerical attitudes regarding homosexuals—their promiscuous behaviour, their capacity to disrupt community harmony, their embedded neuroses, their narcissism. To that end, his observations are grounded in pre-scientific assumptions, prejudices, and fears that work against the creation of a healthy and emotionally integrated workforce for the church. In many ways, Francis is simply implementing the thinking that emerged from a 2005 Vatican document by the then Congregation for Catholic Education titled *An Instruction Concerning the Criteria for the Discernment of Vocations with Regard to Persons with Homosexual Tendencies in View of Their Admission to the Seminary and to Holy Orders*. One professor serving in a major Canadian seminary at the time, and who has requested anonymity, told me that the faculty were convulsed by the document and its impact on both seminarians and their priestly instructors. He explained,

> More and more, the students we received at the seminary were disciples of John Paul II's "Theology of the Body," with its emphasis on complementarity of the sexes, its unbending traditional reading of the natural law theory, its vigorous reaffirmation of the teaching of *Humanae vitae* with its opposition to all forms of artificial birth regulation, as well as its explicit rejection of any legitimization of homosexuality or same-sex relationships which combined to create an often adversarial atmosphere in the seminary. At the same time the document appeared, Canada became one of the first countries to legalize same-sex marriage under, ironically, its observant Catholic prime minister, Paul Martin. Many of the seminarians saw this as the opening salvo of a battle for the soul of Canada in which they were engaged and which only the Theology of the Body could adequately answer.

The battle lines were drawn. The most sensitive and pastoral of seminary faculty found themselves walking on hot coals. Subsequent directions from Rome compounded the difficulties of working in an environment in which gays were being identified as the source of the clerical sex abuse scandals and Catholic morality was perceived as running amok. The American prelate William Levada, the prefect-elect for the Congregation for the Doctrine of the Faith, and therefore Joseph Ratzinger's successor in the job now that he was elected Benedict XVI, used the occasion of an installation address of the new rector of the North American College in Rome to remind the seminarians that the scriptures define God's love for his people as the love of a husband for his wife. Levada went on to say that because Jesus is the Bridegroom of the church, and because homosexuals desire men and not women and therefore cannot marry, gay priests cannot represent Christ in a female-gendered church. He also lambasted gay priests who, outraged by the 2005 *Instruction*, had self-outed and thereby affirmed the wisdom of the *Instruction* itself.

One of the key shapers of Vatican thinking on the subject at the time was the French priest-psychotherapist Monsignor Tony Anatrella, who wrote that "candidates who present deep-seated homosexual tendencies, that is, an exclusive attraction with regard to persons of the same sex (a structural orientation)—independently of whether or not they've had erotic experiences—may not be admitted to seminaries and to sacred orders." In a bizarre twist of events, this enterprising rigorist, hell-bent on keeping gays out of the priesthood, was involved in his own peculiar "conversion therapy," working with gay seminarians sent to him by various French dioceses with the intention of helping them suppress their homosexuality. One seminarian, who subsequently went public with the *Nederlands Dagblad* in 2006, alleged that Anatrella's therapy included having sex with his male client as a way of curing him of his sexuality. Numerous accusations followed, although church authorities were slow to respond, with André Vingt-Trois, the archbishop of Paris, opening a canonical investigation as late as 2016. His successor, the physician-prelate Michel Aupetit, formally removed Anatrella from priestly ministry in 2018. The Vatican issued its own full suspension of Anatrella's work as a psychotherapist in 2023. Pope Francis was now completely apprised of the evolving scandal, and his thinking on the matter itself had evolved.

But before that evolution there was the scalding precipitated by the Claretian interview, with public reactions that were swift and driven by an emotional as well as moral urgency. Alarmed by the prospect that those who have advocated for a scouring of the seminaries and houses of formation would now be once again emboldened to purge the ministry of gays—those publicly self-confessed and those cloaked in secrecy—critics of Francis's comments deluged the media with their shock, alarm, and outrage.

Francis himself was stunned. Like many prelates, he had concluded that the wide spread of clerical sexual predation was to some degree the result of active gays in church structures. This conviction, still held resolutely in some Catholic quarters, has been totally discredited by extensive research, especially that of the John Jay College of Criminal Justice in New York: it fully demonstrated that there is no correlation between homosexuality and pedophilia, that the number of pedophiles in Catholic clerical life is not disproportionate to other professions, and that celibacy does not cause sexual abuse.[21] There are certainly reasons why clerical sex abuse has flourished in Catholic institutions—including the psycho-sexual maturity of many priests, the role of clericalism in guaranteeing access to victims and ensuring high-level cover-ups, the greater preponderance of young males as prey—but reducing it to the presence of gays in seminaries, the priesthood, and religious life is dangerously simplistic and contrary to the evidence.

Were his strictures to be implemented, someone like the influential spiritual writer, psychologist, and pastor Henri J. M. Nouwen would have been prevented from entering the seminary on the simple grounds that it would have been an unwelcome environment in which sexual self-honesty would have been discouraged. Nouwen, the author of some forty books, an Ivy League professor, a prolific correspondent with multitudes drawn from a broad spectrum of religious beliefs, and a very popular retreat giver, was serious about his own vow of celibacy and the call to be chaste. He lived as authentic a life as one could, replete with turmoils, burdens, and failures, and he struggled to integrate his gay sexuality into his self-understanding and growth in priestly ministry. This ministry was characterized mostly by an extraordinary gift for friendship, a heart marked with an endless capacity for compassion, and a gift for deep spiritual-psychological insight.[22]

And, yet, if Nouwen (who died in 1996 and was a contemporary of Bergoglio prior to his papacy) were to seek admission to a diocesan seminary, or a novitiate operated by a religious order, it is highly likely that he would be discouraged, his presence in the seminary feared as a moral contagion.

This unwanted state of affairs undercuts the pope's call for the presbyterate to be shorn of its isolating and destructive clericalism, with its culture of careerism and entitlement. But how do you change the process of educating future priests—and Francis has addressed many seminary rectors, exhorting them to improve the quality of admission, the quality of the curriculum, the quality of pastoral oversight—when at the same time you foster, even if inadvertently, a hostile environment toward gays? And how do you usher in a new era of transparency in formation when you actually frustrate honesty, reduce intimacy to genital activity, and create an environment of guarded affection and sexual repression?

This is at the heart of Francis's efforts at seminary reform: cultivate a pastoral sensitivity to the marginalized while at the same time harbouring misconceptions around gays, and encouraging a healthy display of emotion while at the same time surveilling the terrain for those with an "ingrained tendency" to same-sex love. It can't work.

Nouwen provided Francis with a model of priestly integrity. He was a man of the Eucharist, a confessor of uncommon attentiveness and empathy, and, most especially, considering Francis's professed priorities, a priest who internalized the call to non-judgment and mercy.

Francis would have known of Nouwen's work—but not of his sexual orientation—through his highly popular books, many translated into Spanish and not a few with a commanding relevance around issues of pastoral leadership, social justice, and contemplation.[23]

Although the Claretian book reflects Francis's thinking around the gay issue and the priesthood in a traditional way—more bureaucratic and regulatory than pastoral—his later encounters with gays, as already chronicled, display a continuing openness to the complexity of the issue and a growing conscientization and sensitivity to the personal and communal ramifications around the church's conventional morality, with its censorious and judgmental attitudes.

Although new guidelines around priestly formation have

emerged from the Dicastery for the Clergy, and they move beyond the replication of an older template with its emphasis on Thomistic formation, gaps remain around the human formation component. The seminary is an inadequate tool for the training of contemporary priests in large measure because it is the womb out of which comes the fully formed cleric. Clericalism, the bane of the priesthood, finds its genesis and gestation in the seminary, an enclosed, all-male setting, buoyed by feelings of exceptionalism and expected privilege. Precisely the kind of environment that runs counter to the Bergoglio efforts to humanize the priesthood, to make it "real" rather than ideal and detached from human commerce. In an address to Calabrian seminarians, their formators and rectors in March of 2023, the pope once again warned the priestly candidates present that they were to avoid the plague of clerical careerism, not to aspire to be "clerical priests who don't know how to knead the clay of our suffering humanity [but] instead to be like Jesus, a sign of the Father's tenderness. It is very sad when you find priests who are functionaries, who have forgotten they are pastors of the people and have turned into state clerics, like those of the French court, le Monsieur l'Abbé."

But such noble calls are often stillborn in the very structure designed to nurture their healthy birth: the seminary. It is similar to squaring the circle when looking to the very institution that creates new clerics to self-erase and then emerge as a new and vital reality in the shaping of new generations of priests in the Francis model, with the "smell of the sheep." And when you add to that the presence in the current structure of gays struggling to avoid detection or living an underground existence, you have a combustible problem.

One way forward can be found in the work of Philip John

Bewley, who argues that Nouwen's phenomenological and pastoral insights around self-availability or *disponibilité* can complement Francis's stumbling but well-meaning efforts to reconnect with queer Catholics:

> For Nouwen, the concept of "self-availability" became the therapeutic means by which homosexual men and women could cultivate a sense of liberation and self-acceptance, and could make right moral decisions for themselves. Only by taking a phenomenological attitude in his pastoral approach to homosexual men and women was Nouwen able to make such a deduction—the very epitome of teaching another as a "living human document" ... The official *Catechism of the Catholic Church* still teaches that homosexuals, by their very nature, are "intrinsically disordered," and that physical expressions of their orientation constitute "acts of depravity" ... Might such words have the capacity (at least in some) to bring about an *indisponible* or non-self-available attitude towards one's sexuality—to the detriment of one's own psychosexual development? As an insult to the core identity of a queer person (which in itself has the potential to affect one's mental health), it certainly does not promote a *disponible* attitude of self-acceptance and integration of one's same-sex orientation into one's own personality ... Undeniably, the Catholic Church itself needs to practice (as an institution) an attitude of *disponibilité*. Only then can the episcopate offer true pastoral outreach towards its own queer members.[24]

Bewley summons the Catholic Church of Francis to undertake a respectful and real *engagement* with its own sizeable gay constituency, its gay clergy, and queer Christians everywhere looking for ways to be reconnected with their faith community. A tall order.

Francis certainly has been apprised of the problems facing gay Catholics, in and out of official ministry, and his efforts have been welcomed by most gay Catholics, although they understandably feel that the pope's *rapprochement*, while genuine and heartfelt, is insufficient.

As the former Benedictine monk, theologian, spiritual writer, Cambridge University academic, and now Anglican priest Luigi Gioia makes clear when speaking of the Church of England's process of learning and discernment around the sacramental validity of same-sex marriages: "In my view, allowing the blessing of same-sex civil marriages is not enough, yet in my experience nothing changes the perception of intractable issues (the ordination of women is another good example) more than incremental steps that take into account the diverse doctrinal sensitivities in the Church, assuage fears, and progressively help people to see things from a different viewpoint."[25]

Although Gioia is speaking explicitly about the Anglican Church and its need to solemnize sacramental marriages for gays—clergy and lay in his adopted church—implicitly, he is challenging the Roman Catholic Church, and Francis in particular, to see the immense value in incrementalism.

Synodality is incrementalism writ large. It is in Francis's understanding of synodality that you see the seeds of potential incrementalism, to the horror of his critics and to the muted exuberance of his admirers.

Synodality, a process of sensitive discernment and full participation by all the constituencies of the church in deciphering God's will for an authentic and harmonious community of faith, argues for the coexistence of different perspectives seeking a deeper unity.

Queer Catholic theologian Andrew Buechel-Rieger of Mount St. Joseph University in Cincinnati discovers that deeper unity when LGBTQ+ Catholics realize in their liturgical identity a rich commonality that transcends all their other identities because

> our unity as Church—as the body of Christ—is rooted in God's activity expressed through the liturgy, not our own. It is not our achievement, nor is it ours to police. Rather, it is ours to live into as a gift given ... Queer or LGBTQ Christians identify differently than many others in the church in terms of our social identities—but our primary identity as members of Christ's body is what holds us together ... I believe Pope Francis is trying to encourage us to remember this reality as we work through the many divisions that exist in the church today. I'll therefore end with words he uses to close his Apostolic Letter *Desiderio desideravi* (2022): "Let us abandon our polemics to listen together to what the Spirit is saying to the Church. Let us safeguard our communion."[26]

Polemics, posturing, and pontificating are the enemies of synodality. It's precisely this widening rift that commands the full attention of the Bishop of Rome, who chooses not to judge but to understand.

THE PEOPLE'S CHAMPION

Francis and the Planet

The common good and human solidarity around environmental issues constitute the ecological game plan laid out in
Francis's 2015 encyclical, *Laudato Si'* (Praise Be to You: On
Care for Our Common Home). The appearance of this papal
letter secures Francis a place among global environmentalists,
including lobbyists and activists who ordinarily would not be
seen associating with a pope or reading papal documents. But
millions have embraced this encyclical not just as one of many
but as *the* strategy for righting our attitudes toward the earth
and all humanity.

In keeping with Saint John Damascene, the eighth-century
monk who once wrote that the "whole earth is a living icon of
the face of God," Francis underscores the sacred at the heart
of planetary matter. And he manifestly holds to the conviction
that humanity, as imperilled by terrestrial ruination as it is,
isn't paralyzed, hopeless, inexorably doomed. This view is in
marked contrast with that of artists like Calvinist filmmaker

Paul Schrader, who announced at a press conference for the debut of his film *First Reformed* at the Venice Film Festival in 2017 that "if you're hopeful about humanity and the planet, you're not paying attention. I don't see humanity outliving this century."

Contra such pessimism—widespread among many who view the world through an apocalyptic lens—Francis's vision is suffused with a life-invigorating hope. He is not unaware of the stark realities that face our collective future; he is not captive to a back-to-the-land romanticism; he is no Luddite; and he has little time for oracular utterances and their empty rhetoric. His bold remedies have garnered not a few critics who see him as dangerous. They include the following, according to Herman Daly, environmental economist and professor emeritus at the University of Maryland School of Public Policy: "Francis 'will be known by the enemies this encyclical makes for him,' among them 'the Heartland Institute, Jeb Bush, Senator James Inhofe, Rush Limbaugh, Rick Santorum.' (Daly could have included the libertarian commentator Greg Gutfeld, who, while discussing *Laudato Si'* on Fox News, characterized Francis as 'the most dangerous person on the planet.')."[1]

Over the years following the release of the encyclical, Francis would gather even more critics drawn from Catholics as well as non-Catholics horrified by the pope's critique of market economics, his seeming deification of nature, his Socialist tendencies, and his apparent departure from papal social doctrine, specifically that of John Paul II.

None of these are legitimate criticisms—more the product of neo-con phantasms than scrupulous scientific analysis—but they are illustrative of the opposition his most popular encyclical generated at the time of publication and since.

As mentioned earlier, Thomas Merton, one of the four moral prophets Francis celebrated when addressing the joint session of Congress during the Obama era, had spoken of the intensifying global crisis in a series of letters published a year before his death in which he highlighted the salient challenges facing us and bemoaned the official church's failed leadership:

> We must not try to prepare for the [new] millennium immolating our living earth, by careless and stupid exploitation for short-term commercial, military, or technological ends which will be paid for by irreparable loss in living species and natural resources. This ecological consciousness can be summed up in the words of Albert Schweitzer: to wit, "life is sacred ... that of plants and animals [as well as that of our] fellow man." And the conservationist Aldo Leopold spoke of a basic "ecological conscience," the source of an ethic that can be stated in the following expansion of the Golden Rule: "A thing is right when it tends to preserve the integrity, stability, and beauty of the biotic community. It is wrong when it tends otherwise." ... The ecological consciousness is not predominant, to put it mildly, in business, in the armed services, in government, in urban and suburban life, in the academy. It tends to receive some notice from humanist philosophers, artists, psychoanalysts, poets, conservationists, hippies, etc. I regret to say that it is something about which the Church apparently couldn't care less, at least today. But in the past people like St. Francis of Assisi have stood for it in a primitive sort of way.[2]

The gap in church awareness Merton rightly laments has been greatly offset since his correspondence with Barbara Hubbard and ecological visionary Rachel Carson by the

influential and substantial work of Passionist priest Thomas
Berry, Franciscans Richard Rohr and Ilia Delio, and Notre
Dame Sister Kathleen Deignan, to name the most prominent,
as well as work by John Paul II and Benedict XVI.

But the impact, timeliness, passion, and moral clout of
Laudato Si' are without parallel in Catholic discourse. Not
surprisingly, Francis uses as his spiritual lodestar the very same
friar and poet Merton invoked in his concluding sentence:
Francis of Assisi.

The witness of Francis, the appeal of his nature mysticism,
the enduring popularity of the friar-minstrel himself, his election
of the poor as his premier spiritual priority, and his simplicity
of style have special meaning for the other Francis—Bergoglio.

Although enamoured of the original Franciscan and his
ecological savvy, poetic sensibility, and Gospel-inspired simplicity of life, the other Francis, modern pope and former chemistry
teacher, has taken full advantage of contemporary science to
strengthen his position as an informed commentator on the
earth as our common home.

He comes by it naturally. His own interest in science was
there at the beginning of his life; it was further nurtured in
his friendship and conversations with the biophysicist Rabbi
Abraham Skorka,[3] and it was built into his Jesuit DNA. Jesuits,
after all, have been in the vanguard of scientific study and exploration since their founding. As the Canadian Jesuit forester
John McCarthy notes, quoting the Canadian bishops in their
2018 document *Science and Catholic Faith*: "If Christianity is
against science ... why are 35 craters on the moon named after
Jesuit priests?"

And still counting.

Speaking as a Jesuit scientist, McCarthy reminds us that

the first Jesuit colleges, besides offering the traditional programs in humanities, theology and philosophy, gave special attention to the teaching of mathematics and astronomy. Missionaries to the "new world" became interested in studying the geography, flora and fauna of the Americas, Asia and Africa. Between 1814 and 1970, the Jesuits created a remarkable network of astronomical, meteorological, geomagnetic and seismological observatories on every continent, including in many regions of the world where scientific capacity was in its infancy or simply non-existent. All this to say that the Jesuit scientific tradition has served as a significant nexus of the faith-science dialogue at the service of the Church.[4]

This is Francis's tradition. It isn't foreign to him. He knows the history of his order, an order that includes the likes of Giovanni Riccioli, Johann Deckers, and Albert Curtz, the latter two collaborators of the great astronomer Johannes Kepler; Austrian court astronomer Maximilian Hell and his confreres Joseph Stepling, Christian Mayer, and Johann Metzger; Ignaz Kögler, president of the Tribunal of Astronomy in Peking; as well as recent and current astronomers and astrophysicists George Coyne, Christopher Corbally, Guy Consolmagno, and Adam Hincks.

But it isn't only astronomy in which the Jesuits excel. When I was president of St. Jerome's University, I was approached by two of my mathematics professors, one of whom held a chair of quantum computing at the University of Waterloo, with which St. Jerome's is federated. These professors were flummoxed by a question posed to them by the chancellor of the University of Waterloo, the celebrated co-founder of the BlackBerry smartphone, Mike Lazaridis, who wanted to know why a Catholic university would have a mathematics faculty.

My mathematical colleagues lobbed the question into my court.

I informed the chancellor that in the eighteenth century, the foremost mathematicians in Europe were Italian Jesuits, and that in the early nineteenth century, the continent's premier cryptographers were Jesuits; I chose to leave out mention of the seventeenth-century polymath and devout Blaise Pascal, inventor of the first calculator, because he was a formidable anti-Jesuit. Why complicate things?

This illustrious history of Jesuit science constitutes a major plank on which Francis builds his passion for faith and reason and seeks in the work of professional scientists partners in his own papal mission. Besides his friendship with Rabbi Skorka and the score of scientists working in Jesuit universities and laboratories, Francis can also rely on the diverse expertise to be found in the Pontifical Academy of Sciences. This body consists of eighty scientists of outstanding calibre and reputation who are appointed for life. They operate under "the exalted and direct protection of the Supreme Pontiff" and are elected by the Academicians irrespective of ethnicity, nationality, or political or faith affiliation. Many of them are Nobel Prize laureates.

An august body. And they are the pope's.

So, when it came time for Francis to pen *Laudato Si'*, he had his own private resources: a community of eminent scientists at his exclusive service, and a joint encyclical letter, *Lumen fidei* (The Light of Faith), issued in the first year of his papacy, 2013. Unusual in its authorship, it was the continuation of a work begun by Benedict XVI and brought to fruition by his successor. It contains an unwavering commitment to the role of faith and reason in Catholic life and shows how the light of faith illumines the material world, trusts its inherent order and knows that it calls us to an ever widening path of harmony and understanding. The gaze of science thus benefits from faith: faith encourages the scientist to remain constantly open to reality in all its inexhaustible richness. Faith awakens the critical sense by preventing research from being satisfied with its own formulae and helps it to realize that nature is always greater. By stimulating wonder before the profound mystery of creation, faith broadens the horizons of reason to shed greater light on the world which discloses itself to scientific investigation.[5]

And so, Francis is primed to do the work—the expert consultations, the vast resources available to him in his various congregations or dicasteries, councils, institutes, religious orders spanning the globe with headquarters in Rome, papal ambassadors, the Jesuit network, et cetera, the pertinent readings, the numerous drafts—that would result in *Laudato Si'*. He would bring the "gaze of science" and the "light of faith" to work in unison toward a deeper understanding of the planet's struggle for survival. And offer a way forward.

From the outset, the reader is left in no doubt who the abiding presence is, the spirit that hovers over the composition of the encyclical, as Francis quotes from *Canticle of the Creatures*:

"Laudato Si', mi' Signore—Praise be to you, my Lord." In the words of this beautiful canticle, Saint Francis of Assisi reminds us that our common home is like a sister with whom we share our life and a beautiful mother who opens her arms to embrace us. "Praise be to you, my Lord, through our Sister, Mother Earth, who sustains and governs us, and who produces various fruit with coloured flowers and herbs."

Not only does the pope quote from the Umbrian mendicant at the very beginning of the encyclical, but he identifies his own indebtedness to him:

> I do not want to write this Encyclical without turning to that attractive and compelling figure, whose name I took as my guide and inspiration when I was elected Bishop of Rome. I believe that Saint Francis is the example par excellence of care for the vulnerable and of an integral ecology lived out joyfully and authentically. He is the patron saint of all who study and work in the area of ecology, and he is also much loved by non-Christians. He was particularly concerned for God's creation and for the poor and outcast. He loved, and was deeply loved for his joy, his generous self-giving, his openheartedness. He was a mystic and a pilgrim who lived in simplicity and in wonderful harmony with God, with others, with nature and with himself. He shows us just how inseparable the bond is between concern for nature, justice for the poor, commitment to society, and interior peace.

For both Francis the friar and Francis the pope, all are bound together: "We are not disconnected from the rest of creatures, but joined in a splendid universal communion." How to make this global truth a global reality embedded in the consciousness of individuals, governments, business corporations, as well as religious institutions is the goal of this most Franciscan of papal documents.

First, this bracing fact: "Caring for ecosystems demands far-sightedness, since no one looking for quick and easy profit is truly interested in their preservation ... We can be silent witnesses to terrible injustices if we think that we can obtain significant benefits by making the rest of humanity, present and future, pay the extremely high costs of environmental deterioration."

The papal gauntlet has been cast. Global corporations and their national allies acting with relative impunity, plundering the planet to turbocharge their economies, placating restive investors by enhancing their dividends, and securing their financial futures by holding lesser powers captive to their fiscal juggernaut are now under papal judgment.

No wonder that many CEOs and their neo-liberal underwriters looked on with rising anxiety as this increasingly very popular pope had no reservation naming the culprits of our ecological malaise.

He is not, as many of his critics categorize him, a diehard opponent of capitalism. He understands how it works but is no slave to its shibboleth of "trickle-down economics" and the purported enlightened philanthropy of the global superclasses. The poor are his priority, and their fate is inextricably linked to the defoliation of the planet. They are the human collateral damage of economic policies that deem them of secondary interest. The market is the true god that governs.

But not so, argues the pope from Argentina. Quoting from the Fifth General Conference of the Latin American and Caribbean Bishops and their *Aparecida Document* of 2007, Francis urges us to counter "the interests of economic groups which irrationally demolish sources of life and should not prevail in dealing with natural resources."

Bergoglio was archbishop of Buenos Aires at the time of the 2007 conference, and he served on the committee that drafted the concluding document. He thought at the time that the emphasis many other bishops, particularly those from Amazonia—Brazil, Peru, Bolivia, Ecuador, Colombia, Venezuela, Guyana, Suriname, and French Guiana—placed on the perils faced by Amazonia were excessive.

But then he called in 2017 for a Special synod on Amazonia and things changed utterly. Between Aparecida and Amazonia, between 2007 and 2017, Pope Francis's thinking evolved. As he says in his book-length dialogue with papal biographer Austen Ivereigh,

> After Aparecida, I started to see news stories: for example, the government of a well-known island in the South Pacific bought lands in Samoa to transfer its population there, because in twenty years' time the island will be underwater. Another day, a missionary in the Pacific told me of when he was travelling by boat and saw a tree sticking up from the water. He asked: Was that tree planted in the sea? The man steering the boat told him: No, that was once an island. And so, through many encounters, dialogues, and anecdotes like these my mind was opened ... That was my process: serene and calm ... until I became convinced of the seriousness of the thing ... it was a spiritual experience of the sort Saint Ignatius describes as like drops on a sponge: gentle, silent, but insistent ... I started to see the harmonious unity of humanity and nature, and how humanity's fate is inseparably bound up with our common home.[6]

And so, in his own words, the pope's ecological awareness emerged. Neither ideological nor partisan, he was conscientized by incident, story, dialogue, and reading, all masterfully realized through the Jesuit spiritual alchemy that is Ignatian discernment.

Francis is now primed for action. He has his Pontifical Academy of Sciences, his cohort of consultants, the *Aparecida Document*, and the prophetic ministry of Francis of Assisi.

In "The Gospel of Creation," the second chapter of *Laudato Si'*, Francis distances himself from an approach to the earth that has in no small part contributed to the ravaging of the planet:

> We are not God. The earth was here before us and it has been given to us. This allows us to respond to the charge that Judaeo-Christian thinking, on the basis of the Genesis account which grants man "dominion" over the earth (cf. *Gen* 1:28), has encouraged the unbridled exploitation of nature ... This is not a correct interpretation of the Bible as understood by the Church. Although it is true that we Christians have at times incorrectly interpreted the Scriptures, nowadays we must forcefully reject the notion that our being created in God's image and given dominion over the earth justifies absolute domination over other creatures. The biblical texts are to be read in their context, with an appropriate hermeneutic, recognizing that they tell us to "till and keep" the garden of the world (cf. *Gen* 2:15).

Having forsworn, then, an exegesis that justified for centuries the equivalence of dominion with domination, Francis pursues a critique of technology that draws heavily on his early mentor Romano Guardini, particularly his *The End of the Modern World*, in which the naturalized German theologian-philosopher bemoans the inability of "contemporary man" to use power well, to think of power and its use in terms of utility or security and not in terms of human freedom. Pope Francis includes Guardini's critique of the "technocratic paradigm" in his own thinking about the environment, the relationship of the corporate world with its economic engineers the new priesthood, using technology and its myriad variations to advance a business agenda:

> Since the market tends to promote extreme consumerism in an effort to sell its products, people can easily get caught up in a whirlwind of needless buying and spending. Compulsive consumerism is one example of how the techno-economic paradigm affects individuals. Romano Guardini had already foreseen this: "The gadgets and technics forced upon him by the patterns of machine production and of abstract planning mass man accepts quite simply; they are the forms of life itself. To either a greater or lesser degree mass man is convinced that his conformity is both reasonable and just." This paradigm leads people to believe that they are free as long as they have the supposed freedom to consume. But those really free are the minority who wield economic and financial power. Amid this confusion, postmodern humanity has not yet achieved a new self-awareness capable of offering guidance and direction, and this lack of identity is a source of anxiety. We have too many means and only a few insubstantial ends.[7]

The impact of technology on human self-understanding, on human worth in the black sea of instrumentalist thinking, is the major substratum running through *Laudato Si'*.

The global prevalence of the "techno-economic paradigm" magnifies the need to ensure that life itself is not suborned. Francis writes: "Life gradually becomes a surrender to situations conditioned by technology, itself viewed as the principal key to the meaning of existence. In the concrete situation confronting us, there are a number of symptoms which point to what is wrong, such as environmental degradation, anxiety, a loss of the purpose of life and of community living. Once more we see that 'realities are more important than ideas.'"

Francis's disinclination to rank thinking over doing, ideas over realities—a marked feature of the Ratzinger papacy—first surfaced in official papal literature with his 2013 apostolic exhortation *Evangelii gaudium* (The Joy of the Gospel). The perception that Francis is not a thinker—frequently asserted by his critics as a demeaning assessment intended to stand in sharp contrast with his intellectually formidable predecessors—is a sad caricature. He is quite capable of serious thinking and can rise to the occasion when necessary, but his impulse is always to choose to address things on the ground and as they are rather than as conceptual entities.

An integral human ecology, with its respect for human dignity at every stage, its heightened sense of the connectivity of all Creation, its sensitivity to the unique cultural fabric and diverse systems that constitute the human family, must be an ecology situated in the "common good, a central and unifying principle of social ethics."

Francis is interested in an alternative model to the "techno-economic paradigm," and the common good model serves that purpose with its emphasis on subsidiarity, social peace, the flourishing of the family as the "basic cell of society," and its commitment to distributive justice.

If it was in any way unclear where Francis stood on the liberationist dogma of the "priority of the poor," *Laudato Si'*, in unabashed consistency with *Evangelii gaudium*, affirms his commitment to the poor, irrespective of any theological critique with which he might have some nuanced disagreement. The poor *demand* our attention; in obedience to the Gospel, we have no other option than to respond. Reality supersedes ideation.

> In the present condition of global society, where injustices abound and growing numbers of people are deprived of basic human rights and considered expendable, the principle of the common good immediately becomes, logically and inevitably, a summons to solidarity and a preferential option for the poorest of our brothers and sisters. This option entails recognizing the implications of the universal destination of the world's goods, but, as I mentioned in the Apostolic Exhortation *Evangelii Gaudium*, it demands before all else an appreciation of the immense dignity of the poor in the light of our deepest convictions as believers. We need only look around us to see that, today, this option is in fact an ethical imperative essential for effectively attaining the common good. (section 158)

Putting the pieces together, then, we can see that the common good is indispensable to an integral human ecology and that the preferential option for the poor is indispensable to the common good. This means radical adjustments to our goals: it is not enough to speak sympathetically about the plight of the poor, to exhort governments to build social solidarity, to propound ideas that lack flesh. We need to *act* because the well-being of the poor and the future of the planet are inseparable realities. Governments are naturally indisposed to unravelling their machinery of state, and so a politics of full inclusion must be a *sine qua non* of environmental flourishing. The alternative is calculated stalling with our collective futures—environmental and social—compromised unto death.

A politics concerned with immediate results, supported by consumerist sectors of the population, is driven to produce short-term growth. In response to electoral interests, governments are reluctant to upset the public with measures which could affect the level of consumption or create risks for foreign investment. The myopia of power politics delays the inclusion of a far-sighted environmental agenda within the overall agenda of governments. Thus we forget that "time is greater than space," that we are always more effective when we generate processes rather than holding on to positions of power. True statecraft is manifest when, in difficult times, we uphold high principles and think of the long-term common good. Political powers do not find it easy to assume this duty in the work of nation-building. (section 178)

This maxim of "time is greater than space" first appeared in *Evangelii gaudium* and is shorthand for a papacy of reform: when Francis prioritizes process over position, he is speaking not only of the need for serious political and social reform—the exterior entities (*ad extra*)—but of ecclesial reform as well— the interior entity (*ad intra*). The Jesuit Disruptor's ambitious agenda, his theological strategy, entails more than a new integral human ecology; it entails a new ecclesial ecology. In fact, they are intimately linked.

These take time; they are grounded in processes that enable dialogue and freedom to help the human community pivot toward a deeper humanism, an integrated spirituality. And the umbrella term for this Francis will call *synodality*. More of this in a later chapter.

Of special need of radical restructuring in our environment-threatened geopolitical universe is the market and its ready companion the banking system. Their tentacles of control and regulation embrace every nation—from democratic to autocratic and everything in between—and their abuses cry out for correction.[8]

In concluding *Laudato Si'*, Francis invokes Bernard Lonergan's notion of conversion: intellectual, moral, and religious. It is connected to his concept of horizon and firmly roots Francis's efforts to situate serious climate change in a philosophical-theological framework:

> In its literal sense the word "horizon" denotes the bounding circle, the line at which earth and sky appear to meet. This line is the limit of one's field of vision … As our field of vision, so too the scope of our knowledge and the range of our interests are bounded … So there has arisen a metaphorical or perhaps analogous meaning of the word "horizon" … the movement into a new horizon involves an about-face; it comes out of the old by repudiating characteristic features; it begins a new sequence that can keep revealing ever greater depth and breadth and wealth. Such an about-face and new beginning is what is meant by a conversion.[9]

Lonergan's epistemological language around horizon and conversion is much more layered than an about-face might suggest, but it is a creative heuristic for an embattled time when communal harmony is elusive and planetary survival uncertain.

Francis argues that the "ecological conversion needed to bring about lasting change is also a community conversion" and that such a conversion "entails gratitude and gratuitousness, a recognition that the world is God's loving gift" (section 219) as well as a "loving awareness that we are not disconnected from the rest of creatures, but joined in a splendid universal communion" (section 220).

At the end of his encyclical, he circles back to the Francis of the beginning, the Italian saint of ecology whose vision of the unity of all Creation and whose tenderness toward all animate, indeed also inanimate, matter is cause for praise—*laudato Si'*.

Francis's multivalent approach to the environment, to the ravages perpetrated against the marginalized as a consequence of the rapacious greed of powers political and economic, is more than a moral broadside, a *cri de coeur* by the Successor of Peter. It is a means of recapturing what Catholic theologian Johann Baptist Metz once termed "mysticism with open eyes." Irish Jesuit writer and spiritual director Brian Grogan uses Metz's arresting insight when speaking of what Francis is doing with *Laudato Si'*:

> Genuine mystics are moved by what they see, whether it be painful or pleasant ... God was in disguise in the passion of Jesus and is likewise in the contemporary passion of sister earth. To catch this dimension theologian J. B. Metz coined the striking phrase "mysticism with open eyes." An enlisted German teenager during the Second World War, he was reacting to the fact that the eyes of many good Christians were closed to the reality of the Holocaust ... He lamented the absence of prophetic voices who would scream in protest at the genocide that was grinding systematically on. How, he wondered, might wooden doctrines and practices be transformed so that believers could pour out mercy on a suffering world and bind up the wounds of a savage passage of history? His generation has passed but today our situation is not dissimilar ... We cannot stand idly by while nature suffers ...

Mysticism with open eyes begets deep feeling for suffering of whatever kind. An integral ecology is needed, made up of simple daily gestures which break with the logic of violence, exploitation and selfishness.[10]

To help achieve this integral ecology, Francis needs allies. And he has them in bountiful numbers. The Swedish youth Greta Thunberg is just one of them rallying the young around the world to a common cause of survival, castigating paralyzed politicians, unimaginative business leaders, and a demoralized public and aligning herself with the papal agenda—if only from a tangentially remote theological distance.

Another ally is Canadian forest ecologist Suzanne Simard of the University of British Columbia, author of *Finding the Mother Tree*, whose scientific research has explored the symbiotic relationship that exists between forests and ectomycorrhizal fungi establishing a subterranean network that shares nutrients and information across species.

We are all deeply connected: our collective health and flourishing depends on acknowledging this interdependence. This is the Franciscan sensibility writ large.

Although Pope Francis's thinking about Creation is informed by many rivers and rivulets—scientific, philosophical, theological, and spiritual—he remains firmly within a Catholic intellectual tradition that is as wide as it is deep. Two thinkers whose work closely approximates the vision of *Laudato Si'*, and in one instance informs it, are the Irish nature poet, ecologist, and spiritual visionary John Moriarty and the French Jesuit scientist and mystic Pierre Teilhard de Chardin.

It is a certainty that Francis would not have heard or come across Moriarty during the very short period he was in Ireland in 1980 trying to improve his English at Milltown Institute, as Moriarty would not begin to emerge as a publicly recognized savant and nature apologist until the 1990s. However, the many points of convergence around their shared thinking on matters ecological and spiritual are illustrative of the synchronous, fecund, synthetic thinking shaping the Catholic sensibility in the post-conciliar period.

Moriarty (1938–2007) was variously a traveller, storyteller, philosopher, landscape gardener, RTE television and radio personality, university teacher (he spent six years, from 1965 to 1971, as a professor at the University of Manitoba), prolific writer, and polymath.

In a lecture given at the Massachusetts Institute of Technology titled "Prometheus and the Dolphin," Moriarty challenged his rapt audience to rethink the way they engage with the universe. He argued that our current way of thinking, designed to shape the universe to suit us—the Promethean path—was leading us to destruction, whereas we must allow the universe to shape us to suit it. That is the path of the Dolphin, for as he said in *Invoking Ireland, Ailiu Iaith n-hErend*, our souls are not only in us but also in the felled tree and the clubbed seal, for we are not only situated in the world, the world is situated in us. Damage inflicted on the world is damage inflicted on us.[11]

To truly know himself and his role to correct the course humanity was on—Moriarty was not messianic in his ambitions but was possessed with the confidence born of a visionary's sense of vocation—he had a task at hand that drew on his C/catholic reading, finely tuned sensitivity to nature, and native mystical proclivities.

With the world spinning madly toward self-destruction, Moriarty wrote with a manic passion trying to summon humanity to its senses as he was "obsessed by the thought that Western Civilization had come to an end."[12] Neither delirious nor crazed, although his insights could be troublingly subversive and counter-intuitive, Moriarty was doing what other ecologists, nature mystics, and poetic visionaries were doing: sounding the alarum-bell. Although he wrote that his time in Canada helped him to unfold his new cartography of mind and spirit, it was back in Ireland—he would return in the early 1970s and remain until his death—where he would don the mantle of a new Patrick: "By the time he died in 2007 he had provided a new vision, a dreamtime—a creative commingling that seeks to bind in a fertile unity the immanent and the transcendent, the geological and the mystical, in a post-binary quest for a universal integration of matter and spirit, a pan-Christic labour that incorporates the wisdom traditions of all faiths. Nothing less than this."[13]

Moriarty lamented the disconnectedness that has riven our culture, our history, our Christianity: we are suffering from "somatically sensuous deprivation," and we need to recover our "bush soul." Although Francis would have some difficulty with the language, syncretistic theology, and unbridled Celticism of Moriarty's vision, he would be open to its expansiveness, spiritual extraterritoriality, and tenderness of heart.

And he would recognize in it a similar vision to that of his fellow Jesuit, a thinker he would quote approvingly in *Laudato Si'*: Pierre Teilhard de Chardin, whose ideas infused his own reflections.

The ultimate destiny of the universe is the fullness of God, which has already been attained by the risen Christ, the measure of the maturity of all things. Here we can add yet

another argument for rejecting every tyrannical and irrespon-
sible domination of human beings over other creatures. The
ultimate purpose of other creatures is not to be found in us.
Rather, all creatures are moving forward with us and through
us towards a common point of arrival, which is God, in that
transcendent fullness where the risen Christ embraces and
illumines all things. Human beings, endowed with intelligence
and love, and drawn by the fullness of Christ, are called to
lead all creatures back to their Creator.

Teilhard, a French paleontologist, evolutionist, and mystic
who lived from 1881 to 1955, was shortly after his ordination as
a priest of the Society of Jesus assigned to graduate studies at
the Museum of Natural History in Paris. His studies having
been interrupted by the First World War, in which he served
on the front as a *brancardier* or stretcher-bearer, he resumed
them after the war, wrote his dissertation on the mammifers of
the lower Eocene in France, and was elected president of the
Geological Society of France.

From the beginning, he sought a fresh merger of science and
religion in the light of evolution. This was fine as long as he
limited himself to his work as a scientist, but when he began
synthesizing the two in some quite original ways, the Jesuit
authorities became skittish. Under pressure from the ultraconservative Vatican hierarch Cardinal Merry del Val, the Father
General of the Jesuits, Wlodimir Ledóchowski, ordered Teilhard
to withdraw from his position at the Institut catholique, cease
writing articles on theological subjects, and restrict himself to
matters of scientific inquiry only. He complied, but in a letter
to a friend—written before the censure—he indicated the kind
of attitude that would define his relationship to the church up

to his death: an attitude of obedient compliance coupled with a heroic tenacity to the truth of his vocation and vision:

The church represents so powerful a channeling of what constitutes the moral and sublimating lifeblood of souls, a conduit dug so deep into the whole of man's past, in spite of certain accidental and ephemeral lapses from generosity, she has to so marked a degree the faculty of encouraging human nature to develop itself fully and harmoniously, that I would feel guilty of disloyalty to life if I tried to free myself from so organic a current as the church provides. In spite of the unvoiced and instinctive wish I have at certain times experienced, the wish to find a positive reason for dropping everything, I cannot shut my eyes to the fact that it would be a biological blunder for me to leave the religious current of Catholicism. I believe that the church is still a child. Christ, by whom she lives, is immeasurably greater than she imagines.[14]

If Teilhard was tested in 1921 and found himself issuing the above statement, what was in store for him was likely beyond his imagination, and yet he remained deeply faithful to the spirit of this stalwart affirmation. His many books—*The Phenomenon of Man*, *The Future of Man*, *The Heart of Matter*, *Building the Earth*, *Christianity and Evolution*, *The Divine Milieu*, and many more besides—were all suppressed, never seeing the light of print during his life, and he had no empirical grounds to believe that his research and insights would survive his death. But they did. And there was a remarkable flurry of publications, symposia, and official endorsements—even if still accompanied with a *monitum* or warning—in the 1960s that ushered in a period of rehabilitation for a committed Jesuit who spent the majority of his life on the margins.

For Teilhard, all matter and spirit are immersed in a forward-moving process with regression and stasis but never devoid of that innate dynamism peculiar to life. From instinct to thought to reflection to love. That is the evolutionary dynamic. Using his neologisms, Teilhard saw biogenesis to noogenesis to cosmogenesis to Christogenesis as all part of an evolutionary system that is best understood as a coiling, an *enroulement*. In other words, evolutionary progress for Teilhard was not a straight line but a coiling, the same cycle being repeated, but each time a slow advance. Like W. B. Yeats's gyre.

The coiling process is the occasion for new crises to arise because each crisis is the product or result of a previous achievement. In other words, as soon as you have an achievement, an evolutionary threshold, you move up the coil to a new crisis. Teilhard's ultimate vision, *the Christic*, was completed one month before his death: it remains his final statement about the cohesion of spirit with matter, mysticism with evolution. It was his final testament to the transforming and creative power of the Divine Milieu:

> God can in future be experienced and apprehended, and even in a true sense completed by the whole ambient totality of what we call Evolution. "In Christo Jesu." This is still, of course, Christianity, and always will be. But a Christianity reincarnated for the second time in the spiritual energies of matter. It is precisely the ultra-Christianity we need here and now to meet the ever-more urgent demands of the ultra-human.[15]

Teilhard is not thinking of the Terminator or AI but of the ever-evolving humanization of the species moving forward in its coiling fashion to Christ the Omega. Bergoglio would agree, but not use the same terms, as he is more Guardinian than Teilhardian in his philosophical and theological discourse. But he buys the vision of the French evolutionist, and *Laudato Si'* provides evidence of that.[16]

He also understands that earth, our common home, is at another crisis point. Because of that, in the midst of the COVID-19 pandemic, and years after the appearance of *Laudato Si'*, he returns to the themes that underline the encyclical's argument for an integral ecology that embraces the common good under the shadow of imminent planetary disaster. And he does so in a different format: an extended interview with a sympathetic and informed interlocutor and his most insightful biographer. In response to the question of how we cope with the numberless "hidden pandemics" of the world—hunger, violence, climate change, political upheaval, and massive migration displacements—Francis invokes a German poet:

> There's a line in Friedrich Hölderlin's *Hyperion* that speaks to me, about how the danger that threatens in a crisis is never total; there's always a way out. "Where the danger is, also grows the saving power." That's the genius in the human story: there's always a way to escape destruction. Where humankind has to act is precisely there, in the threat itself; that's where the door opens. That line of Hölderlin's has been by my side at different points in my life.[17]

Let Us Dream is a continuation of the passionate advocacy of *Laudato Si'*. Francis upholds the dignity of all life—from conception to natural death—making it abundantly and unequivocally clear that it is never right to eliminate a human life to resolve a problem, whatever its origin or moral category: political, social, economic, disability, abortion, medical assistance in dying. He embraces the "seamless garment" model of Catholic morality so vigorously and controversially promoted by the former cardinal archbishop of Chicago, Joseph Bernardin.

Francis insists that *now*—this time of crisis—is the time when we can advance a new humanism, create a new unity out of the havoc wrought by cruel hegemonies of economic and political domination, reshape the priorities of the planet for sustainable existence, foster an informed and engaged citizenry, redeem our global destiny.

It is *all* connected.

And the energy and commitment he has unleashed in the young through *Laudato Si'*, and subsequent pronouncements and publications urging the implementation of its vision, continue to reverberate everywhere. Francis's moral urgings and personal witness effortlessly cross the boundaries that separate the young, religiously disengaged, and justifiably alienated youth who find ecclesial structures incredible and uninviting and inspire them to marshal their hope and energy to a radical reshaping agenda. One such inspired young adult is Nolan Scharper: "In 2016, a little over a year after the release of *Laudato Si'*, I thought I had left the Catholic Church far behind. I was twenty-two years old, had just moved to New York City, and viewed Catholicism with a mix of anger and confusion. I could not, I thought, untangle my faith from the history of colonialism and imperialism that are woven into the legacy of the Church."[18]

Scharper worked in Highbridge Park in Manhattan, disentangling the vines that are choking the living trees and beginning the restoration of a natural ecological balance to the forest. As he did this work, he felt "the old cynical prejudices strangling my faith begin to uncoil. Miraculously, I began to pray again—something I had not done seriously in years … Ecological and spiritual restoration are not separate endeavours. They are interwoven into [Francis's] 'new social fabric,' threading together the mending of Mother Earth with the healing of the human soul."[19]

This is precisely what Francis was hoping to achieve: connectivity, community, integration of prayer with action, spiritual solidarity, the privileging of reality over abstraction.

Scharper's concrete faith in action—shorn from its pious roots, maturing and socially aware—is just one example of what has been called "the Francis Effect."

The near mythic Argentine footballer Diego Maradona has been dubbed "the People's Champion." That appellation can just as easily apply to his fellow Argentine, Jorge Mario Bergoglio, about whom Maradona has said that because the pope cares about the marginalized, the hungry kids, those on the periphery, he has restored the football legend's own Catholic faith.

Still, as environmentalist and professor Simon Appolloni astutely notes, there is a stunning deficiency at the heart of *Laudato Si'* that diminishes its effectiveness and speaks to a deeper deficiency in papal leadership:

Despite its marvellous pastoral insights as an encyclical on the environment, some find it insensible to the downcast role it assigns women. Ecofeminist theologian Nichole M.

Flores points out that while Francis' use of the sibling/mother metaphor of Earth as our sister and mother can help bestow a certain intimacy with creation, Earth is cast as the feminine victim. The Church is cast as the father figure, the *paterfamilias*, who is responsible for the direction of the family. Such language, Flores underlines, only perpetuates women as being dependent on male governance. Such language will suppress full engagement with the document from women.[20]

Francis has to move beyond describing women as "the strawberry on the cake." Such language is indigestible papal patronizing and Francis, of all popes, should know better.

He needs to know better.

THE "STRAWBERRY ON THE CAKE"

The "Feminine Genius" Is a Tough Sell

FROM THE VERY BEGINNING of the Bergoglio papacy, Francis sent the message that women mattered as much as men in the life of the church. He demonstrated his equalitarian approach when he chose to sit among the leaders of women's religious orders in a circle at a meeting in the Vatican rather than in the traditional placement on a dais. The nuns loved it and he loved them. He listened to them—their complaints about an ongoing curial investigation into their post-conciliar lives that cast a shadow over their ministry, their anger around the distrust of male clerics regarding their more experimental and daring pastoral activities—and he followed up on many of the items on their collective agenda, including closing down the curial investigation.

The women had an ally in the See of Peter.

But they quickly discovered that it would not be smooth sailing. Although Mao Zedong said that "women hold up half the sky," a quick assessment of Chinese Communist life on the ground reveals that noble sentiments of equality get easily eclipsed in deeply embedded patriarchal organizations. Beijing and Rome, although ideological and strategic adversaries, have this in common.

And patriarchy is not just a governance system; it is an attitude.

Pope Francis's comment at a meeting of the International Theological Commission in Rome in 2014 that female theologians are the "strawberry on the cake"—the titters of laughter were mostly his own—highlights the tone-deaf approach to women characteristic of most prelates.

Still, Francis got it right when he said, returning from Bahrain in November of 2022, during a plane interview session—his often preferred venue for saying aloud things that scripted sessions in the Vatican constrain—that a "society that does not give women the same rights as men will become impoverished. Women are a gift. After God made man, he didn't create a lapdog for him to play with. No, he created two who are equal, a man and a woman."

To better appreciate Francis's understanding of women and their role in the church, it is imperative to step back a bit and consider the role of the laity in the church. Period. Women, women religious, and men who are not clerics (deacons, priests, and bishops) constitute the laity, and we are a formidable majority of the global membership. And it has been forever thus.

The laity have, however, been the huge neglected component of the Catholic mosaic. The rediscovery of them—us—by the Second Vatican Council has been both liberating and disheartening at the same time. Liberating in that the gifts and ministries of the laity are being rediscovered and valued, and disheartening in that this liberation is subject to canonical battles, bouts of inexplicable censure, institutional dread around creeping democracy, and that always predictable standby: power-centric anxiety over diminution.

As improbable as it may seem at first, it was Eugenio Pacelli, that most august and imperial of pontiffs, Pius XII, who noted just after the Second World War that "the laity are the frontline of the church's life ... They, above all, ought to have an ever-more clear consciousness, not only of belonging to the Church, but of being the Church ... They are the Church."[1]

There was a time when a sentiment such as this would have produced howls of derision in the very bosom of orthodoxy. Monsignor George Talbot (1816–1886), a British papal chamberlain to Pope Pius IX, observed in a letter to his friend Henry Edward Manning that the role of the laity was "to hunt, to shoot, to entertain. These matters they understand, but to meddle with ecclesiastical matters they have no right at all."[2]

Cardinal Aidan Gasquet, in his essay "The Layman in the Pre-Reformation Parish," listed three positions for the layperson: kneeling before the altar, sitting below the pulpit, and putting his hand in his purse. This patronizing view of the laity is epitomized, argues English author Margaret Hebblethwaite, in the picture dominating Brian Power's schoolroom when he was a child and which he recounts in *The Ford of Heaven*:

> At the top of heaven, the Holy Trinity sat on white clouds, surrounded by angels and saints with haloes. They were receiving a long queue of good people who climbed up towards them. First came popes in tiaras and cardinals in red hats, followed by bishops and priests in golden vestments. Then came religious brothers and white neck bands. At the bottom of the picture were the ordinary people. They were led by a

family holding each other's hands as they stood patiently in the queue, their eyes shining with devotion. The children looked up at their mother, she looked up at her husband, and he looked up towards the Holy Trinity.[3]

This is an accurate portrait of a fixed and monarchical model of the Catholic Church—resplendently patriarchal with Catholic domesticity set in aspic, Catholic deference to clerics enshrined in the very DNA of lay Catholics, all enveloped in an ambiance of unshakeable devotion. This was the reigning model prior to the Second Vatican Council, but the council changed that model with its revolutionary Dogmatic Constitution on the Church, *Lumen gentium* (Light of the Nations), and replaced it with an ecclesial model more suited to the early church. The *ecclesia* or assembly is now described as the pilgrim people of God. The church is on a joint journey toward holiness where office or ordained function is secondary to that great equalizer of Catholic life: baptism into the common priesthood of believers. But this new vision that captured the imagination of the council fathers, the bishops of the church, along with their retinue of theological experts, hasn't been so easily incorporated into the life of the church. As Francis is wont to say: abstraction is one thing and reality another.

The picture of the laity as supportive, acquiescent, at the very bottom of the faith community stubbornly persists more than half a century since the council's close in 1965.

No figure in the Catholic Church promoted the laity more than Cardinal John Henry Newman (canonized as a saint by Pope Francis), and Newman didn't have an easy time of it. He had to fight on several fronts: Rome itself, where he was regularly traduced by fearful English clerics; English bishops, who wanted

him to constrict the rebellious Catholic intellectuals keen on fresh
thinking; unsympathetic Irish senior clergy, suspicious of his new
university plan in Dublin shorn of clerical oversight and with
lay professors calling the shots; and a Catholic culture shaped
by the controversies of the Reformation and the reforms of the
Counter-Reformation with little or no knowledge of the early
church, and with a near invincible ignorance of church history.

In the midst of these struggles, Newman penned what is the
magna carta of a lay theology: *On Consulting the Faithful in
Matters of Doctrine*.[4] In this work Newman drew on a careful
assemblage of relevant historical incidents to show that the laity
not only *receive* the faith, they help to *shape* and, on occasion,
correct the tradition itself. He termed this *sensus fidelium*, or
sense of the faith, and argued that on specific historical occasions, the laity held firm when the bishops and theological
contestation among warring factions of the clergy collapsed
into the din of Babel. Newman asserted that there is a voice for
the laity, a place for the laity, not only in articulating the sense
of the faith but in providing an informed and not just supine
acceptance of church teaching drawing from the rich reserves
of their wide experience:

> I think I am right in saying that the tradition of the Apostles,
> committed to the whole Church in its various constituents
> and functions *per modum unis*, manifests itself variously at
> various times: sometimes by the mouth of the episcopacy,
> sometimes by the doctors, sometimes by the people, some-
> times by liturgies, rites, ceremonies, and customs, by events,
> disputes, movements, and all those other phenomena which
> are comprised under the name of history. It follows that none
> of these channels of tradition may be treated with disrespect.[5]

He also cautions the church authorities that there is a serious danger in neglecting to consult the laity—one of the channels of tradition worthy of respect—on all matters that touch on faith: "I think certainly that the *Ecclesia docens* [the magisterium] is more happy when she has such enthusiastic partisans about her ... than when she cuts off the faithful from study of her divine doctrines and the sympathy of her divine contemplations, and requires from them a *fides implicita* in her word, which in the educated classes will terminate in indifference, and in the poorer in superstition."[6]

Newman is dear to Francis's heart; the cardinal's injunction to consult the laity has been heard by this pope loud and clear. The problem is that only half of the laity feel that they are valued for something beyond their baptism. For women, it is only their motherhood, devotionalism, and natural gift for compassion that seem to earn the church's respect. The perception that women are second-class citizens in the Catholic Church may be poorly rooted in theology, but at the ground level it remains true for many women, young and old, formally educated or otherwise.

Catherine Mulroney, a journalist and editor with a veteran's history of survival in the church, highlights the myopia that defines much in church leadership:

> Since the promulgation of *Lumen Gentium*—and in spite of its reiteration that we all have gifts to bring to the Church—the institutional Church has issued periodic pointed reminders of gender roles. For example, as the reforms of Vatican II rolled out post-council, we began to see girls serving as altar servers, something that could not even have been imagined a few years earlier. But as recently as 1980, instructions were issued from

the Vatican expressly stating that females could not routinely serve Mass, pointing to the 1917 Code of Canon Law, which forbade female altar servers except in instances when males were not available, and only if they "give the responses from a distance and in no way approach the altar." Only when the revised code was issued in 1983 was this changed, and girls were allowed to participate in an important way in many parishes.[7]

However, it was not until 1994, when the Vatican body charged with responsibility for liturgy, the Congregation for Divine Worship and the Discipline of the Sacraments, ruled that indeed the use of the term "laypersons" in the new Code of Canon Law included females in that designation. In other words, laypersons were both male and female. It took a decade to settle the inclusivity of the nomenclature.

The arguments advanced by ultraconservative clerics and their lay sympathizers for the continued exclusion of females from serving as altar servers includes such specious and desperate reasoning as follows: altar boys constitute a traditional recruitment pool for future seminarians; boys would not welcome girls into their hitherto exclusive club; priests could be sexually distracted by having young girls assisting at the celebration of Mass (this argument was also used by anti-feminist Catholic factions when it came to allowing women to serve as readers at Mass). None of these arguments holds water. There have been no demonstrated instances of parish outrage or altar boy hostility when altar girls were first introduced, and the practice has been universally widespread, although it has taken decades before the Vatican finally moved to have women in formal instituted ministries. And it was Francis who did it.

The ministries of acolyte (altar server) and lector (reader of the non-Gospel selections in the sacred liturgy) were canonically confirmed as stable ministries open to both men *and* women in Francis's *motu proprio* letter *Spiritus Domini* (The Spirit of the Lord) in January 2021. These ministries are entrusted "to individual members of the faithful, by virtue of a particular form of exercise of the baptismal priesthood."

Question settled. But not quite. Not by a long shot.

Questions around the freedom of women in the Catholic Church, their specific charisms, the patriarchal attitudes and structures that inhibit their full flourishing, the embedded toxin of clericalism, and the rampant strains of sexism are not so easily exorcized. A Vatican statement installing women in ministries that they have exercised for decades smacks of paternalism. Francis's liberating initiative, however, to secure in law what has been pastoral practice for years was a smart and necessary move. It has, perhaps, bought him some time.

The struggle—and it has been a struggle—to get church leadership to listen to the concerns of women has had its high and low points even within the same jurisdiction. For instance, going back as early as 1971, six years since the council's close, the archbishop of Winnipeg, Cardinal George B. Flahiff, on behalf of the Canadian delegation to the Rome synod and speaking for the Canadian Catholic Conference, approached the question of ministries and women with characteristic Canadian caution— tentative in its tone, respectful of the times, and gently warning of the consequences of inaction:

> We do not wish to prejudge the question. We do not know if further action should follow. And we certainly have no recommendations regarding the time and mode of such action. But despite a centuries-old social tradition against a ministry of

women in the Church, we are convinced that the signs of the times (and one of those signs is that already many women perform many pastoral services and this with great success) strongly urge a study at least both of the present situation and of the possibilities for the future. Unless such a study is begun at once, we may find ourselves behind the course of events.[8]

The Canadian bishops returned to the theme of women nine years later when Robert Lebel, Bishop of Valleyfield, Quebec, addressed the Rome synod of 1980 celebrating feminism and moving the question of women and their diverse roles further along the path set by Flahiff in 1971:

The Church must ... in fidelity to the word of God, recognize the modern feminist movement as a positive reality. We are dealing, on the whole, with an advance in civilization; and it is a forward step in the establishment of the kingdom ... one must not limit a woman's role in the Church to her influence through the family. A woman is more than a wife and mother, even if these two roles embody an immense human and supernatural reality. How can women, by virtue of what they themselves are as human persons, play a role in the Church which is just as important as men's?[9]

The Canadian bishops made one final and especially forceful contribution when the Canadian Primate, the archbishop of Quebec City, Louis-Albert Vachon, spoke about the sins committed against women:

Let us recognize the ravages of sexism, and our own male appropriation of Church institutions and numerous aspects of the

Christian life. Need I mention the example of the masculine language of our official—and even liturgical texts? In our society and in our Church, man has come to think of himself as the sole possessor of rationality, authority, and active initiative, relegating women to the private sector and dependent tasks. Our recognition, as Church, of our own cultural deformation will allow us to overcome the archaic concepts of womanhood which have been inculcated in us for centuries.[10]

Subsequent interventions by Canadian bishops at the Roman synods held during the pontificates of John Paul II and Benedict XVI never rose to the level of passion and conviction on the roles and Christian witness of women that culminated with the Vachon intervention.

The Canadian bishops clearly got the message that ministry and women, inclusive language in liturgy, and moving beyond a history-conditioned paradigm privileging womanhood in domestic terms were not high priorities during both the Wojtyla and Ratzinger papacies. The popes saw the need to address the issue of women not by way of reparation, new anthropological insights, or more expansive readings of scripture but by strengthening the church's backbone, forbidding even discussion around women and the presbyterate. As if that would work.

Certainly, pontifical thinking was built on the foundation provided by Pope Paul VI in his Council Message to Women in 1965, when he declared that "the hour is coming, in fact has come, when the vocation of women is being achieved in its fullness, the hour in which woman acquires in the world an influence, an effect and a power never hitherto achieved. That is why, at this moment when the human race is undergoing so deep a transformation, women impregnated with the spirit of the Gospel can do so much to aid mankind in not failing."

It is understandable, then, that the Canadian bishops would be emboldened to speak on behalf of women and to call for further study of women in ministry given Paul VI's message, but the Vatican was not ready for the deeper implications that follow on a review of its tradition-encrusted teachings on women.

John Paul II had his own views on women. They would be addressed in various ways, primarily through his comprehensive teaching on the sexes, *Theology of the Body*; in his apostolic letters *Mulieris dignitatem* (The Dignity and Vocation of Women) in 1988 and *Ordinatio sacerdotalis* (Priestly Ordination) in 1994; and in private addresses at *ad limina* visits by bishops (the quinquennial trips bishops are to make to head office).

John Paul II was especially fond of speaking about what he called the "feminine genius":

Pope John Paul II's appraisal can be summed up into four salient points. First, feminine genius implies respecting women's dignity and rights. He recognized society's failure in the course of history by relegating women to secondary social roles. Second, feminine genius means service out of love. Women have the unique contribution of love that nurtures humanity; in this capacity, even men discover their capacity for manhood and fatherhood. Third, feminine genius exposes the evils of violence and exploitation of women that ought to change by appealing to governments to address this injustice. Finally, John Paul idealized the woman. He spoke of the genius of a woman (in the singular) and linked her virtues to motherhood and virginity.[11]

Francis also uses the phrase "feminine genius" or "the genius of women" in several places—scrum interviews, formal statements, papal pronouncements—indicating that he subscribes in great measure to the teaching of his immediate predecessors on this matter.

Fearful of creating a false feminism, a "female ideology of machismo," Francis is trying to craft an understanding of the feminine genius that takes into account the role of the Blessed Virgin Mary as a prototype of a Christian feminist and which ensures an understanding and respect for the uniqueness of women as a model of the church: a nurturing mother with a capacity for compassion and empathy and with a gift for intuition that surpasses their male counterparts.

He has explicitly called for the development of a *profound* theology of women, shorn of ideology, ecclesial factionalism, and disruptive debates over gender. Francis knows that allowing females to serve on the altar, read at Mass, and serve in canonical tribunals is fine as far as it goes, but it is insufficient: more needs to be done, and therein lies the trap.

Francis is boxed in by his predecessors, defined by his Latino culture, and intellectually and emotionally hostage to his perception of women as a *typos* that is often laced in that strange admixture of religious romanticism and idealization characteristic of bachelor-clerics.

Still, he flexes his papal muscles, tries to find new openings to settled ideas, and balances received teaching by his predecessors with a wholesome receptivity to empirical experience and the breadth of operations characteristic of the freedom of the Holy Spirit. For instance, the notion of sexual and gender complementarity in the thinking of John Paul II is a substantial, if not philosophically persuasive, teaching that embraces several dimensions: natural complementarity that is subdivided into heterogenital and reproductive complementarities; ontological or affective complementarity; biological and personal complementarity.

John Paul's philosophical personalism and close reading of the Book of Genesis combine to create a seemingly unassailable anthropology, what he calls an "honest anthropology," securing in nature and metaphysics a principle of complementarity that unites a wife and husband in a pact, a "unity of the two," that brings into the nuptial fusion—physically, psychologically, and ontologically—all the parts that constitute the whole.

No place in this scheme for gays, other-gendered individuals, and trans persons. All is settled, natural, and normative. The notion of complementarity was expounded at length in John Paul's thinking, and he used every appropriate occasion to allude to it. Not easy to skirt around, and Francis doesn't dispute or revoke the teaching, but he does a bit of fancy choreography in his opening address to a colloquium, "The Complementarity of Man and Woman in Marriage," sponsored by the Congregation for the Doctrine of the Faith in 2014.

He speaks of complementarity as a dynamic and evolving idea rather than as a "simplistic idea that all the roles and relations of the two sexes are fixed in a single, static pattern," and he makes the case that a real as opposed to an abstract complementarity "will take many forms as each man and woman brings his or her distinctive contributions to their marriage and to the formation of their children—his or her personal richness, personal charisma."

And as is customary with Francis, he eschews fixed abstract categories in favour of lived experience, moving the teaching on complementarity away from some of its procrustean tendencies for apriorism and apodictic judgments. As Creighton University theologians Michael G. Lawler and Todd A. Salzman note, Francis's focus on the family as an anthropological reality and not as an ahistorical one is a welcome departure from settled papal teaching:

> Worldwide experience shows that family is defined and influenced culturally, historically, socially, and legally. While one can certainly conceive and present an "ideal" notion of family like one man, one woman and their children, the history and reality of family are much more complex. There are now single-parent families, stepparent families, adoptive-parent families, foster-parent families, polygamous- and monogamous-parent families, and same-sex parent families. In each of these cases, "family is family," and we must engage the reality we find, not what we would like it ideally to be. We must also evaluate the nature of the relationship between parents and their children based on sound scientific evidence, not on unjustified speculative prejudgment.[12]

Engaging the *reality* we find, not an ideology or abstract system, is precisely the Bergoglio *modus operandi*. But no matter how Francis nuances the Wojtyla teaching on complementarity, he will not abjure it. His own instincts rebel against what he dubs a "machismo feminism," he is the product of a culture and history that minutely socializes the role and status of women, and he is part of a clerical tradition that has often prized virginity over marriage.

Still, we should remember that Francis spoke openly of gays and their right to be part of a family, and he has changed canon law to allow for greater efficiency and fairness around the canonical process that issues decrees of nullity allowing divorced Catholics to remarry sacramentally. His palpable affection for families is on display regularly in his weekly audiences, in his journeys to war- and famine-ravaged regions of the world, and in his outspoken advocacy for migrant and refugee families caught in the vise of political ego and cupidity.

The family—its thriving a papal priority regardless of its global iteration—and the enhanced role of women in society at every level—a pressing need in a male-dominated church—continue to command Francis's attention in spite of concerted efforts to shift the focus onto diaconal and sacerdotal ministries.

In other words: the ordination of women.

From the outset of his papacy, Francis has been clear that the teaching of his predecessors—Paul VI, John Paul II, and Benedict XVI—on the exclusion of women from the priesthood remains in force. He cannot do otherwise. In an airplane interview returning to Rome from a World Youth Day event in 2013, he was adamant about respecting the role of women, at the same time insisting that church teaching on women and priesthood is not negotiable:

> I believe we have much more to do in making explicit the role and charism of women. This needs to be better explained. All we say is: they can do this and they can do that; now they are altar servers, now they do readings, now they are in charge of Catholic charities. BUT. There is more! We need to develop a profound theology of womanhood. On the ordination of women as priests, that door is closed. But on this issue, I want to tell you something. I have said it and I repeat it. Our Lady, Mary, was more important than the Apostles, than bishops, priests and deacons. Women in the Church are *more*

important than bishops and priests. *How?* This is something we have to try and explain better, because I believe that we lack a theological explanation of this.

As a pledge of his earnest on this matter, he established in 2016 a commission of experts to determine—historically, canonically, and theologically—whether women can be ordained to the diaconate. The results of the commission were inconclusive, and so he felt incapable of moving forward with any change to the current practice. But, undaunted, he formed another commission in 2020 composed entirely of new members and tasked them to study the possibility of women deacons. Again.

At the heart of the debate for the ordination of women—diaconal and sacerdotal—are cultural and theological concerns that can't be reduced to a simple formula of human rights and equity. These ordinations would constitute a dogmatic shift, but Francis may be open—*just*—to the ordination of women as deacons were he persuaded on historical and patristic grounds that such existed in the past and that he was engaged in a *recovery* of an ancient practice rather than in an *innovative departure* from the tradition.

Continuity assured; unity protected. Doing his job as Peter.

The ordination of women to the priesthood is a different matter. To approve such ordinations would rupture the unity of the Catholic Church, and no pope is going there, Francis included.

Popes have been fretting about this since the 1970s, when the push for greater involvement of women and ministry began to be heard in the aulas of the Vatican. Cardinal Flahiff's bold intervention at the 1971 Synod—a boldness encased in tentative and respectful discourse—is an early example of institutional attention. Scholars—biblical, historical, and theological—were raising issues around women in the early church that were previously unexplored. And other Christian denominations—the Anglican Church specifically—were wrestling with the challenge of female ordination, forcing Rome to react.

And react it did.

Pope Paul VI instructed the Pontifical Biblical Commission to study the question: the commission concluded that there may be reasons for the continued inadmissibility of women to the presbyterate, but such a justification cannot be grounded in scripture. Not the answer Paul was looking for. One of the members of that commission, the Canadian Jesuit biblical scholar David Stanley, told me that the unanimity of the commission shook the pope; when Pope Paul moved ahead with the publication of a formal document closing discussion on the matter, Stanley resigned from the commission.

That formal document, *Inter insigniores* (Among the Noteworthy), was issued by *La Suprema*, the Sacred Congregation for the Doctrine of the Faith, under the mandate of the pope on January 27, 1977.[13] It left little uncertainty about the church's definitive thinking: NO.

This *Declaration on the Question of Admission of Women to the Ministerial Priesthood* affirmed that the "Catholic Church has never felt that priestly or episcopal ordination can be validly conferred on women" and proceeded to make the case on the basis of several considerations: the priest acts *in persona Christi* and Jesus was male; Jesus did not call women to be apostles; the church's practice has been secured by a constant tradition in both the East and the West. The document includes, not without sympathy for those who will be disappointed by its judgment, that women who express a desire for the ministerial priesthood are doubtless motivated by the desire to serve Christ and the church. And it is not surprising that, at a time when they are becoming more aware of the discrimination to which they have been subjected, they should desire the ministerial priesthood itself. But it must not be forgotten that the priesthood does not form part of the rights of the individual, but stems from the economy of the mystery of Christ and the church. The priestly office cannot become the goal of social advancement; no merely human progress of society or of the individual can of itself give access to it: it is of another order.

So, the question was settled: "it is of another order." If the pope and his doctrinal officials thought this would actually resolve the matter, they were to be quickly enlightened otherwise. It was not settled in the minds of many and subsequent popes. John Paul II, especially in *Ordinatio sacerdotalis*, sought to close down all debate on the matter as it was futile, contra-ecclesial, and divisive:

> Although the teaching that priestly ordination is to be reserved to men alone has been preserved by the constant and universal Tradition of the Church and firmly taught by the Magisterium in its more recent documents, at the present time in some places it is nonetheless considered open to debate, or the Church's judgment that women are not to be admitted to ordination is considered to have a merely disciplinary force.
>
> Wherefore, in order that all doubt may be removed regarding a matter of great importance, a matter which pertains to the Church's divine constitution itself, in virtue of my ministry of confirming the brethren (cf. *Lk* 22:32) I declare that the

Church has no authority whatsoever to confer priestly ordination on women and that this judgment is to be definitively
held by all the Church's faithful. (section 4)

Because the matter "pertains to the Church's divine constitution itself" and is not a disciplinary or legal issue, the church's
inability to ordain women to the priesthood is indisputable.
Except for many in the church it was not, and whatever flames
John Paul intended to douse were persistent and are still fiercely
aglow. Hence, Francis's dilemma.

Church authorities have great difficulty advancing an argument that simply stands the test of enduring credibility. The
Vatican, prior to issuing *Ordinatio sacerdotalis*, tried to enlist
prominent prelates to take a stand that would support the
church's unalterable position and in doing so advance some
new and convincing argumentation.

One of the prelates approached was Cardinal Gerald
Emmett Carter of Toronto, a powerful churchman, much
respected in the corridors of corporate and political power,
feared if not loathed by Catholic dissidents, influential in the
Vatican especially in matters of finance, capable of dominating
the Canadian national hierarchy by sheer dint of his outsized
personality. Rome saw him as the right man for the job of
selling the church's increasingly unpopular position. He was
less sure.

Cardinal Ratzinger leaned on him, and Carter obliged. And
so, in 1983, *Do This in Memory of Me: A Pastoral Letter upon the
Sacrament of Priestly Orders* was issued by the cardinal's office,
and controversy erupted. Theologians disparaged its arguments,
feminist activists lamented its tired repetition of old nostrums,
other Canadian bishops looked for cover, and the cardinal's

friends in secular high places admired its political adroitness but wondered about its authorship. For sure, Carter—an able, lucid, smooth stylist whose previous books and sermons were models of concision devoid of jargon and dense reasoning—this very Carter seemed absent in the text. *Do This in Memory of Me* was a marked departure from his usual authorial qualities.

Investigative journalists and keen theologians conversant with the literature on priesthood and women unearthed an article by an American Jesuit, "Sacramental Sexuality and the Ordination of Women" by Donald J. Keefe of Marquette University; the cardinal demonstrably depended on that article, as the terminology, the issues, and, to a large degree, the very sequencing of the argument bear more than a passing resemblance to Keefe's text.

Still, Carter claimed it was entirely his work, and he strenuously defended it in public through interviews, sermons, and public addresses, although the language of the document was at striking variance with Carter the educator and natural communicator.[14]

His conclusion admits of no ambiguity:

> The Catholic tradition concerning the priesthood, its indispensability and restriction to men, is not frivolous, nor is it merely cultural. The debate, centered mostly in North America, will be long and bitter. The only thing that is absolutely clear is that it cannot be concluded or resolved on the basis of sociological surveys, political extrapolations or anthropological necessities. The enabling power which permits a man to offer the sacrifice of Christ *in persona Christi* can be regulated only by the authority of His Church, an authority which Catholic tradition places firmly in the hands of the

successors of the Apostles in communion with the Successor of Peter.[15]

This pastoral letter was penned almost midpoint between *Inter insigniores* and *Ordinatio sacerdotalis*; it echoes the arguments of the former and anticipates the certitude of the latter. Carter repeats the position of every pope who has spoken on the subject, insisting that "we're overdue for a whole rehabilitation of women in what we might call the power structure of the church, the administrative structure. I am always telling them that when I go to Rome."[16] In addition, Carter advocated for change in those areas of church life and law where there is consensus as he viewed the debate, although far from false and irrelevant, as strategically misplaced. Go for what you can get rather than fight for what is not possible—at least now. In fact, Carter hedged his bet on the future when he wrote to his co-biographer Douglas R. Letson that when it comes to the ordination of women, it doesn't disturb him that the issue is being debated in public. He added, "I am not sure that the last word has been said on this subject and a counter position to what the Church has taught so far is not, in my view, heretical, at least not yet … My position is, I think, a little more advanced than the Pope's and therefore I should not parade it in public."[17]

If Carter thought he had some manoeuvring room, he was soon to be disappointed by John Paul II's authoritative 1994 apostolic letter reinforcing the church's teaching and allowing no room for change.

Roma locuta est; causa finita. Rome has spoken; the matter is settled.

Still, the issue did not go away. Instead, it intensified. Roman Catholic women were ordained, and Rome declared their ordinations illicit and invalid and excommunicated both the women priests and those who took part in the ceremonies. Debates in the academy and in learned publications refused to be silenced. Women organized to champion causes that caused Rome more than a little discomfiture. Religious orders of women balked at Roman efforts to suppress free discussion. Sympathetic bishops and priests who defied the Vatican were censored and disciplined.

This is the state of the art that Francis inherited. Although many Catholic women reconfigured their organizations and goals to shift away from ordination as their *sine qua non* to broader issues of women's equality in the Catholic Church as a consequence of Rome's intractability,[18] the issue of ordination centred on the potentially achievable goal of women in the diaconate rather than the priesthood. In addition, global awareness of other pressing issues for Catholic women was on the ascendant: human trafficking, domestic violence, migrant women and children, and, as a consequence, strictly *ad intra* ecclesial issues waned.

But did not disappear.

While the scholars are studying women as deacons, and commissions are formed seemingly ad infinitum, Francis has moved decisively on the empowering of women in the highest echelons with his *Predicate evangelium* (Preach the Gospel), an apostolic letter promulgated in 2022. This document radically reconceives, renames, and restructures the Vatican Curia, allowing laywomen and laymen to exercise leadership positions in the various departments or dicasteries that previously they would have served at only a secretarial or consultancy level, if at all. With this startling structural innovation, Francis has moved the laity to the very centre of power.

Convinced that women can bring to the church gifts that do not require clerical status, that the struggle to access holy orders is misconceived as the varied ministries exercised by women are unique to them, women do not require ordination oils as their grace, capacity for compassion, and nurturing and mediating skills are best deployed in the service of the church outside the restricted male ministries. In an interview with *America* in 2022, Francis insisted that the fact that women cannot "enter into the ministerial life is not a deprivation." He once again spoke of the paucity of thinking around the role and natures of women, this time invoking the thinking of the controversial Swiss theologian Hans Urs von Balthasar, who wrote of the Marian as distinct from the Petrine principle when speaking of the charisms of women and men. Von Balthasar's principles are not simplistically gendered, are not perceived as oppositional, and are constitutive of church life. But they do have unique symbolic qualities: the Petrine is related to authority, order, and judgment, and the Marian to a love that is concretely against abstraction and beyond the boundaries of structure, a propulsive love steeped in reflection. Although Francis *is* Peter and therefore a special historical embodiment of the Petrine Principle, his heart and his spirituality of mercy are perfectly attuned to the Marian.

However, such nuancing didn't surface in the pontiff's *America* interview, and international reaction was swift and merciless. The former president of Ireland, Mary McAleese, a distinguished civil jurist and canon lawyer, dismissed Francis's comments as "misogynistic drivel," and one of the leading feminist Catholic theologians in the world, Tina Beattie of England, lambasted the pontiff for getting it persistently wrong on the matter of a theology for women:

When Pope Francis explained the Marian principle to the journalist from *America* he went on to say: "We have not developed a theology of women that reflects this." The church does not lack a theology of women. It lacks a theological anthropology, for if half the human race made in the image and likeness of God is waiting for the other half to develop a theology to explain its existence, then all we have is chaff. That is not much to offer individuals and cultures that are being torn apart by confusion over what it means to be male and female, created in the image and likeness of God.[19]

Francis seems deadlocked in his efforts to build bridges of understanding, stymied by his predecessors, derided by his conservative adversaries for selling out Catholic priestly identity, and reprimanded by his legions of supporters who see his position on women as irredeemably traditionalist and indeed clericalist.

But Francis's end game is more subtle than opting for a false irenicism. He understands what is at stake. Change, but not now.

First of all, the soil must be skillfully tilled. Although Francis shares with many prelates the realization that simply repeating the prohibition against the ordination of women to the priesthood is ultimately ineffective, he cannot change the church's teaching by papal fiat. Second, by keeping the question of the ordination of women to the diaconate alive and current, he is prioritizing recovery of a long-lost pastoral practice over an innovation—ordination to the priesthood—that would rupture church unity and compromise his ministry as Peter.

So, in the meantime, he does what he can: appoint women to positions of senior responsibility in Vatican governance, augment the pool of first-order specialists with an enhanced female presence—including economists of high calibre like Mariana Mazzucato of University College, London, and Kate Raworth of Oxford—and position women in key decision-making operations that are personally close to his heart, as in the appointment of French religious sister Nathalie Becquart as a co-undersecretary of the Synod of Bishops' office. Major breakthrough.

Francis supports these moves with the understanding that it will be one further nail into the coffin of clericalism:

> because of clericalism, which is a corruption of the priest-hood, many people wrongly believe that church leadership is exclusively male. But if you go to any diocese in the world you'll see women running departments, schools, hospitals, and many other organizations and programmes; in some areas, you'll find many more women than men as leaders ... To say that they aren't true leaders because they *aren't* [my emphasis] ordained is clericalist and disrespectful.[20]

In fact, Francis is on record for saying, on many occasions, that women have a gift for administration that is superior in kind and performance than that of men.

They do the work and they do it differently. He would agree with actor Emma Thompson, who, when speaking of female heroism to theatre critic John Lahr, commented that "women will look around and often be aware of what others need. They have to be like that because no one else will fucking do it. Women look after everyone endlessly—and without them there would be nothing."[21]

Francis would concur—*sans* the expletive—and although

debates continue to rage fiercely around gender gifts, nature-versus-nurture roles in the socialization of females, et cetera, the Argentine pope does his bit to move beyond stereotypes when enabling women to rise above the glass duomo, as it were, but clerical casteism remains a near insuperable obstacle.

Priesthood shorn of clericalism is a high priority for Francis, and it is connected to his thinking around the inclusion of women in the sacrament of orders. After all, those non-Catholic churches, specifically those in the Anglican Communion, that have ordained women are still dealing with clericalism, and for Francis that is the more immediate challenge. The tradition allows him to deal with this without shaking the very foundations of universal church unity.

What for many may appear as a cynically calculated delay upon close inspection reveals the pope's thinking around the creative contraries that define the human project: the ecclesial perichoresis that allows for a careful balancing and interplay of discrete entities and concepts grounding everything in the experience of encounter. Listening, genuine dialogue, patience, earnest respect for the position of competing views, and reverence for the *other as other* combine to create an environment where an emerging truth can surface. In this, Francis thinks like the one he sainted, John Henry Newman, whose *Letter to Pusey on Occasion of His Eirenicon* (1866) underscores the English intellectual's tolerance for novel or conflicting ideas, his sturdy faith in the evolutionary capacity of ideas to serve as markers of the Holy Spirit in human affairs, and his unassailable conviction that truth need fear nothing, for "Truth is wrought out by many minds working together freely." For Newman, Catholic intellect in collision with Catholic intellect provides the way forward. Although, in his letter to his fellow Tractarian and friend Edward Bouverie Pusey, Newman is debating Marian doctrines and devotions, he advances an argument that will surface in other contexts as well and that provides a rationale for looking at truth the way we should look at life itself, a way that is Bergoglian in its approach:

> Life in this world is motion, and involves a continual process of change. Living things grow into their perfection, into their decline, into their death. No rule of art will suffice to stop the operation of this natural law, whether in the material world or in the human mind. We can indeed encounter disorders, when they occur, by external antagonism and remedies; but we cannot eradicate the process itself, out of which they arise. Life has the same right to decay, as it has to wax strong. This is specially the case with great ideas. You may stifle them; or you may refuse them elbow-room; or then again you may torment them with your continuing meddling; or you may let them have free course and range and be content, instead of anticipating their excesses, to expose and restrain those excesses after they have occurred. But you have only this alternative; and for myself, I prefer much wherever it is possible, to be first generous and just; to grant full liberty of thought, and to call it to account when abused.[22]

Francis may not appear to be giving the idea of ordained women to the priesthood "free course and range," for after all he has repeated the position of previous popes on the issue, but by leaving open the role of free and transparent speech in synodal sessions he creates an environment wherein the collision of intellects can move truth forward. Not all is foreclosed. A strategy of incrementalism or gradualism ensures that new ideas are not expunged but given airtime, even if that means their potential for polarizing moves them to peripheral rather than central status. And we know what Francis thinks of the peripheries—geopolitical and spiritual. As Francis says in *Fratelli tutti*, "a healthy openness never threatens one's own identity."

The words of war correspondent Martha Gellhorn can serve as a cautionary warning for Francis and his church: "a wonderful New Year's resolution for the men who run the world: get to know the people who live in it."[23] The women who live in the Catholic Church are by every measure the largest and most productive component of its life and outreach; the men who run the church must get to know them in ways that don't reduce them to a holy mystery in need of their own justificatory theology, to an abstraction rather than an encounter, to a principle rather than an enfleshed reality.

Francis's strategy is to purge the abstraction and embrace the reality. He is halfway there.

- 7 -

THE SUNDERING SCANDALS
The Hot-Button Issues That Roil the Papacy

WHEN THE ARCHCONSERVATIVE CARDINAL of Genoa, Giuseppe Siri, observed after the death of Pope John XXIII that his pontificate was "the greatest disaster in recent ecclesiastical history,"[1] and by recent he actually meant the last five hundred years, he was undoubtedly aggrieved by the years of tumult John had initiated with the Second Vatican Council. What is true for John XXIII is sure to be true of Francis. Already, protocol and discretion cast to the winds, several churchmen have displayed varying degrees of dissatisfaction with the Bergoglio papacy. Some have done so publicly, as in the case of cardinals Raymond Burke and Gerhard Müller and archbishops Georg Gänswein and Carlo Maria Viganò, and many more have done so under the cover of serving as the loyal opposition to the pope, writing letters obliquely critical of Francis, as in the case of the "Fraternal Open Letter to Our Brother Bishops in Germany," with seventy-four signatories (four of them Canadian). These are in addition to the various *dubia* or critical questions seeking clarity on points of doctrine and polity designed to embarrass the pontiff and issued with customary attestations of loyalty to the person of the pontiff. Cardinal George Pell, the bellicose and blustery Australian prelate enmired in sex abuse controversies and their lingering reputational damage, even when cleared, was less than forthright and kind when dealing with Francis. More than any other churchman, Pell, under the pope's instruction, struggled to get Vatican finances in order and to a considerable degree did so successfully. Still, he dismissed his boss's tenure as a disaster.

But no one is fooled. Least of all Francis. When you take on the historically encrusted structure you are head of and introduce new directions for recovery of the original animating spirit of the institution, purging the dross in the process, you will make enemies. John XXIII did, and so does Francis.

The biggest institutional challenge calling out for purification and reform is the universal toxin that is clerical sexual abuse.

Although he has denounced sex abuse as a deleterious product of clericalism, which he once described in a lecture to seminarians as the church's "ugliest perversion," he does not limit the sins of clericalism to matters sexual alone. It is a corruption of the priesthood, a power model that diminishes all that it touches, the preserve of a false entitlement, an attitude and structure that diminishes human freedom, a negation of the humility that Jesus calls for in those who exercise authority. The reach of clericalism is vast and is not limited to those in holy orders. It is a blight on the body of Christ, a spiritual pathology that compromises the very mission of the church.

As the spiritual writer, priest, and popular retreat director Daniel O'Leary has noted of mandatory clerical celibacy, the linchpin of clericalism: "Clericalism is a collective malaise which keeps vibrant, abundant life at bay; it quarantines us for life from the personal and communal expression of healing relationships, and the lovely grace of the tenderness which Pope Francis is trying to restore to the hearts of all God's people: all who are trying to be more like the One most beautiful, divine and human heart that ever lived."[2]

Although compulsory celibacy for parochial clergy remains a canonical requirement for priesthood and continues to be debated widely in church circles, Francis retains the discipline for the global church. Certainly, as O'Leary demonstrates from his decades-long spiritual accompaniment with priests, mandatory celibacy has not been good for a multitude of priests, but there is no empirical evidence that establishes that it has directly contributed to sex abuse, the most egregious and ruinous expression of clericalism.

If it is true, as Catholic University of America theologian Christopher Ruddy has observed on a different matter of neuralgic intensity for the church, that "it will take decades, possibly centuries, to heal the liturgical wound in Roman Catholicism," the wound inflicted by systemic clerical sex abuse doesn't have the luxury of decades for its healing. The extirpation of the toxin is of the highest pastoral priority, and Francis knows that, mostly.

The time is now. But "now" was a long time in coming, and a moral urgency that attends to the sex abuse crisis calls out for quick surgical action. And Francis knows that, too, mostly.

Before I examine the Francis record, however, some context is critical. Conscientization around clerical sex abuse is a late-twentieth-century phenomenon: it has certainly existed in the church for centuries, but wide public awareness of this psychological and spiritual disorder with its deeply corrupting aftermath is a recent development.

It was not crusading clerics, moral reformers, or enlightened bishops who led the campaign to address this rot in the bosom of the church, but rather brave survivors, diligent investigative journalists, and caring pastoral outsiders. The institutional church, much like its secular equivalents in politics, media conglomerates, global entertainment empires, sports syndicates, and corporate elites, when once confronted by the many instances of abuse by its personnel, moved with uncommon alacrity to limit damage by deploying a legion of lawyers, actuaries, spin doctors, stalling tactics, and righteous spasms of outrage mixed with denial, all designed to protect the reputation and well-being of the institution *qua* institution. The priority was the institution; the complainants were a problem to handle.

The Roman Catholic Church's response to the explosion of clerical abuse cases was inadequate at every level.

When cases first began to emerge publicly in the United States in the 1980s, in Louisiana and Massachusetts particularly, I recall a conversation I had with John Wilkins in Rome while reporting on the Extraordinary synod of 1985. He was the editor at the time of the *Tablet*, an accomplished journalist of the highest standards, and he told me that these cases were really symptomatic of the North American Catholic Church and in no way reflective of the universal church's experience. Wouldn't happen in the United Kingdom, he wagered.

Wilkins was wrong. The United States was to prove the tip of the iceberg.

A tsunami was on the horizon, and the church was ill prepared. The mighty wave really broke during the pontificate of John Paul II, and as pontiffs go, he was the least equipped to deal with the scandals, the ecclesiastical reverberations, and the besmirching of the priestly profile. Accustomed to the devious strategies of the Communist regime that sought to undermine the moral credibility of the Catholic clergy in Poland, but not only in Poland, by spreading rumours of priestly depravity, John Paul read many of the accusations surfacing throughout the church as simply another iteration of the Communist play-book of deceit.

I can attest to this nefarious strategy from my own experi-ence in Cuba, when I was there ostensibly interviewing Fidel Castro for *Grail: An Ecumenical Journal* (it never actually happened; after a week's calculated delay, the president sent Jose Carneado, one of his long-time associates, in his stead). I discovered from an interview with the recently appointed archbishop of Havana, Jaime Lucas Ortega y Alamino, that it was a common practice of the Castro regime to jail priest dissenters on the grounds that they were homosexual deviates. He had been incarcerated on such a trumped-up charge himself.

John Paul's experience in Poland sensitized him to Communist efforts to discredit Catholic clergy, and so when allegations of clerical sexual abuse arose, he was deeply suspi-cious of their provenance and intention. He fiercely defended his bishops and priests and saw such attacks, in addition to being a Communist ploy, as a strong illustration of a resurgence of anti-clericalism in secular Europe and as a serious undermin-ing of the unique dignity of the priesthood.

John Paul's own highly romanticized concept of the priest as a heroic figure, a concept drawn from his deep reading of Polish literary culture and religious history and as evidenced by his own highly dramatic embodiment of the priest as selfless witness/martyr/spiritual warrior, made it very difficult for him to countenance the anti-image of the priest as dissolute predator.

His stubborn refusal to heed mounting charges of abuse percolating throughout Europe and the Americas created profound crises in local churches wrestling with the charges and the subsequent public outcry. Vienna is just one instance.

In Europe, the Hans Hermann Groër affair dominated the Catholic ecclesiastical scene throughout the 1990s. The cardinal archbishop of Vienna and a former Benedictine abbot, Groër was accused of having molested young seminarians while in charge of a prominent Austrian Marian shrine years before his appointment to Vienna. As archbishop, his tenure was mediocre—in sharp contrast with that of his immediate predecessor, the intellectual and charismatic Franz Koenig—and he did not enjoy the confidence of his priests or fellow bishops, with the exception of the conservative and combative Kurt Krenn, who was himself the subject of controversy around porn in his seminary and who resigned subsequently as a bishop.

When Groër was confronted with his own allegations of abuse, he stalled, refused to acknowledge their legitimacy, resisted calls for his resignation, and relied on Rome to back him. John Paul did not ask for his resignation; as a consequence of the cardinal's intransigence, hundreds of thousands of Austrian Catholics were alienated, the episcopal conference was riven, and the bishops' authority and credibility compromised. Faced with an insoluble problem—diminishing numbers of Catholics practising and financially supporting their church— John Paul did what he very rarely did: reverse his position.

But the damage done by the Vatican's tardiness in responding to the scandal left a bad taste in the mouths of many hitherto devout Austrians and seriously diminished public regard for the episcopacy in secular as well as religious circles.[3]

The Groër affair was merely a forerunner of the more salacious and structure-shaking crisis that unfolded in the Boston of Cardinal Bernard Law. Throughout the 1980s and 1990s and into the twenty-first century, Cardinal Law, close ally of John Paul II, Harvard graduate, and friend of President George H. Bush and his family, was a classic example of the all-powerful Irish Catholic prelate whose social and political influence in Boston and beyond were seemingly unchecked or never contested. That is, until the *Boston Globe*, determined on a course of investigations by their Spotlight Team following up on leads, disclosures, and survivor tenacity, unearthed an ecclesial regime of shame-inducing magnitude. Law dealt with numerous cases of sex abuse—some clearly meeting the clinical and legal definition of pedophilia—by imposing silence on victims, transferring priests who were abusers to other parishes, intimidating the media and civil authorities when rumours began to circulate, and ultimately shielding some of the more egregious offenders by sending them to other dioceses or abroad, and all of this to protect the church from scandal, vicarious liability, and institutional decline.

Law's sins were on full display, and he was facing possible legal indictment by the attorney general of the state when John Paul whisked him off to Rome, gave him an honorary position at the Basilica of Santa Maria Maggiore, and managed to outrage Catholic and non-Catholic Boston in the bargain.

Canada fared no better.

The Mount Cashel Orphanage for Boys scandal that rocked Newfoundland in the last quarter of the twentieth century was to be the first but by no means last suppurating wound of the

church in Canada. Mount Cashel, a nineteenth-century apostolate of the Irish Christian Brothers, was first investigated by the
Royal Newfoundland Constabulary in 1975 as a consequence of
sexual and physical abuse allegations resulting in the removal of
two staff members. This was followed in 1982 by a second investigation, with one Christian Brother being convicted. But it was
not until 1989, when a torrent of media revelations demanded
a full investigation, that matters intensified. Commissions were
established, there was a flood of lawsuits, allegations levelled
against the clergy of the Archdiocese of St. John's eventually
prompted the resignation of Archbishop Alphonsus Penney,
Mount Cashel itself was demolished, and an air of despair and
horror, more impervious to light than the province's storied fog,
settled over the Catholic community on the Rock.

The Canadian church was to be battered by other scandals—
Antigonish Bishop Raymond Lahey's jailing over possession of
kiddie porn being the most prominent—and Catholics were
left reeling from the cascade of revelations that seemed to spare
no part of the country.

Both in Canada as well as in other jurisdictions around
the world, no one was prepared for what was to unfold. The
bishops and superiors of religious orders of men and women
hadn't seen anything of this magnitude before, and they relied
on civil lawyers, canon lawyers, accountants, psychiatrists, and
pastoral psychologists to give them direction. They became
dependent to a great degree on the expertise of others; some
of that expertise, in retrospect, was erroneous, short-sighted, or
inadequate. Few, including the professionals, fully grasped the
essential incurability of pedophiles, with their high recidivist
rate. Church authorities failed to distinguish between pedophiles and ephebophiles, predation and failures of chastity as

a consequence of psycho-sexual immaturity. As a result, they often appeared to be scrambling desperately from one solution to another, making life difficult for the vast majority of priests untouched by personal scandal but living under the shadow of a general scandal that in the public mind attached to them all.

It was a malaise that would not lift.

It remains as an unexorcisable spectre hanging over the John Paul II pontificate. His failure to take quick and decisive action against the malefactors, to believe those who came forward with complaints, to remove bishops derelict in their duty, and to get ahead of the problem by prioritizing it as a pastoral crisis combine to tarnish the reputation of a genuinely heroic and visionary pope.

Although his successor, Benedict XVI, was prefect of the Congregation for the Doctrine of the Faith during the majority of John Paul's papacy and was aware of the problem and more proactive in dealing with it, it was when he became pope that he worked to stem the tide of disclosures and the reputational damage inflicted on the church. He was only partially successful. It was during his papacy that the Irish church imploded. In a pastoral letter to the Catholics of Ireland in 2010, Benedict attempted to ameliorate some of the pain and anger directed toward the church by acknowledging serious errors made by the leadership, calling all to repentance, renewal, and reform, and placing the needs of the abused children at the centre of the church's pastoral attention.

And then, in 2011, following the release of the Cloyne Report, the Furies of hell were unleashed. The Cloyne Report—in addition to the earlier ones, like the Murphy and Ryan reports—provided a merciless and comprehensive account of ecclesiastical failure listing figures throughout the entire church personnel apparatus who were culpable: bishops, priests, brothers, sisters. It spared none, alienating countless Catholics, resulting at one point in a public chastising of the church and the Vatican by Prime Minister Enda Kenny: "the rape and torture of children were downplayed or mismanaged, to uphold instead the primacy of the Institution, its power, standing and reputation." Never before were such words by a Catholic politician in Catholic Ireland uttered in public. Rome reacted by recalling its nuncio to Ireland; shortly afterward, the Irish foreign minister, Eamon Gilmore, announced the closure of the Irish embassy to the Holy See. Gilmore denied that the closure was due to the recent incendiary exchange of words between Rome and Dublin, saying that it was a budget matter only. The explanation didn't mitigate the outrage it occasioned in the Vatican.

Diplomatic relations were eventually restored, new embassy quarters were opened, and governing parties changed. But no one has forgotten the boldness of the prime minister and that his outburst tinged with righteous anger represented the mood of the people. The folks in Rome didn't forget either.

Benedict was successful, however, in bringing to an end the decades-long sordid business known as the Maciel Affair. Marcial Maciel Degollado was the Mexican priest who in 1941 founded the Legionaries of Christ, dubbed by Britain's *Independent* as a "shadowy but powerful Catholic sect." During the time in which Maciel led the Legionaries of Christ, the organization certainly had structural and ascetical similarities with a sect: unquestioned obedience to and reverence for the founder; a heavy cloak of secrecy around its internal and external operations; interventions into the private lives of its members; severe sanctions for perceived disloyalty; lack of transparency concerning all fiscal matters. The Legionaries of Christ was and, after serious reforms, remains a canonically established community.

During Maciel's tenure, they had numerous property holdings, large reserves of cash, lucrative international investments, many seminaries and universities, a significant and influential lay affiliate body called Regnum Christi, and an intricate network of social and political connections in many countries, especially Mexico.

Most importantly, they were admired for their devotion to the Holy Father, "orthodox" spirituality, and financial largesse. They were favoured sons, and they revelled in the status this accorded them.

However, for many years, dating back to the 1950s, a cloud of suspicion hung over the founder's head, although variously dissipated and scattered. Maciel was frequently the object of allegations of sex abuse by seminarians, ex-seminarians, priests, and former Legionaires, but no progress was ever made confirming their validity.

It seemed that he was protected property, close to John Paul's heart, and Maciel rested secure in what he saw as a privileged relationship to the pontiff.

But pontiffs come and go; once Benedict ascended to the papacy, he suspended Maciel from the public exercise of his priestly ministry, consigned him to a penitential place, and watched carefully as the fabric of skillfully woven lies unravelled with unsettling speed following the founder's death in 2008.

The rumours proved to be true; the accusations were confirmed; the length and breadth of Maciel's perfidy were exposed to all. The Father, as he insisted on being called,[4] led a double life: he had numerous lovers with whom he had many children, and he abused nephews, seminarians, and priests while at the same time amassing a private fortune.

He was John Paul's Rasputin.

But Benedict would not be his tsar.

Benedict—even posthumously—was tarred by his distant connection with the priest offender Peter Hullermann, who was allowed upon request from the Diocese of Essen into the Archdiocese of Munich to receive psychiatric treatment for his abuse of minors during Ratzinger's time as archbishop. A far from prudential decision by the usually cautious Ratzinger: there remains some debate as to Ratzinger's degree of involvement in the decision, but it happened on his watch.

Even death does not shield you from controversy around clerical sex abuse, as both John Paul and Benedict demonstrate.

Undoubtedly, a thought that continues to cross the mind of their current successor. Francis must have wished that the clerical sex abuse disease would have been fully diagnosed and appropriate remedies employed to ensure that it was addressed once and for all upon his election as Peter. After all, there are other matters pressing on papal attention—the plight of migrants, widening economic global inequity, the survival of the planet, the critical need for focused attention on the plethora of peripheries that connect the church with its Gospel imperative, et cetera. Without downplaying the seriousness of the systemic abuse crisis, strategies have been engaged to "eliminate the filth," as Benedict once said, and it is time to move on.

Not so, Francis quickly discovered.

Allegations from across the world continue seemingly unabated. And Francis has found himself at centre stage. In 2018, he became entangled in the Bishop Barros imbroglio and needed to extricate himself from the self-induced furore.

Juan Barros had been appointed a bishop in Chile in 2015; his appointment was decried by many Chileans because of Barros's association with the notorious serial abuser Monsignor Fernando Karadima. Francis was adamant that there was no proof of misdeeds by Barros and that he was being maligned. As he abruptly said to a group of journalists: "The day they bring me proof against Bishop Barros I will speak. There's not one piece of evidence against him. It's calumny."

And then, following a report prepared by two prelates he dispatched to Chile to conduct a thorough investigation of the Barros and Karadima connections, as well as the larger abuse issues in the country, Francis was confronted with an embarrassing situation. The prelates—the formidable Maltese archbishop and canon law investigator Charles Scicluna, and his associate from the Congregation for the Doctrine of the Faith, Jordi Bertomeu—delivered a damning 2,300-page report outlining a series of now recognizable abuses: widespread cover-up, the complaints of victims either discounted or minimized, priest offenders reassigned, episcopal duplicity or denial. And all in abundant evidence. Francis needed to do something. And he did. Vaticanologist and historian John Cornwell, author of many books on Catholic life and papal leadership, including the controversial *Hitler's Pope: The Secret History of Pius XII* and the Pope Francis–friendly *Church Interrupted: Havoc and Hope—The Tender Revolt of Pope Francis* has no hesitation in saying that Francis's apology was unprecedented, shattering a mystique around the papacy that will be impossible to reverse. In Cornwell's words: "Francis made a public apology, unprecedented in any modern pope ... Anybody who has studied the culture and behavior of the papacy in the modern period will realize the astounding disruption of this admission … The day Francis made that admission a mystique evaporated. It may take some years, and several papacies for it to sink in; but the papacy could never be the same again."[5]

Whether Francis's apology actually changed the papacy forever may be debatable, but what is not debatable is the hard impact the Barros misjudgment had on Francis personally. He learned several lessons he would not forget: submit to scrutiny the advice he receives from parties with much to lose from revelations of complicity; listen to critics and victims with an open mind; take to heart his own injunction to clergy that they lead with humility; grasp the enormity of the abuse issue and the fact that it constitutes the severest threat to the church's credibility.

Francis would soon act further by issuing his *Letter to the People of God* on August 20, 2018, in which he acknowledged the devastating impact of clerical sex abuse, asserted the indispensable role of the victims in bringing us to the awareness that things *must* change, and reminding the church that its canonical procedures and norms, although important, were by their nature limited and designed mostly to protect the church, whereas immersion in the problem by recognizing its provenance in a culture of clericalism was essential for effective personal and institutional purgation.

Still, as Francis biographer and collaborator Austen Ivereigh observes in light of the worsening situation in the United States, as countless cases emerge in Pennsylvania and other states where statutes of limitation were being lifted, allowing victims to sue the church, Francis's initiative had a less than enthusiastic reception:

The letter went down poorly among conservatives in the United States, where many asked indignantly why *they* should do penance for the sins of errant clergy and corrupt bishops. Others complained about the lack of "concrete measures" in the pope's response. For their part, the US bishops were remarkably silent about it. Their best-known communicator, YouTube star Bishop Robert Barron, recorded two widely viewed videos on the abuse scandals a few days after it was released, without once mentioning the letter.[6]

Frustration with the continued failure to get on top of the abuse issue—a hydra that seemingly cannot be tamed—is especially acute in the United States, the epicentre of the worst excesses. In spite of many legal and political moves to accept responsibility through episcopal and financial accountability, some of which have been successful, bankrupt dioceses have become common, the media remains relentless in its pursuit of exposing corruption, and allegations and complaints persist, although their number is dramatically down from the peak period at the turn of the twenty-first century. The continued controversies sap energy and paralyze the preponderant number of clergy whose lives are untouched by the scourge of abuse.

US frustration is compounded by what they see as Rome's inaction in formulating guidelines that can be universally and consistently applied. In 2019, Francis issued *Vos estis lux mundi* (You Are the Light of the World), a *vade mecum* or manual that clarifies the existing rules on the sex abuse scandal. In it he noted that

the crimes of sexual abuse offend Our Lord, cause physical, psychological and spiritual damage to the victims and harm

the community of the faithful. In order that these phenom-
ena, in all their forms, never happen again, a continuous and
profound conversion of hearts is needed, attested by concrete
and effective actions that involve everyone in the Church.
Therefore, it is good that procedures be universally adopted
to prevent and combat these crimes that betray the trust of
the faithful.

In many ways this is papal boilerplate, but its contents
need to be repeated and appropriated again and again, in every
chancery, canonical tribunal, parish community, and episcopal
conference. Francis has strengthened the legal norms to ensure
that bishops who are guilty of sex abuse themselves or who
have failed in oversight by engineering a cover-up will not be
given a pass. Accountability will be implemented at every level
of the hierarchy. Cardinals will not be exempt from the most
demanding sanctions.

As Theodore McCarrick discovered in 2020.

Cardinal Theodore McCarrick, both affectionately or mock-
ingly referred to as "Ted," was a bishop-maker, an unequalled
money machine for Vatican coffers, a senior prelate of liberal
leanings in an American hierarchy known for its stolid conser-
vatism, and a clerical bon vivant who consorted comfortably
with both ecclesiastical and secular elites.

Variously the first bishop of Metuchen, New Jersey, and
auxiliary bishop of New York, then archbishop of Newark,
his church promotions culminated with his appointment as
cardinal archbishop in Washington, DC.

And then it all spectacularly collapsed.

McCarrick was credibly accused to have abused seminarians
over his long career, selecting the chosen ones, inviting them

into his confidence and then into his bed at his cottage on the Jersey Shore. This is a classic predation pattern: cultivate the prey with charm and power.

Once again, John Paul II paid little heed to the rumours circulating in the highest church circles about McCarrick's alleged behaviour with seminarians and young priests. In fact, it was John Paul who created McCarrick a cardinal in 2001. At the time, there were no complaints coming forth from victims, only the suspicions—already long in duration—that activities at the cottage consisted of more than cribbage, chow, and clerical chitchat.[7]

Following a stream of public accusations in 2017, McCarrick resigned from the College of Cardinals; in 2018, Francis instructed the Vatican's secretary of state, Cardinal Pietro Parolin, to conduct a comprehensive examination of "all the records preserved in the Archives of the Dicasteries and Offices of the Holy See regarding McCarrick, in order to ascertain the relevant facts, placing them in their historical context and evaluating them objectively." The result appeared in 2020: *Report on the Holy See's Institutional Knowledge and Decision-Making Related to Former Cardinal Theodore Edgar McCarrick (1930 to 2017)*.

The significance of this document cannot be underestimated. Francis opted for a level of disclosure hitherto unknown in Vatican circles: no stone was to be left unturned. The investigation did not spare ecclesiastical sensitivities and identified failures in the hierarchy's closed culture. It also exposed political lobbying in Vatican factions, serious flaws in the promotion process, broken communications between relevant dicasteries, and minimally informed pontiffs. In the end, the Francis-ordered report outlined in great detail a sordid record of institutional blindness, addressed individual culpability, provided a long list of sexually abused victims, many of whom spoke with uncensored openness to the Vatican investigators, and in no way sugar-coated the reputational consequences for McCarrick and the church.

For McCarrick, it was a catastrophic career-killer. Stripped of his cardinalate, he was also laicized and thereby deprived of his priesthood. He remains a tragic reminder of the sorry cost of hubris, institutional laxity, and the corrosive and ever-lingering effects of clericalism.

For Francis, it was an opportunity to assert control over the mismanaged clerical sex abuse crisis at the top and in doing so defend his record against the volleys of vituperation levelled at him by his former nuncio to Washington, Carlo Maria Viganò. No ordinary disgruntled Vatican careerist, Archbishop Viganò has been a thorn in the papal flesh for years: he regularly denounces Francis for all the excesses in the church, its collapse of discipline, its blanket liberalism, its weakening of identity in the face of the assaults of postmodernity, its hidden socialist agenda, its morally dissolute bishops protected in office by an ideology-fixated pope. You name it, according to Viganò, Francis has done it.

With Viganò, it all came to a head with his publicly distributed *Testimony* of August 2018: part screed, part jeremiad, but written, as he would have it, under obedience to his conscience and because the church is foundering badly under his boss, Pope Francis. Viganò's detailed letter of complaint touched a chord among many conservative laity and was silently applauded by those bishops who were in agreement but not yet bold enough to take on Peter.

Although no longer in office, Viganò spends a great deal of

his time marshalling Catholic malcontents in the corporate and political world, dissident bishops opposed to the Francis papacy, right-wing leaders and influencers distraught by Francis's revolutionary efforts to change his church, all in the hope of discrediting the pope and forcing his resignation. He also goes after Francis in personal terms and has publicly berated him for allowing corrupt bishops like McCarrick to thrive. His allegations of inaction by Francis in the face of manifest evidence of sexual immorality by McCarrick were rigorously refuted in the Vatican report. That report persuaded many, but not Viganò. The retired ambassador is not for turning.[8]

But if Francis has made headway with the reform of the church's practices regarding sexual abuse and clergy—both those traditionally called the high clergy, as in the episcopacy, and the low clergy, as in the diocesan and religious order priests—his track record remains dangerously spotty.

For sure, he has listened to survivors, and they in turn have been moved by his personal remorse and pain over their treatment, demonstrating again and again how his personal credibility as an attentive pastor through these one-on-one and group encounters has been in ample evidence.

Early in his papacy, he established the Pontifical Commission for the Protection of Minors. He called a global summit of bishops to address the abuse crisis. The Institute of Anthropology: Interdisciplinary Studies on Human Dignity and Care was created in the Jesuit Gregorian University with his approval, and bishops and professional experts were exhorted to be proactive on this file. No more invoking pontifical secrets as a stratagem of avoiding accountability; no more stonewalling.

And then, reality set in.

In spite of his personal sensitivity to the complainants, his compassion for their suffering and anger, as well as his determination to root out the rot and hold senior prelates directly to account, the abuse crisis refuses to abate. The Sauvé Report that emanated from France brought on a new wave of litigations, outrage, firings, and internal tumult.

At the end of September 2021, the pope met with the archbishop of Paris, accompanied by many other French hierarchs, as a prelude to the release the following month of the explosive Sauvé Report. This investigation was commissioned by the French episcopacy in 2018 following a series of clerical sex abuse scandals that included the French Primate, the cardinal archbishop of Lyon, Philippe Barbarin, who though never accused of sex abuse himself failed to report the abuses of a chronic offender, the former priest Bernard Preynat. Barbarin was held to account and sentenced to a six-month suspended prison sentence, which was overturned on appeal. Barbarin tendered his resignation to Francis, which the pope declined to accept at the time, and all of the country wrestled with the confusion, pain, and anger generated by the trial and its outcome.

The Sauvé Report was conceived as a pledge of the French hierarchy's earnest resolve to deal with the aftermath of the sex abuse disclosures. But if it was designed to mollify the public, it failed, as it actually revealed even more shocking news. Francis had instructed his French bishops at the September meeting to "look truth in the face."

It was their Dorian Gray moment.

It was a morally shattering picture.

The statistical tally recorded in the report was staggering. Although there has been subsequent debate over the veracity of the numbers—216,000 people sexually abused by clerics since 1950, an additional 114,000 abused by lay people in ecclesiastical

service, with the number of priest abusers conservatively esti-
mated at 3,000—the scope and seriousness of the data has been
accepted as valid by the commissioners, the bishops themselves.[9]

Jean-Marc Sauvé, a retired senior civil servant, judge,
and committed Catholic berated his church for showing a
"profound and total, even cruel, indifference to the victims." He
also disclosed publicly that he had to seek psychological coun-
selling himself after spending so much gruelling time listening
to the experiences of the survivors. His report is not simply a
compilation, historical analysis, and sociological summary: it
is personal.

The report's team drew on numerous experts in jurisprudence, history, psychology, sociology, and theology, interviewed
more than 6,000 victims, and then "presented their findings to
a church still capable of shock."[10]

The Jesuit theologian-rector of the Centre Sèvres in Paris,
Étienne Grieu, was moved to ask in *La Croix International*:
"how is that we did not dare say aloud what we were witnessing
in secret? And how is that we did not give credit to those who
had the courage to alert us?"

Trying to find answers to these questions has bedevilled
Catholic authorities for decades now. But we actually *do* know
how these pathologies have been enabled; we actually *do* know
what needs to be done beyond the reactive and restorative strategies we have adopted. And Francis knows, too, even if his
bishops do not.

A month before the Sauvé Report was issued, Tomáš Halík,
a Czech psychotherapist, sociology professor at Prague's Charles
University, philosopher, and priest-theologian (he is also a
recipient of the coveted Templeton Award), delivered an address
in Warsaw about the scandal of abusive priests in which he

noted—and in this he joins Italian author and church historian Massimo Faggioli, among others—that "the situation of the Catholic Church today strongly resembles the situation just before the Reformation ... It is necessary not just to change structures but to change the mentality, to change the culture of relationships within the Church."

If we are to seal the coffin of clericalism for good, then we must take action: we must, as Francis told the French bishops who met with him, "look the truth in the face."

But how that plays out in the context of the universal church and the universal pastor is much more complex than the worthy exhortation to look truth in the face. As Francis has discovered again and again.

Before France, there was Germany, England, Wales, Ireland, the United States, Australia, Chile, Canada, and so it goes. Before the Sauvé Report, there was the Winter Report (Canada), the Ryan Report (Ireland), the Nolan Report (England), and these are only a fraction of them. The number of plays, documentaries, novels, and scholarly studies are legion—*Fall, Deliver Us from Evil, The Boys of St. Vincent, Doubt, The Bishop's Man, A Lost Tribe, Smile, Snow, Old God's Time, Faith, A History of Loneliness, Pedophiles and Priests: Anatomy of a Contemporary Crisis, A Tragic Grace: The Catholic Church and Sexual Abuse, The Post-Pandemic Church: Prophetic Possibilities* ... and this is the short list.

Francis is making great strides on some fronts—stricter canonical requirements for reporting, removal of errant and negligent bishops, private encounters with survivors, and heightening of the moral and spiritual consequences of this dread toxin in the body of Christ—but on other fronts, he is failing to deliver.

Marie Collins, the Irish survivor, public advocate for church redress, and principal spokesperson on the issue for the Irish church, resigned her position on the Pontifical Commission for the Protection of Minors in protest over the resistance she faced from the curial administration; and Baroness Sheila Hollins, a prominent former member of the commission and past president of the Royal College of Psychiatrists in the United Kingdom, has expressed strong concern over the direction of the pontifical commission that Francis himself created. Most distressing, however, was the resignation of the Jesuit expert on child protection, theologian-psychologist Hans Zollner, who identified in his letter of resignation the shortcomings prevalent in the protocols of "responsibility, compliance, accountability and transparency."

The internal squabbles, dicasterial jostlings for power, and attendant budget allocation disputes have diminished Francis's ability to get on top of this file. High-level resignations, curial inertia, and clerical opposition to lay oversight set up barriers to Francis's efforts to eradicate clericalism. In addition, the institutional failure to see the clerical sex abuse crisis as something more than a catalogue of sins that can be absolved, of renegade priests that have been brought to heel, of media overreaction and lawyerly venality, all stoked by a societal and visceral anti-Catholicism, combine to make for a near insurmountable resistance.

Francis recognizes the inadequacies of a mentality of entitlement that still prevails in seminaries and theologates; he knows that as long as the priesthood is held captive to the spiritually and emotionally ruinous culture of clericalism—a culture that renders priestly renewal compromised at its core—his efforts are hobbled.

For those Catholics who call out for immediate, meaningful, and transparent reform—and their number is growing by the minute—patience for Francis's Sisyphean cleansing has been replaced by a crushing demoralization. And Francis knows that it isn't just the laity who are demoralized. Countless priests, brothers, nuns, and monks persisting with personal fidelity to their lives of religious service under the shadow of this dark history continue to carry their own overwhelming feelings of shame and betrayal. No less a figure than the German bishop Franz-Josef Bode, vice-president of the German bishops' conference, remarked that during his many conversations with sex abuse victims, there were times when he nearly lost his own faith. There are many in and out of the hierarchy who share this experience, and Francis acknowledges this pain in addition to the far greater pain of the survivors.

Sex abuse and emotional predation are not the exclusive preserve of the clergy, of course, as the Jean Vanier affair demonstrates. Vanier, a Canadian icon whose lineal pedigree and universal acclaim as a great humanitarian were once without parallel, was discovered after his death in 2019 to have abused several women who sought his counsel. Vanier, a spiritual eminence, Companion of the Order of Canada, was the co-founder of L'Arche, the international movement that creates communities for people with and without intellectual disabilities.

Because of his work with the L'Arche communities, his reputation as a man of unassailable spiritual calibre, his extensive influence as a writer, and his international religious presence, the disclosures of abuse wracked the Catholic world—and beyond. The former president of Ireland, Mary McAleese, in a letter to Pope Francis in 2020 that was made available to the press, highlights the level of anger and anguish many Catholics felt:

> Vanier was consistently lauded by the Church at the highest level without the remotest suggestion that there was anything worrying in his character ... I am one of those who regarded Vanier as inspirational for decades. Hearing the awful story of his sexually and spiritually abusive conduct was devastating. Even worse was learning that the Holy See had been aware since the 1950s of his malevolent proclivities and those of his colleague Père Thomas Philippe ... Many times in recent years I have had reason to despair at the failures at papal, episcopal and curial levels regarding the protection of vulnerable children and the vindication of victims.

McAleese was justified in her fury but premature in its expression. And her deep suspicion of Vatican involvement is not entirely justified, as revealed in a 900-page L'Arche International report, *Control and Abuse: An Investigation on Thomas Philippe, Jean Vanier and L'Arche*, published in January of 2023 following a two-year-long no-holds-barred investigation into the allegations and disclosures. The report explores every aspect of the affair—psychoanalytical, sociological, psychiatric, theological, juridical, and historical—with the commissioners of the report given access to every pertinent document and record, including the Vatican's. Not *entirely* justified, as I say, but not without foundation.

Vanier's "spiritual father" was the Dominican friar Thomas Philippe. The latter's eccentric Mariology, charismatic personality, and mesmerizing charm held sway over Vanier's life for decades. The general introduction of the L'Arche report notes that "the mystique of T. Philippe is based in particular on the affirmation of incestuous sexual relations between Jesus and Mary during their earthly life and continuing in their heavenly life. This religious vocabulary encloses people in a gangue." The executive report declares Vanier and Philippe's relationship the core of "a perverse mystico-sexual and toxic nucleus." As late as 2009, Vanier recalled how "listening to him and in his presence, I had a taste for God, to love Jesus and Mary ... I felt transformed in his presence ... This shows how deeply Jesus used him to enter into me."[11]

The Holy Office of the Inquisition had already investigated the charges against Thomas Philippe in a major report of 1956, severely restricted his ministry, and imposed hard sanctions on him. In a subsequent report by the now renamed Congregation for the Doctrine of the Faith in 1975, the Vatican office noted the punishment of Philippe "for serious offenses of a pseudo-mystical nature" and called Vanier "*il piu fanatico dei discepoli P. Philippe*" (the most fanatical of Père Philippe's disciples).

But in spite of these censures, Thomas Philippe was enabled by Vanier to continue his ministry at L'Arche headquarters in Trosly, France, up to his death in 1993.

The commissioners of the L'Arche report underscore the Vatican's diligence and thoroughness in investigating Père Thomas's morally and legally untoward behaviour but also note that that diligence was not always exercised with appropriate rigour, with its conclusions and judgment remaining under secrecy. They have no hesitation in rebuking the Vatican, however, and in particular John Paul II:

Given the many people who suffered from Thomas Philippe's spiritual and sexual abuse, directly or indirectly via followers who shared his delusion and reproduced his actions, and in the first instance his brother Marie-Dominique and Jean Vanier ... the photograph of these three men received by Pope John Paul II speaks volumes about their ability to infiltrate, seduce and deceive, whereas the Vatican was supposed to be aware. *It also speaks volumes about the dysfunctions of the ecclesiastical institution* [italics added].

So, McAleese is right to hold the Vatican to account but incorrect in assuming that the Vatican was complicit in covering up the history of abuses. Its failure lies in insufficient vigilance, intra-curial operations conducted in a culture of secrecy, and misplaced trust in the Dominican order to enforce the canonical sanctions.

Pope Francis's admiration and affection for Vanier—expressed effusively on the occasion of his death—speaks to his own ignorance regarding the Vatican's previous investigations. After all, as the L'Arche commissioners write in *Control and Abuse*: "Vanier for many years passed as a most saintly man, the living embodiment of the Gospel, a man whose charisma was there for all to see, a *starets*, the lodestar of the Catholic renewal of John Paul II's pontificate." We now know that Vanier's strategy of holy self-effacement was really a concerted strategy of self-erasure. Less spiritual and intellectual humility and more optics spin-doctoring.[12]

The case of Vanier and Philippe, as well as other recent eruptions of scandal, duplicity, and violation of vows—the lay liturgical musician and widely popular Catholic composer David Haas, with a history of sexual exploitation, and Marko Rupnik, the celebrated mosaicist and artist, expelled from the Jesuits for sexually manipulating a community of Slovenian nuns—highlight the larger challenge facing Francis: the misalliance of an ossified spirituality with a patriarchal anthropology preventing an integrated sexuality and life-affirming spirituality from flourishing in tandem.

Confronted with the seemingly endless spate of sexual misdeeds by those called to serve the church, frustrated by the in-house recalcitrance of prelates querying the severity of the sex abuse crisis and minimizing its impact, and crippled in his efforts to effect change because of power struggles at home and abroad, Francis *has* been successful in modelling a pastoral approach that has gained some momentum as a template for genuine reparation and healing.

This approach was much in evidence when Francis intervened directly by contacting superiors of the Comboni Missionaries (also known as the Verona Fathers), instructing them to work with abuse survivors of St Peter Claver College in Mirfield, England. He met with the victims himself in Rome and has repeatedly insisted that the church move beyond a legalistic and adversarial approach to one marked by compassion.

For Francis, this is best understood in the context of his thinking of life "for all its confrontations as the art of encounter." Francis spoke to a "culture of encounter" in *Fratelli tutti* and the "art of encounter" in his opening address on October 10, 2021, launching the Vatican's ambitious Synod on Synodality. That launch inaugurated a two-year process culminating with the Synod in Rome in two parts: in October 2023 and October 2024.

In his 2021 address, Francis offered the art of encounter as an antidote to the art of the deal, underscoring that "every encounter ... calls for openness, courage and a willingness to let ourselves be challenged by the presence and stories of others ...

Let us not soundproof our hearts." The only way forward as a church, an ecclesial body resistant to the status of a museum, determined to be a dynamic organism rather than an atrophying one, is the incorporation of the art of encounter in all our dealings *as* a church.

This pastoral strategy offers the only genuinely hopeful way out of the morass created by the sex abuse scandals. Francis will have plenty of opportunity to display this strategy's possibilities of effecting reform when he turns his attention to the unfolding nightmare of the Indian residential schools moral debacle in the Canadian church.

May 27, 2021, was a dark day in Canadian history. That's when there was a public announcement indicating that some two hundred unmarked graves had been discovered on the grounds of the Kamloops Indian Residential School in British Columbia, a school that operated since its inception in 1890 until its transfer to government administration in 1969 under the supervision of the Oblates of Mary Immaculate, a Catholic missionary order of priests and brothers. Although rumours of these unmarked graves had persisted in the Indigenous communities for decades, and although the Truth and Reconciliation Commission Report of 2015 had indicated that some six thousand children died while attending schools like the one in Kamloops, the impact of the ground radar discoveries had a seismic impact on the country. It became a cumulative horror as more discoveries at other schools across the Prairie provinces and Ontario exponentially augmented the nightmare of systemic abuse. There was no escaping the ugly truth of centuries of neglect and complicity of churches and governments in a process that is now identified as cultural genocide—while many Indigenous people and groups use the term "genocide."

Globe and Mail columnist Andrew Coyne summed up the outrage of the country when he wrote that the residential schools policy

> could not have been sustained all those years without the tacit support, or at least acquiescence, of prime ministers, members of Parliament, civil servants and ultimately the general population. The shame of it—the immense, unspeakable shame—must be worn, not solely by the individuals most directly responsible, but by Canada … even a great nation—especially a great nation—must acknowledge its sins, and more than that, atone for them.[13]

For sure, the country as a whole must carry the opprobrium of the residential schools policy, the cruel incarceration and forced separation of children from their parents by authorities determined to assimilate the Indigenous Peoples—First Nations, Inuit, Métis—and in the process extirpate their language, spirituality, communal rituals, and cultural identity. A form of death.

But the churches took the brunt of the attack following the Kamloops discovery, as they were the oversight bodies contracted by the federal government to administer the schools. These churches included the Anglican Church of Canada, the Presbyterian Church of Canada, the United Church of Canada (the largest of the Protestant churches), and the Methodist Church.

But by far the biggest player was the Roman Catholic Church, with responsibility for more than half of the schools and with dozens of religious orders exercising on-site administration. Such orders included the Oblates, the Jesuits, the Grey

Nuns, and the Sisters of St. Ann. The majority of their schools were concentrated in the West.

The award-winning poet and essayist Tim Lilburn, a former Jesuit seminarian with an acute philosophical sensibility, rightly situates our intellectual and spiritual malaise in epistemology:

> Roman Catholics must identify what attitudes in Catholicism instigated the vicious, thanophilic culture in residential schools that religious orders ran for over a hundred year period in North America. These dispositions, missiological, ecclesiastical, spiritual, inter-personal and the thought-worlds backing them up, *must be purged*: much will disappear if this exercise is performed with conviction. Parts of hegemonic whiteness will be disabled and a certain form of religion will become uncomfortable to practice.[14]

Indeed, as Lilburn says, it is a matter of knowing, a matter of intellectual apprehending, a matter of emotional seeing, and we need now to do this differently. Our moral and existential survival depend upon it. And key to this alternative way of knowing, this different epistemology, is the realization that the *other* remains the *other* in our understanding, is respected and valued precisely because the differences that exist in the face of the *other* define the *other* and are not to be eradicated.

Although official Catholic thinking on matters of missiology, interfaith dialogue, and religious freedom have changed profoundly as a consequence of the Second Vatican Council, centuries of encrusted prejudice, racial superiority, and ecclesial triumphalism retain their residual power.

This must change. The Kamloops unmarked graves have ushered in this change, or at least brought the nation, and the

Catholic Church in particular, to a new awareness: new in its moral urgency and new in its conscience-driven imperative to act.

The discovery of The Missing, *Le Estcwicwéy* in the language of the Tk'emlúps te Secwépemc, can lead to what Garry Gottfriedson calls *Tsqelmucwílc,* or "circling back to our humanity." But it requires both a change of heart and a resolve to repair the fissures and fractures of our relationship to the First Peoples of this land in order to succeed.

Catholic educator and deacon Harry Lafond of Muskeg Lake Cree Nation in Saskatchewan, who once pursued priesthood in the Oblate order, highlights the historic significance of the Kamloops revelations and the challenges now facing settler Catholics and their bishops: "the graves at Kamloops have really awakened Canadians and generated renewed interest in knowing what happened ... *Wahkohtowin* in Cree refers to building relationships and connections; we have laws of behavior about how to treat human beings. To reset the relationship between the Catholic Church and Indigenous peoples, we have to follow processes that take us there."[15]

A signal item in that process is the 2015 report of the federally established Truth and Reconciliation Commission of Canada (TRC), a body whose express purpose was redressing the "legacy of residential schools." Included among the ninety-four Calls to Action is number 58:

> We call upon the Pope to issue an apology to Survivors, their families, and communities for the Roman Catholic Church's role in the spiritual, cultural, emotional, physical, and sexual abuse of First Nations, Inuit, and Métis children in Catholic-run residential schools. We call for that apology to be similar

to the 2010 apology issued to Irish victims of abuse and to occur within one year of the issuing of this Report and to be delivered by the Pope in Canada.

It would take not one but seven years for Recommendation #58 to be enacted.

And beforehand, there would be much skirmishing among the players: the church hierarchy, Indigenous leaders, and the federal government. In a 2017 visit to the Vatican, Prime Minister Justin Trudeau cited this recommendation when requesting that Francis come to Canada to deliver the apology. A year later, the pope wrote and declined. Trudeau expressed public disappointment with the papal decision, including his personal dismay as a Catholic that the Indigenous request was being denied. This intensified the already cool relations between the Canadian Conference of Catholic Bishops (CCCB) and the federal government. Following the Kamloops revelations, things got much worse. The Catholic laity were stunned and shamed by what they perceived as episcopal inaction. There was a cascade of further discoveries of unmarked graves. The Canadian media and public at large were puzzled and agitated by the lack of leadership among the country's Catholic bishops. Anger spilled out in several places, with churches being torched, statues toppled, cathedral steps and doors splattered with red paint, Catholic sacred places defaced.

It looked to many as if the CCCB was keen on keeping the pope out of the country for fear that his presence could complicate church–government–Indigenous relations. Given that the religious orders that ran the schools have apologized, made financial restitution, and provided other services as stipulated by the TRC report, the majority had provided full access to private records and accounts, and those that had not yet done so pledged to comply, the CCCB's defiant stance threatened to compromise the moral leadership of the full Catholic community.

After all, other popes in the past had met with Indigenous leaders either in Canada, in the case of John Paul II, or in the Vatican, in the case of Benedict XVI. In addition, palpable goodwill existed between the Holy See and the Indigenous Peoples of Canada for years. And still the CCCB chose to do battle with Trudeau over his personal attempts to pressure for compliance with Recommendation #58. The decision for the pope not to come to Canada—more homemade than Rome-bred—did not play out well on the national scene. Trudeau, ever adept at shifting with enviable facility between being the Catholic *homo religiosus* and the Catholic *homo politicus*, read the national temper far better than the CCCB did.

Hypercaution, defensiveness, and legerdemain rather than pastoral openness and transparency largely defined the church's response. While it met its financial obligations per the Indian Residential Schools Settlement Agreement, providing $29 million in cash for the Aboriginal Healing Foundation and $25 million for services in kind to various Indigenous communities, it raised an embarrassing fraction of an additional $25 million for healing and reconciliation and, because of a legal loophole, was able to secure a release from the government for that full sum. It did so in part by claiming that the Roman Catholic Church as constituted exists as a church *in* Canada and not as the church *of* Canada, that it is in both canon and civil law *not* a national church, as are her sister denominations the Anglicans and United Church; as a result, negotiations over reparations, compensation, and apologies must be worked out with the fifty Catholic legal entities that comprise the various religious orders and dioceses directly affected.

Many of the bishops in the CCCB saw no reason why they should be involved in areas that fell outside their jurisdiction. They had plenty of sympathy, of course, but their priorities included basilica and cathedral repairs and renovations, seminary upgrades, and pious initiatives designed to reawaken an older Catholic sensibility. Other bishops, facing severe financial reordering of their dioceses because of falling attendance and aging clergy, saw Indigenous issues as legitimate but not of first-order concern. The Catholic Church in Canada may not be a national church, but had it *acted* nationally: it would have gone some way to insulate the hierarchy from a situation that has devastated its credibility.

But some bishops responded differently and with prophetic force—they knew there was both a local *and* national obligation for leadership.

Regina Archbishop Don Bolen, a one-time Roman curial official whose archdiocese includes the Cowessess residential school, which was as infamous as Kamloops, publicly and swiftly acknowledged that the discovery of the unmarked graves "brings us face to face with the brutal legacy of the Indian Residential School System ... I know that apologies seem a very small step as the weight of past suffering comes into greater light, but I extend that apology, and pledge to do what we can to turn that apology into meaningful concrete actions." In addition, the metropolitan archbishop of Vancouver, J. Michael Miller, was forthright in acknowledging past atrocities and church complicity in his "Expression of Commitment": "The church was unquestionably wrong in implementing a government colonialist policy which resulted in devastation for children, families and communities. If words of apology for such unspeakable deeds are to bring life and healing, they must be accompanied by tangible actions that foster the full disclosure of the truth. Truth comes before reconciliation."

Catholics, however, were not to be easily mollified. Pressure to bring the pope to Canada, to have him reconsider his decision, to arrange for a delegation of Indigenous leaders to meet him personally in the Vatican, to get the CCCB to honour its full financial obligations as the other Christian churches had already done was augmented by relentless and critical media coverage.

As Elder Sam Achneepineskum, a member of Marten Falls First Nation, said to journalist Tanya Talaga: "They hire lawyers and then more lawyers to convince themselves they didn't do wrong. Yet it is easy to take the good road. It is Jesus's teachings—it is not about image and creating a false sense of self. How can anyone who calls himself a Christian not see that?"[16]

Time to take the good road.

And so, the Indigenous Peoples were on the road to Rome in March and April of 2022 to see the Successor of Peter under the theme of "walking together toward healing and reconciliation." They came to him so that he would come to them. And it worked.

When he gave his much-sought-after apology in the Vatican's majestic Sala Clementina for the church's participation in the residential schools, following intense listening to the various representative groups—First Nations, Inuit, and Métis—all of whom he met with separately, and now collectively in the Clementina, Francis did not avoid the painful; he embraced it: "I have said this to you and now I am repeating it. Sorrow and shame: for the role that a number of Catholics, particularly those with educational responsibilities, have had in all these things that wounded you, in the abuses you suffered and in the lack of respect shown to your identity, your culture and even your spiritual values. All these things are contrary to the Gospel of Jesus Christ."

Francis listened to the Indigenous leaders and to the Canadian episcopal reps who accompanied them. He also sought the counsel of the senior Canadians in the Roman Curia: Cardinal Marc Ouellet, prefect of the Dicastery for Bishops, and Cardinal Michael Czerny, a fellow Jesuit who worked in the area of integral human development and who would become an increasingly trusted confidant of the pope.

He would come to Turtle Island.

And he would do in Canada what he did on his 2015 trip to Bolivia, when he humbly asked for forgiveness for the "crimes committed against the native peoples during the so-called conquest of America." He would set the tone for the Canadian church's obligations, embody the model to be used, and summon the believing community to forswear any alignment of the "logic of the sword with the power of the Cross."

Francis listened to the Indigenous leaders when they were in Rome. He listened to their legends, tasted in his skin their history of suffering, their struggles to preserve their heritage, their special affection for their elderly and their ancestors. He was inspired by their capacity to see Creation whole, not subservient to a species hierarchy that relegates all non-human life to a subordinate functionalism. These are a people, after all, who treasure our common home. In a way, they are *his* people.

When the details for the papal visit were worked out— acute time constraints, juggling priorities and requests from all the players, an immobilized pontiff due to knee and sciatica problems, an international media jockeying for locales and interviews, and cost allocations—it was a bit of miracle to pull off anything of this nature in less than four months. But the CCCB, Indigenous communities, and government did manage to work together to achieve a qualified success.

Francis came to Canada, arriving in Edmonton, Alberta, on July 24, 2022, and returning to Rome from Iqaluit, Nunavut, on July 29. During those intense six days, he met with thousands of former residential school inhabitants in Maskwacis, home to the former Ermineskin Residential School. He visited the Sacred Heart Church of the First Peoples in downtown Edmonton. He presided at Mass in Edmonton's Commonwealth Stadium on the feast day of Saint Anne. He participated in a prayer service at Lac Ste. Anne, site of an annual pilgrimage for tens of thousands of Indigenous participants. He met with Canada's first Indigenous governor general, Mary Simon, in Quebec City. He celebrated Mass at Sainte-Anne-de-Beaupré; participated in a Vespers service for clergy, religious, and ecclesial lay workers in the Cathedral-Basilica of Notre-Dame de Québec; had a private meeting with fellow Jesuits; and concluded his "penitential pilgrimage" with Inuit on their own land.

Francis came as a penitent: he came to publicly apologize for the history of abuse inflicted on the Indigenous Peoples and to model a way of healing and reconciliation.

He also came as a missionary. Not the kind of missionary who brings his culture with him, imposing faith on an unreceptive audience, transplanting a Christo-European notion of church on a noble and foreign reality. Not that kind of missionary. But a missionary like the sixteenth-century Italian Jesuit Matteo Ricci, who adopted the Chinese way of living, became fluent in the language and dialects of the land, was the first European to enter the Forbidden City, befriended courtiers and scholars, and is honoured as a conduit for dialogue and peace between cultures. For Francis, Ricci was a "champion of the culture of dialogue and a man of encounters," a model Jesuit, a model missionary, a model Christian. So much the model that Francis has begun the process of sainting him.

If Francis's response to the clerical sex abuse crisis has been uneven, spotty, bold in some instances, preservationist in others, ruthless in scouring out miscreants in the episcopacy, if only selectively, his record on Indigenous issues is more of a piece, even if controverted. And Canada is where it is playing out. It is the drawing board for a revamped apostolate.

Francis embraced the journey to the Indigenous Peoples on their lands on his terms. Certainly, he was apprised by the CCCB of the potential political pitfalls of the trip, and certainly he was not unaware of the grieving and intergenerational trauma on display at his private encounters with the Indigenous delegations in Rome. And so, he was primed for his on-site moment of repentance.

> Here, from this place associated with painful memories, I would like to begin what I consider a penitential pilgrimage. I have come to your native lands to tell you in person of my sorrow, to implore God's forgiveness, healing and reconciliation, to express my closeness and to pray with you and for you …
>
> Today I am here, in this land that, along with its ancient memories, preserves the scars of still open wounds.
>
> I am here because the first step of my penitential pilgrimage among you is that of again asking forgiveness, of telling you once more that I am deeply sorry. Sorry for the ways in which, regrettably, many Christians supported the colonizing

mentality of the powers that suppressed the Indigenous Peoples.

I am sorry. I ask forgiveness, in particular, for the ways in which many members of the church and of religious communities cooperated, not least through their indifference, in projects of cultural destruction and forced assimilation promoted by the governments of that time, which culminated in the system of residential schools.

Reaction to the apology varied dramatically. Many who heard it on-site were deeply moved by the pope's authenticity and remorse. Many Elders and survivors professed their appreciation and approval. But there were caveats among those whose view was predominantly positive, perhaps best articulated by Daryold Winkler, an Ojibwe priest: "I was very disappointed that at the public liturgies in Edmonton and at Ste. Anne de Beaupré, there were missed opportunities to integrate and celebrate Indigenous cultures and spiritualities; it could have been a sign—a time to model reconciliation on a liturgical level—to see the Pope surrounded by survivors at these liturgies, rather than being surrounded by bishops."[17]

By opting for traditional Latin Rite liturgies—including the use of Latin, the lingua franca of Christendom—the planners massively mismanaged an opportunity to showcase liturgical celebrations laced with First Peoples' symbols and rituals, thereby underscoring the true nature of being catholic or universal. The architects of this folly demonstrated a tone-deafness to religious culture at the very moment the pope was moving in the opposite direction.

The pope's apology was scrutinized also for what it omitted. "The Irish victims of abuse apology was included as an example in the Call to Action [Recommendation #58] outlining what the apology should sound like. That apology acknowledged the Church's culpability as a whole, as an institution, whereas in this one [delivered in Edmonton] the Pope strategically avoided saying that."[18]

One of the electric issues of the entire visit was the Doctrine of Discovery, a leitmotif running through much of the public commentaries, a festering wound that prompted demonstrations, cries for restitution, and abrogation by the Holy See of the doctrine itself. Archbishop Bolen of Regina spoke to the criticism:

> While Pope Francis did not directly address the papal bulls of the fifteenth century often associated with the "Doctrine of Discovery," his address communicated a strong critique of colonization and cooperation within the Christian community with policies of assimilation. At the Basilica of Quebec City, he stated strongly: "Never again can the Christian community allow itself to be infected by the idea that one culture is superior to others, or that it is legitimate to employ ways of coercing others." It was communicated during the course of the papal visit that the Holy See would in due course be issuing a further statement on the Doctrine of Discovery.[19]

But what precisely is the Doctrine of Discovery?

The doctrine has its beginning in a series of papal bulls issued by Nicholas V—*Dum diversas* (1452) and *Romanus pontifex* (1455)—and by Alexander VI—*Inter caetera* (1493)—all of which deal with trading rights, rival territorial claims, and missionary jurisdictions in the interests of their Catholic majesties of Spain and Portugal. It is the bull by the Spanish

Borgia pope, *Inter caetera*, that has become the focus of the controversy swirling around the doctrine. Subsequent popes took a sharply different direction when speaking of the so-called New World and its pre-European inhabitants, with Paul III's *Sublimus Deus* (1537) declaring that the Indigenous were not in any way subhuman, that their property should not be seized, nor should they be subject to any form of enslavement. He also declared that any previous authorizations should be understood as null and of no effect. Abrogation pure and simple.

In a statement issued by the Permanent Observer Mission of the Holy See to the United Nations on April 27, 2010, the Vatican made clear that *Inter caetera* was *first* abrogated by the Treaty of Tordesillas in 1494, by numerous encyclicals and decrees subsequently, as well as by Canon 6 of the 1983 Code of Canon Law.

But no matter how many times it has been revoked, superseded, rescinded, or abrogated, it simply won't go away. Why?

Part of the answer can be found in the "advice to white people" given by Black novelist and essayist James Baldwin, who said, "Go back to where you started, as far back as you can, examine all of it, travel your road again and tell the truth about it."[20] That is precisely what Indigenous people are asking the Canadian Catholic Church to do. So, despite the work of the CCCB's own Commission for Justice and Peace, which produced a credible and historically balanced overview of the Doctrine of Discovery in 2016, despite the formal response of the CCCB as well as the Canadian Catholic Aboriginal Council on the Doctrine of Discovery and *Terra Nullius*,[21] and despite the Permanent Observer Mission Statement to the United Nations earlier in 2010—all making clear that the doctrine is *not* Catholic teaching, that it has no enduring legal status in the church, and that it has been formally repudiated on numerous occasions and in numerous jurisdictions—the Vatican, in keeping with Francis's promise to issue a further document on the doctrine, released a joint statement of two dicasteries, Culture and Education as well as Promoting Integral Human Development, on March 30, 2023. The document reiterated earlier statements on the nullity of the papal bulls, authoritative documents that failed to "adequately reflect the equal dignity and rights of indigenous peoples [and that were] manipulated for political purposes by competing powers." The dicasteries quote Francis himself declaring that "never again can the Christian community allow itself to be infected by the idea that one culture is superior to others, or that it is legitimate to employ ways of coercing others."

One irenic development coming out of this joint statement is the pledge by the CCCB and its US equivalent, the USCCB, to collaborate with the Pontifical Committee for Historical Sciences to find ways to deepen historical understanding of the doctrine itself, drawing on both Indigenous and non-Indigenous scholars.[22]

But the real test will be in the political arena. Phil Fontaine, a former chief of the Assembly of First Nations, made that clear in an interview with the Associated Press when he shifted the focus from Rome to Ottawa:

The Holy Father promised that upon his return to Rome, they would begin work on a statement which was designed to allay the fears and concerns of many survivors and others concerned about the relationship between their Catholic Church and our people, and he did as he said he would. Now the ball is in the court of governments, the United States and in Canada—but particularly in the United States, where the doctrine is embedded in the law.[23]

It is largely because of its controversial legal status that the doctrine continues to command attention. In US jurisprudence, the case known as the Johnson v. M'Intosh decision of 1823 codified the doctrine and established the precedent or principle in American common law that private citizens could not purchase land from Native Americans: such purchases could be authorized only by the United States, which in turn "had received this exclusive right of sovereignty from Great Britain, which had obtained it by discovery."

Bruce McIvor, a Métis historian and lawyer from Manitoba and the author of *Standoff: Why Reconciliation Fails Indigenous People and How to Fix It*, advances the argument that although it is true that the church has invalidated the doctrine, the state continues to use its secular legal iteration, with its underpinning argument for property law, as a way of asserting Crown sovereignty. McIvor wryly observes that the doctrine is not really on life support when you see RCMP officers and their attack dogs cordoning off women and children protestors or manhandling young male Indigenous or minimizing the disappearance or unsolved murders of Indigenous women. The doctrine lives still.

But for the church, there is a way forward—modelled by Pope Francis—that moves beyond acts of abrogation, formal statements of contrition, and pledges of financial reparation. This way forward is sensitively captured in the words of Canadian theologian Jean-Pierre Fortin: "For the controlled and controlling words of pre-formulated and self-justifying apologies and requests for forgiveness to lead to authentic repentance and decolonizing reform, the church must now make itself vulnerable and listen in order to learn about itself (as an agent of colonization) from Indigenous peoples and their stories directly encountered and heard (and to be re-encountered and reheard)."[24]

In other words, repetition and ritualized remorse are made authentic by attentive listening to the *other*, a real encounter in which all presuppositions of superiority, all expectations of entitlement, are suspended in humility—personal and institutional—and cloaked in the mercy of God.

In his address at Vespers in the Cathedral-Basilica of Notre-Dame de Québec, Francis adroitly acknowledged the special significance of such Quebec-born Catholic thinkers as Bernard Lonergan and Charles Taylor. When quoting Taylor on secularization, Francis noted that it represents a challenge for our pastoral imagination, "an occasion for restructuring the spiritual life in new forms and new ways of existing." In applying this bold exercise in pastoral imagination to the specifically Canadian context, in the entire New World context, Francis is calling for nothing less than a spiritual revolution. The question he poses is stark: How do we address the corrosive effects of colonization, the deliberate and systematic effort to eradicate the cultures and spiritualities of First Peoples, the appalling record of Eurocentric hegemony with its presumed civilizational superiority in a way that moves *beyond* theory, exhortatory rhetoric, and deft political manoeuvring?

Theologian Frederick Bauerschmidt concisely encapsulates the options: "Christians must take as their model not Sepúlveda [the Spanish Renaissance humanist], who justified the conversion by conquest of the Americas, but the martyred Trappist monks of Tibhirine, who died because they would not abandon their Muslim neighbors."[25]

232 | THE JESUIT DISRUPTOR

The option, in other words, is either aggressive proselytizing or authentic witness. For centuries, we chose the former, and the consequences are clear. In contrast, Francis repeatedly calls for the recognition of the unique genius of the Indigenous Peoples, their harmony with Creation, the richness of their languages (which we have ruthlessly suppressed), and the paramount need to move *through* truth to reconciliation and forgiveness.

Throughout his "penitential pilgrimage," Francis relished the tactile moments: the moments of connection; the gestures of embrace; the kissing of the hand of an Elder; receiving a headdress with genuine humility. For sure, the political squabbling and internecine ecclesial disagreements with media professionals jockeying for favoured treatment that described the background noise did not diminish Francis's preferred approach of engagements shorn of pomp, script, and tight control. As with airplane scrums.

On his way home, Francis was asked by Brittany Hobson, an Indigenous journalist working for the Canadian Press, a question that electrified the country he had *just* left:

> You often say that it is necessary to speak clearly, honestly, and with *parrhesia*. You know that the Canadian Truth and Reconciliation Commission described the residential school system as "cultural genocide," and then it was modified as genocide. The people who heard your words of apology this past week expressed their disappointment because the word genocide was not used. Would you use that term to say that members of the Church participated in genocide?

The pope did not hesitate to respond in as direct a manner as his interlocutor:

It's true, I didn't use the word because it didn't come to my mind, but I described the genocide and asked for forgiveness, pardon for this activity that is genocidal. For example, I condemned this too: taking away children, changing culture, changing mentality, changing traditions, changing a race, let's put it that way, an entire culture. Yes, genocide is a technical word. I didn't use it because it didn't come to my mind, but I described it ... It's true, yes, yes, it's genocide. You can all stay calm about this. You can report that I said it was genocide.[26]

But many were anything but calmed by the pope's use of the word "genocide." Debates raged over the accuracy of the word's application to the residential schools issue, the consequences of collapsing cultural genocide and physical genocide into the one word "genocide," and the potential fiscal and political ramifications involved if the word acquires general currency and acceptance as a given term of historical verity. There were also efforts to actually suppress its usage in some Catholic circles.[27]

For Cassidy Caron, the Francis-sympathetic and articulate president of the Métis National Council, the pope got it right:

With each new revelation, we have ... taken another collective step toward objectively meeting the United Nations' conditions for the recognition of genocide, which include: killing members of a group; causing serious bodily or mental harm to members of a group; deliberately inflicting on a group conditions of life calculated to bring about its physical destruction in whole or in part; imposing measures intended to prevent births within a group; and forcibly transferring children of a group to another. It is with all of this knowledge, understanding and recognition in mind that we must now and forever move beyond qualified statements about "cultural genocide" … Genocide occurred—period. There is no turning back.[28]

Clearly, the pope had no hesitation in speaking his mind. However, his hosts—the CCCB—are skittish about using the term and have avoided it in subsequent official discourse. Their anxieties are not entirely misplaced, as there are obligations to be honoured: recognizing the role of the many priests, nuns, and lay people whose behaviour, by the conventions of the time, were not without altruism and compassion; the historical debates around whether physical genocide was the endgame or an inadvertent evil; the degree of culpability that has to be rightly apportioned between government and church.

For prominent Indigenous Catholics like Graydon Nicholas—social worker, educator, national leader in Ignatian spirituality and the Christian Life Community, chancellor of St. Thomas University, lawyer, judge, former lieutenant governor of New Brunswick, and respected voice among the Maliseet—it is crystal clear in the end: "I know that there are a lot in the hierarchy who were hit hard by this … I am sure there's going to be some saying, 'No, we didn't commit genocide.' But by destroying languages, transferring people from their communities, destroying their culture and everything else—all the abuse they took, sexual, physical and psychological—all that amounted to genocide. It's not a pretty thing, but it *happened*."[29]

What lies in store for the church—local and universal—once the unqualified acceptance of past sins penetrates beyond the defensive response, beyond the denialism, is the immediate legacy of the papal visit. Francis not only listened, he provided an adumbration for change. As he said in Quebec City: we need a "restructuring of the spiritual life with 'new ways of existing.'" And that is precisely what he has in mind with his church-altering Synod on Synodality, his premier project. In many ways, it is at the heart of the Bergoglio papacy, at the core of the Jesuit disruptor's pastoral vision.

RAGGING THE PUCK

Synodality Is the Apex

WHEN I PUBLISHED MY essay "Is Pope Francis, a polarizing figure for Catholic hard-liners, ready for the coming schism?"[1] in the *Globe and Mail* on April 15, 2022, my editor and others were persuaded that the assaults on the Bergoglio papacy from *within* the church were getting too rowdy and relentless to ignore.

I received the usual splenetic smatterings from the outraged—the anti-Francis, anti-any-pope, anti-Roman crowd—but also a surprisingly high number of personal emails, letters, and phone calls where people expressed dismay, disbelief, and outright skepticism around a Catholic rift perpetrated by their favourite pope.

One email in particular struck me, mostly because of the source. Historian Peter Warrian—Canada's lead authority on the steel industry, a recognized expert on knowledge networks, supply chains, and engineering labour markets, as well as a former assistant deputy minister of finance and chief economist of the Province of Ontario—was more importantly the lead of an international research team for a joint project of the International Labour Organization and the Vatican on AI, robotics, and the future of work.

In other words, Warrian is no stranger to this pope and his religious order (Warrian also chairs the governing council of Regis College, the Jesuit graduate school at the University of Toronto), so when he observed on a recent trip that Francis looked and sounded tired, he quipped that "we can't have two retired popes, for they will unionize." Given Warrian's union track record, that is something. But the questions he asked were also something, not only because they arose out of his theological literacy and deep commitment to the church but because they represent the views of many Catholics and non-Catholics alike: Where are we going as a church? Is there an end game?

Warrian's questions around church governance, women and the priesthood, the environmental crisis, and the pope's endless travails with moneyed Catholic conservatives from the United States are legitimate, but his speculation is that the pope may be "ragging the puck," a hockey ploy whereby the player in possession of the puck skates and stickhandles with finesse and skill without trying to actually score a goal. In other words, is Francis stalling, holding onto the puck and biding his time, leaving it for other popes to score?

That would be to misread how this clever and subtle Jesuit thinks. In spite of rumours to the contrary, Francis is in it for the long haul. Elected in part by his fellow cardinals to reform the Curia, Francis has opted for a greater reform: that of the whole church—and not a few of those who marked their ballot for the Argentine have come to rue their choice.

Francis is unafraid, as we have seen, of chaos, of making a

mess, of upending the comfortable and the complacent. In this he is like Francis Spufford, the British novelist and apologist—though he might squirm at such a designation—who, when talking of his return to Christianity, could be describing the holy remit of the current pope:

> What you don't want is a little pious bubble that appears to pop any time anybody mentions the bad stuff. But there is a strong thing in me that faith is powerful because it is not for the polite stuff. It is not a clubbable, lowered-voice, best-behaviour, Sunday-best kind of thing at all. It is quite a rugged set of understandings that belong with human life at its most chaotic as well as its most orderly ... As orderly, seemly, beautiful as it sometimes is inside, it is not a denial of the chaos and destructiveness of human experience, but on the contrary an accepting reconciliation of them arms wide open.[2]

Arms wide open, as in the manner of the crucified Jesus, is the defining papal gesture; Francis embraces freely those of all faiths and those of none, the broken and the ostracized, the socially insignificant and the politically ignored, because those are Jesus's loci. That is where he can be found. And that is where Peter should be found also.

Francis understands that alienation from the church—its doctrines, pastoral practices and traditions, and formal pronouncements—continues to be a major problem for effective evangelization. He knows this from his time as a bishop in Argentina, and he knows it from his many visits to the churches of his own diocese of Rome. People are brought back into the regular life of the church—the rhythm of its sacraments, its rituals, its life-nourishing Eucharist—when they feel welcome, unjudged, strangers who are now family, the "holy faithful People of God," as Francis terms them. The American writer Brian Doyle captures that feeling of estrangement and yearning in an especially moving passage that would win easy endorsement by Francis:

> You tiptoe back toward religion, in my experience, cautiously and nervously and more than a little suspicious, quietly hoping that it wasn't all smoke and nonsense, that there is some deep wriggle of genius and poetry and power and wild miracle in it, that it is a language you can use to speak about that for which we have no words; and in my case, as in many others I know, this was so, and I saw for the first time in my life that there were two Catholic Churches, one a noun and the other a verb, one a corporation and the other a wild idea held in the hearts of millions of people who are utterly uninterested in authority and power and rules and regulations, and very interested indeed in finding ways to walk through the bruises of life with grace and humility.[3]

The church as *verb* is the church Francis is birthing for our time. His various instructions and writings, including especially *Amoris laetitia* (2016), highlight the priorities articulated by Doyle—the church as the large tent, the church as field hospital, the church as the bosom of communion. Francis entertains no doubt that the church's hitherto exclusive European provenance is no more; the church is no longer the noble offspring of Imperial Rome; the church's sway and its future lie in the global South. Unlike his immediate predecessor, Benedict XVI, Francis entertains no hope for the retrieval of the faith in once-Christian Europe, and the spotty revivals in parts of the continent do not augur a return of Roman Catholic hegemony. But he also knows that Catholic Europe longs to reconnect in some meaningful way with the faith it has drifted away from. The astonishing success of World Youth Day in Lisbon in 2023—with Francis present as a key attraction—is a dramatic reminder that Catholicism can still command a following when genuine Gospel witness is at the heart of its message as an institution.

The pre-eminence of the church as *noun* is a thing of the past. As Francis told the Roman Curia in 2019: "Christendom no longer exists ... Today, we are not the only ones who produce culture, nor are we the first or the most listened to." This kind of utterance would not surprise most sociologists of religion, mainstream Protestant churches, or contemporary Catholic Church historians. But it is not the kind of thing cardinals—especially those resident in uber-Catholic Rome—would judge self-evident. Surrounded by the trappings and mainstays of power and influence, the Vatican can easily be isolated in its past, ever conscious that although the world changes, Rome remains eternal. For the Argentine pope, this is the stuff of romantic thinking, a nostalgia for a circumscribed "holy" that has no place in the contemporary church. In this, Francis and the prolific, eccentric, and startlingly brilliant offside thinker David Bentley Hart have much in common. As Hart puts it:

> [To] my mind a truly Christian society would be one whose skyline would be crowded not only with churches, but with synagogues, temples, mosques, viharas, torii, gudwaras, and so on ... Curiously enough, it seems to me that such a society would much more naturally incubate a renewal of Christian faith than would the coercive confessional state ... There will

never, for instance, be a revival in Europe on any appreciable
scale of a Christianity of impermeable boundaries; but there
might be a revival of the faith in a form better able to stand
amid the religions of the world without terror or hostility,
and better able freely to draw upon them to understand its
own depths and range.[4]

Putting it even more starkly, poet and essayist Christian
Wiman writes:

> I don't believe in atheists. Nor in true believers, for that matter.
> One either lives toward God or not. The word *God* is of course
> an abyss, bright or dark depending on the day. But there is no
> middle ground, no cautious agnosticism in which to settle,
> no spiritual indifference that is not, even when accompanied
> by high refinement and exquisite intelligence, torpor. I know
> the necessity of religion, I know we need communal ritual
> and meaningful creeds. And yet I know, too, that all of this
> emerges from an intuition so original that, in some ultimate
> sense, to define is to defile. One either lives toward God or
> not.[5]

Wiman's poetic wordsmithing captures the apophatic
mysticism of the Carmelites of the sixteenth century but also
the practical mysticism of Ignatius of Loyola. "To define is
to defile": the Christocentrism of the two Jesuits—Ignatius
and Francis—reminds us that *definition* is not the name of the
game: encounter is.

And that encounter is not only personal, it is communal.
Invoking the image of a polyhedron, Francis expands in *Fratelli
tutti* on what he means by encounter:

I have frequently called for the growth of a culture of encounter capable of transcending our differences and divisions. This means working to create a many-faceted polyhedron whose different sides form a variegated unity, in which "the whole is greater than the part." The image of a polyhedron can represent a society where differences coexist, complementing, enriching and reciprocally illuminating one another, even amid disagreements and reservations. Each of us can learn something from others. (section 215)

Francis, then, is poised to address a world in radical flux, a world peopled by many and diverse religious and cultural traditions, a world in which God may well be omnipresent but is in fact not present in the life of multitudes, a world entangled in political and economic inequities, a world riven by war. This is a world his predecessors knew as well, but their pastoral remedies were different, relying on institutional uniformity, doctrinal and moral clarity—in short, a magisterial church, its lines of authority unalterable, its confidence in its own convictions unassailable.

Francis has opted for a different approach: a synodal church.

Francis defines a synodal church in his address on the fiftieth anniversary of the Synod of Bishops in 2015 as a church "which listens, which realizes that listening 'is more than simply hearing.' It is a mutual listening in which everyone has something to learn. The faithful people, the college of bishops, the Bishop of Rome: all listening to each other, and all listening to the Holy Spirit, the 'Spirit of truth' (Jn 14:17), in order to know what he 'says to the Churches' (Rev 2:7)."[6] Grand ecclesiastical rhetoric, but can such a church be realized? Francis has pledged his papacy on it.

From the outset of his pontificate, he has worked to implement a pastoral strategy that will bring the church back to a pre-Constantinian era, a time of institutional humility and simplicity, shorn of the accoutrements of power, disengaged from political ideologies, with no ties to both the *ancien régime* and ascendant orthodoxies of the current era. In fact, he welcomes a change of era, a *cambio de epoca*, as he calls it, with all that it portends: its uncertainties, its possibilities, its unpredictable eruptions of the Holy Spirit.

Francis needn't go back to the early church fathers for his inspiration. The Second Vatican Council would do. And the seminal American Jesuit historian of the council, John O'Malley, saw the connection:

> In 2008 I published a book on the Second Vatican Council [*What Happened at Vatican II*], and I received a lot of invitations to lecture on it and was very happy to do that, but when I finished the lectures I would think to myself, "I'm really talking about something dead in the water. It's an interesting thing that happened, but it's gone." And then beginning in 2012, with the anniversaries of the council, more invitations came and I felt the same way. However, I don't feel that way today. I don't feel that way at all. I think the council, with Pope Francis, is almost as alive as it was in 1965.[7]

Steeped in the teachings of Vatican II, Francis was well equipped theologically to understand what needed to be done to create a synodal church, but he also needed to turn his attention to structural reforms that would enable his council-generated ecclesiology to take shape. He would need to test the ground with the one universal consultative body left him by his predecessors: the synod. He would make alterations—slowly at first, and then explosively—and the synod would become his primary agent of reform, culminating with his master stroke: the 2023–24 Synod on Synodality.

He was engaged in a multi-year process: first the tinkering, then the programmatic changes, and, finally, structural reinvention.

Pope Francis encountered a wall of timidity rather than a wave of temerity when he convoked his own synods. But he was resolute. In fact, as Francis biographer Paul Vallely writes:

> Pope Francis has said he plans to make changes to the international Synod of Bishops to make it more collegial, as Vatican II intended. That intention had been undermined by the insistence of Benedict XVI, when he was head of the Congregation for the Doctrine of the Faith, that episcopal conferences "had no theological significance," being mere collections of bishops whose collective weight was theologically no more than the sum of their parts. By contrast Francis told the fifteen-member coordinating council of the synod in June 2013: "We trust that the Synod of Bishops will be further developed to better facilitate dialogue and collaboration of the bishops among themselves and with the Bishop of Rome."[8]

This was more than papal boilerplate. He threw down the gauntlet. He was serious about collegiality, he was serious about synodality, and he was serious about implementing these principles in the life of the church in meaningful rather than symbolic ways.

The synod structure that Francis inherited—though permanent—was not in its particulars and processes inured to change. Francis was convinced that it needed jets of oxygen, that it was often an intellectually airless chamber, with its participants engaged more in rote and cautious vocabulary than in bold and dynamic interchanges both among themselves and with the pope. It was a propitious time for change.

Prior to Francis's election in 2013, following the startling and unforeseen resignation of Benedict XVI, the church had hosted sixteen Ordinary synods, two Extraordinary synods, and ten Special synods.[9]

Francis's synodal record includes two Ordinary synods to date: "The Vocation and Mission of the Family in the Church and in the Contemporary World" (2015), with the resulting apostolic exhortation *Amoris laetitia* (The Joy of Love), and "Young People, the Faith and Vocational Discernment" (2018), with the resulting apostolic exhortation *Christus vivit* (Christ Is Alive). He also convoked one Extraordinary synod, "The Pastoral Challenges of the Family in the Context of Evangelization" (2014), and one Special synod on the Pan-Amazon Region (2019), resulting in the apostolic exhortation *Querida Amazonia* (Beloved Amazon).

Both the Extraordinary and the Special synods raised issues of great import for the church, generated controversy within synod halls and in the church at large, ruffled chancery personnel, vexed canon lawyers, upstaged theological purists, and created a level and volume of excitement that no previous synod had ever managed, or even wished, to create.

New pope; new synod.

To make sure that future synods conformed to a different model—not radically different, but substantively different, nonetheless, and enhanced—and to set in place a template that publicly guaranteed a synod grounded in a truly conciliar perspective, Francis issued an apostolic exhortation on the Synod of Bishops, *Episcopalis communio* (Episcopal Communion), in 2018.

The document was the result of incorporating the reflections and analyses by theologians on the topic of "synodality in the life of the church," and it became the foundation stone on which would be built a "constitutively synodal church." Although the bishop-delegates would in no way be supplanted, they would be complemented, as consultations with the faithful and indeed participation by the laity would become the new normal in a clericalized church. Francis emphasized that the bishops, including specifically the Bishop of Rome, were disciples called to listen to "the voice of Christ speaking through the entire people of God."

And *listening* is the operative word.

> The keystone is listening: every synodal praxis "begins by listening to the people of God," "continues by listening to the pastors" and culminates in listening to the Bishop of Rome, called to declare himself "Pastor and Doctor of all Christians" ... *Episcopalis Communio* divided synodal praxis into three phases: preparation, discussion and implementation, and each Synod celebrated during the current pontificate—on the family (2014, 2015), on young people (2018), on the Amazon (2019)—has sought to implement these phases to an increasing extent. As the Holy Father has observed, "the changes introduced so far go in the direction of making the Synods held every two or three years in Rome freer and more dynamic, giving more time for sincere discussion and listening."[10]

There is no doubt—considering the Francis synods to date—that he has succeeded in making these gatherings "freer and more dynamic." Respectfully, the previous synods in my experience, and I was there for three of the John Paul II synods, were neither free nor dynamic, and their impact on the life of the church was accordingly reduced to general irrelevance. The bishops had their own legitimate, even if constrained, experience of collegiality under tight Roman supervision, but the larger communion of Catholics had no taste of the experience, save that mediated by their bishops following their return from the synod. That mediation varied massively, depending on the local bishop's buy-in: the commitment to translating and transmitting the synod proceedings through the agencies of the national episcopal conferences or by means of the bishop-delegates themselves through their own outreach.

Not a satisfactory method of operating.

Francis's way of "synodizing" essentially turns on its head the previous way of operating. Biographer and Bergoglio scholar Austen Ivereigh captures the radicality of it all when he notes in *Wounded Shepherd: Pope Francis and His Struggles to Convert the Catholic Church* how comprehensive and intentional Francis was in ensuring the separate existence of the synod as a permanent body independent of dicasterial control, an open and fully collegial partner with the magisterium, a model of power sharing rather than the traditional model of power consolidation. In doing this, Francis was once again ushering in an epoch-shaping development in Catholic leadership.[11]

This is utterly consonant with the thinking of John Henry Newman, the English cardinal and thinker whom Francis canonized early in his pontificate. Newman had said in his seminal *On Consulting the Faithful in Matters of Doctrine* (1859), concerning the role of the laity:

> I think certainly that the *Ecclesia docens* [the church as teacher or magisterium] is more happy when she has such enthusiastic

partisans about her ... than when she cuts off the faithful from
the study of her divine doctrines and the sympathy of her
divine contemplations, and requires from them a *fides implicita* in her word, which in the educated classes will terminate
in indifference, and in the poorer in superstition.[12]

Francis would have no difficulty agreeing with Newman's
argument that "truth is wrought out by many minds, working
together freely." Newman believed in the vital and free interplay
of intellect and authority, of freedom and discipline in a way
that assured the necessity of *both*—ever poised in tension, but
ever struggling to apprehend the deepest truth.[13] Newman, in
his autobiography, *Apologia pro Vita Sua*, provides the Roman
Catholic post-conciliar church with a model of such exquisite
balance and utter reasonableness that one cannot but be pained
by our contemporary atmosphere of toxic mistrust, visceral
broadsides against the pontiff, and *argumentum ad hominem*
polemics with little regard for facts and tolerance, which are
opening ever-deeper fissures in the communion of Christ. Here
is what Newman says of the church:

> it is a vast assemblage of human beings with willful intellects
> and wild passions, brought together into one by the beauty
> and the Majesty of a Superhuman Power, into what may be
> called a large reformatory or training-school, not as if into
> a hospital or prison, not in order be sent to bed, not to be
> buried alive, but (if I may change metaphor) brought together
> as if into some moral factory, for the melting, refining, and
> moulding, by an incessant noisy process, of the raw material,
> so excellent, so dangerous, so capable of divine purposes.[14]

Admittedly, it is a relief to see Newman switch his metaphor and to concentrate on the "melting, refining, and moulding, by an incessant noisy process," because that is precisely what acting synodally means. It is loud, cacophonous sometimes, spirited, a mess—all that human engagement with different cultural backgrounds, histories, hopes, and resistances cannot but be: part din, part Babel, but also "a vast assemblage of human beings" struggling together to discern the truth, debating with conviction, discerning in the Spirit and listening, listening.

And so, the planning for the October 2023 Synod on Synodality, "Communion, Participation and Mission," was going to include a vast survey of opinion of Catholics all over the world—a survey that would invite Catholics to raise questions around the church, its practices, its beliefs, the institutional mode of operating, leadership credibility, and more. And it would do this in a way that would respect the authenticity of opinion and create a culture of engagement that allows for honest and transparent speech, recognizing that the body of Christ, the church, must be converted to a deeper way of living the Gospel in its teaching and in its lived experience. In this, listening is paramount. This is the synod that would crystallize Francis's thinking around how to incorporate best practices—pastoral, principally, but facilitated by improved and refined governance structures—that would open the entire people of God to a rejuvenated mission of service to the world.

This listening is the prelude to conversion—individual and ecclesial. As the cardinal archbishop of Newark, New Jersey, Joseph Tobin, rightly identifies, the larger context in which synodality is rendered concrete in the lives of Catholics and in the renewal or revitalizing of the church's structures of mediation depends on an experience of conversion:

We cannot deny that for centuries the Church has used synodality [however historically defined] as a way to kick people
out. With every early ecumenical council, we would come
together to repudiate this heresy or to define that dogma,
and the Body of Christ would lumber on. But I submit we
have entered a new stage of the journey. Acts of synodality no
longer function as sweeping dogmatic declarations, but rather
are used to fine-tune how the Gospel is applied to the signs
of the times. And with that comes the next important point
of Francis's long game [following on synodality *as* journey]:
conversion. When I say "conversion," I'm talking about the
Church's own conversion, a new way in understanding and
approaching how we carry out our mission. Francis has rightly
decried the mindset of "But we've always done it this way."
John XXIII famously said that we in the Church are not called
to guard a museum but to tend to a flourishing garden of life.
The same goes for a synodal Church. You can't show up with
an imperious attitude, as if you have all the answers. Indeed,
John XXIII read the signs of turmoil and destruction of the
first half of the twentieth century and saw that the Church had
to be as intentional and missionary as it possibly could with
its witness—and that the way to achieve this was through a
council [a council is technically a synod composed of bishops
and their experts].[15]

From the outset, Francis was determined to do something
with the synod structure he inherited. Abolishing it was not
in the cards, but strengthening it was. And for Francis, to
strengthen meant finding a way of making it—the process of
acting synodally—a more inclusive, free, and dialogue-friendly
gathering wherein delegates speak their minds without fear of a

punitive response from the senior authorities when they go off script. After all, the scrum-loving Francis has set a model for candid and no-holds-barred speaking with his airplane press Q&A's and his easy departure from his prepared speeches, giving ample room to spontaneity and inspiration and thereby generating ample nervousness among his script-adhering aides.

All the previous Francis synods were designed to presage a time and space when the full universal implications of *being* a synodal church were to be fathomed with a new freedom. The previous synods were not simply preparatory, as they had specific pastoral as well as practical goals, but they did pave the way and established the groundwork for the 2023 Synod on Synodality.

The three-year synodal process (2021–2023) involved three phases: diocesan, continental, and universal. The cardinal archbishop of Vienna, Christoph Schönborn, a member of the Council for the Synod of Bishops and a key player at the 1985 Extraordinary synod, neatly summarizes the synodal process—its theological, catechetical, and pedagogical underpinnings:

> The Pope tells us that the Synod is not simply a procedure, a strategy towards a common goal. Synodality is more than that; its purpose is not about pastoral administration or social commitment. What we are being offered is, above all, the experience of the Holy Spirit, as in the New Testament, especially the Acts of the Apostles. During this great ecclesial time, we are all invited to experience reciprocal listening and encounter in the breath of the Holy Spirit, to better discern what God is asking of us today … it is a historical phase as important for the Church as that of the Second Vatican Council, but with a communal and universal dimension, a form of global Gospel School open to all.[16]

Schönborn's identification of the synod as a "Gospel School" is a reminder that the synodal process is not something alien to the Catholic tradition, the reckless insertion into ecclesial affairs of a way of being better suited to a parliamentary democracy, but a school[17] in which, through "reciprocal learning," the entire church body comes together, irrespective of office or rank, to discern the will of the Holy Spirit for *our* time.

Although the selling job on why we need a synodal church is still very much in its infancy—overcoming the comfortable status quo with its perks and settled certainties is never an easy task—Francis is moving forward confident that it is the Spirit that summons, that Catholics are yearning for a church alive to human need and accompaniment, and that modelling via experience will be more successful than a cohort of academic symposia and a cascade of curial decrees.

Daniel Flores, the bishop of Brownsville, Texas, understands the synod as "an enactment that accomplishes great good just in the act of gathering and listening, something simple, something eminently responsible to the love we have received in Christ. Building up our communion is not separate from engaging the mission to the nations, because the witness of this love is essentially what our woundedness seems to need most."[18]

The notion of this kind of synod—a Francis synod—did not originate in the Bergoglio noggin *in vacuo*, synod delegate and theologian Catherine E. Clifford argues in "The Remedy of Synodality":

> The most radical of the remedies that Francis proposes for the renewal of the church and its mission is in his invitation to rediscover how to live as a more synodal church ... the desire for a new culture of synodality is not just a personal wish, but

by leading the church in this direction, he is carrying forward
a mandate entrusted to him by his brother bishops, one forged
in the sometimes-raucous exchanges among the members of
the College of Cardinals preceding the conclave of election
in the spring of 2013.[19]

If the synod that Francis is promoting is the result of his
attentive listening to his brother bishops, it is a testament
to his even deeper listening to the church at large. And that
is why he went further than the previous practice of simply
inviting lay guests as *auditores*; he instituted further changes
in the synod's composition by allowing for the participation
of seventy non-bishop members—ten from each of the seven
global conferences—mandating that young people be included
and that a clear percentage of those named be women.

And he went further still: he granted the right to vote to all
the delegates of the synod—lay and clerical, men and women,
old and young. A global synod will have the face of the globe
about it—anguished, yearning, troubled, and prayerful: the
modern face of humanity in the concrete not cast in abstraction
and ideology.

During the "diocesan phase" preparatory for the Synod
on Synodality, Francis called for an unprecedented degree of
consultation at the grassroots level, where much depended on
the local ecclesiastical jurisdiction: the willingness of the local
bishop to invest time, personnel, money, and personal interest
in gathering consultants, conducting questionnaires, holding
parish as well as diocesan sessions, and preparing thoughtful
summaries for submission to the national bodies and Rome.

Some bishops took the call seriously and engaged passion-
ately in an effort to make this Francis project work. A few

complied with the body charged with managing the synodal process, the General Secretariat for the Synod, when it made its requests for input with the barest minimum investment. But, arguably, the majority did more, however with little in the way of energy and never entirely persuaded of the synod's potential efficacy and relevance. The majority remain the quiet doubters, but they can be brought onside once the synodal dynamic unfolds. Once they are persuaded that the synod is not a destructive remaking of the church they know and that their leadership credibility is not on the line, and once they can see that the summons to gather is designed to provide a lived experience of a genuinely listening church and is not, in the end, a structural threat but the revivification of the Second Vatican Council's multiple pastoral and theological insights, then they can see the challenges ahead and not be daunted or reduced to cynicism.

Added to the official diocesan responses—and, in many ways, more potent and creative in their conception and delivery—is the work of numerous bodies of independent and committed Catholics working with their diverse networks that are cross-diocesan in their reach. Going beyond the limited horizon of the questionnaires, choosing intentionally to go deeper into the causes behind those forces and attitudes that work against rather than for the church of Jesus Christ, many of these unofficial groupings that pepper the body ecclesiastic issued their own reports, whether as addenda to formal diocesan responses to Rome or as discrete submissions.

The summary report of the Catholic Network for Women's Equality (CNWE)—*Embodying a Listening, Inclusive, Synodal Church: The Time Is Now*—is a model example of the genre. In a section titled "A Synodal Church Recognizes the Inherent

Dignity and Equality of Women as Equal Disciples in Ministry and Leadership," the document's authors write:

> With gratitude for the work of feminist biblical scholars and archaeologists, we have learned that co-responsibility is not a new idea. Jesus had women disciples and there also were prominent women in ministry and leadership in the early Church ... We look forward to the day when women and men, according to their gifts, will collaborate in preaching, presiding, and administering sacraments in parishes, when Catholic women and men will work cooperatively in leadership roles at diocesan, national and international levels, and when women and men together will shape Catholic teaching and structures of governance in a synodal Church.[20]

Although this may have a ring of the liberal boilerplate about it, Catholic lay groups deeply unhappy with their church leadership over numerous issues—rarely doctrinal, mostly disciplinary, and often related to clerical sex scandals—have been a feature of Catholic life since the Cardinal Hans Hermann Groër affair of 1990s Austria.[21] Out of crisis is born new visioning or desperate retreat; the former revivifies, while the latter entombs.

The issues raised by the various Catholic lay groups advocating for change and reform surfaced not only at the diocesan phase but at the continental one as well. The work of the North American Working Group is especially noteworthy, consisting of nine experts drawn from across the United States and Canada who conducted detailed interviews covering every conceivable issue on the social justice and ecclesial terrain: Hispanic marginalization, drug addiction, homelessness, Christians in the public square, Indigenous isolation, structural obstacles to the full emancipation of women's gifts in society and in the church, and many more besides. Their final report, *Doing Theology from the Existential Peripheries*, underscores through its extensive interviews, sociological data sifted through a theological prism, and on-the-ground experience admixed with refined theological analysis the clear perspective of the pope:

> As Pope Francis teaches in *Veritatis Gaudium* [The Joy of Truth] theology should not provide pre-packaged answers and ready-made solutions, rather theologians should go to unfamiliar sites with risks and fidelity to the borderline. Theologians, Pope Francis observes, by going out to the peripheries are like "spiritual ethnographers" with the smell of the sheep, whose encounter with people in their cultures, histories, and sites of pain and hope will bring about an inward transformation as they seek for a "hermeneutic of integration" in accounting for the logic of grace and of the signs of God's reign from these sites.[22]

Building on such reports as the above, with their impressive interview density, as well as reports received by the General Secretariat of the Synod that scan the entire globe, a working document for the continental stage was produced with the deliciously biblical title *Enlarge the Space of Your Tent*,[23] with content that can be turgid and yet also arrestingly direct and personal.

For instance, the report, quoting a submission from Argentina—the pope's home country—bluntly calls for a remodelling of ecclesial governance in keeping with the Argentine pontiff's fondness for the inverted pyramid: "It is important to build a synodal institutional model as an ecclesial paradigm of deconstructing pyramidal power that privileges unipersonal managements. The only legitimate authority in the Church must be that of love and service, following the example of the Lord."

Such frank—if infelicitously translated—language speaks loudly in the report. The cries of the ignored, marginalized, and misunderstood colour the report, and the authors honestly record them. The substantial section given over to "rethinking women's participation" is illustrative of the centrality of women's multiple roles in a church that has yet to fully value their diverse contributions. The argument made over the years that women and ministry, whether sacramental or otherwise, was a North American and western European ideological fixation—and that the rest of the global church had no interest in the rarefied feminist theological advocacy that sought the full inclusion of women in the life and governance of the church—is put to bed by this report. Women across all the continents, irrespective of their culture, history, or formation, have a vested interest in the flourishing of the church, and that flourishing needs to be enabled in both the particular and universal church. At the same time, given the multiplicity of voices and perspectives, it should be no surprise that the report does not come to any kind of definitive summary.[24] But the fact that in the vast majority of the listening sessions, and throughout all the written reports, issues around women and their mosaic of contributions call for validation and institutionalization underscores the continent-wide priority of women in the church.

Those who were so quick to dismiss the "women's issue" as an evanescent phenomenon and an ideological product of a human rights–obsessed feminist enclave of theologians that is in no way representative of women throughout the global church got it wrong.

The *Instrumentum laboris of the 16th Ordinary General Assembly of the Synod of Bishops—For a Synodal Church: Communion, Participation, Mission* is the official working document of the synod. It consists of a skillful distillation of the ideas, recommendations, and proposals that surfaced during the two years of consultations and in the various reports that appeared during the diocesan and continental phases. It also provides direction for the synodal discussions, worksheets, and focus questions that constitute the majority time of the sessions. And it recapitulates the heart of the synodal exercise itself when it states that "the synodal assembly was asked to listen deeply to the situations in which the Church lives and carries out its mission. What it means to walk together when this question is asked in a particular context with real people and situations in mind."[25]

Pope Francis has limited interest in self-referential ruminations and debates; he wants to address the anxieties and joys of humanity. Hence the release of the apostolic exhortation *Laudate Deum* (Praise God), on the themes of environmental degradation, the throwaway mentality, the culture of abandonment, and care for our common home, timed both for the opening of the synod and for the feast day of Saint Francis, his namesake and guiding spirit of his papacy. *Laudato Si'* part two.

Still, the synod is about the internal life of the Catholic Church as well. An exhortation addressed to the world to attend with renewed passion and urgency to human justice and planetary issues without including the serious issues of injustice within the church will compromise the document's credibility from the outset.

As one example, we have the cries for justice, penance, and reconciliation emerging from the Indigenous Peoples of the earth. Cries that have been misunderstood, neglected, or suppressed. Francis addressed their history of abuse in Bolivia in 2015 and in Canada in 2022.

As Archbishop Don Bolen of Regina, Saskatchewan, observed:

> The synod is building on the Amazon synod and the pope's visit to Canada, with its emphasis on walking together. In both cases, the special gifts of Indigenous spirituality and culture were showcased ... I am so grateful for Francis's leadership, for his humanity, his humility, his exceptional intelligence, his ability to speak wisely to so many parts; he has humanized the papacy; he has humanized church leadership ... he is creating open spaces in a time of polarization; there is a transparency in his leadership and he admits his mistakes. He is teaching us a way of *being* church.[26]

And so, the first session of the synod that would define his papacy began on October 4, 2023.

I was there in my capacity as an accredited journalist.

It was a relief to get my press badge from the wonderfully alliterative La Sala Stampa della Santa Sede (the Press Office of the Holy See), attesting thereby to the fact that I was not simply a roamer, a wanderer, without access, without a base, and without a network of media connections. This is not the first synod I have covered. It is the fourth—and unlike any other.

And here is how it is unlike:

- Past synods were uni-theme specific, with the General Secretariat of the Synod crafting a *Lineamenta*, or preparatory document, inviting the world's episcopal conferences to initiate discussion around the topic previously decided by the pontiff. Following this consultation and communication with the secretariat, an *Instrumentum laboris* is crafted that would be the guiding document for the bishop-delegates.

This synod had a universal theme and involved years of canvassing, sifting, recording, and refining responses from the entire people of God, with an *Instrumentum laboris* faithfully reflecting the diversity, complexity, and chaotic richness of a global consultation.

- Past synods were traditionally held in the hierarchically tiered *aula del sinodo*, in which the bishops delivered, in sequentially mind-numbing and often monotonous tones, interventions of regulated length, the content crafted by their respective episcopal conferences. There was no reaction to the addresses, just a cumulative pile-up of mediocre and sanitized orations.[27]

This synod consisted of thirty-five round tables with no tiered seating, arranged in the capacious Paul VI Audience Hall. The tables were assigned according to language—English, Italian, French, Spanish, and Portuguese[28]—and were peopled by laity, both women and men, as well as bishops of various rank and dignity, priests, and deacons. All the synod delegates had voting rights, and the composition of the assembly was 364 plus the pope. So, equal to a full year. The delegates were drawn from each of the seven continental assemblies (ten per continent), and their number was to include the young. There were also *ex officio* members drawn from the leadership of religious orders and congregations, prefects of the various curial departments, and others chosen by the pontiff himself—*ex nomine pontificia*.

- Past synods had their own *circuli minores* (small circles) or language-specific discussion groups, but they consisted of clerics only—bishops with a few superiors general of religious orders and *periti* (theological advisors) thrown in.

This synod's smorgasbord-like composition allowed for such a diverse range of experience, background, formation, credentials, and cultural perspectives that the generally uniform coloration of an all-episcopal grouping could not possibly replicate its universality.

An especially singular—actually, revolutionary, by Roman standards—feature of the new *circuli minores* was their manner of proceeding. The discussions were structured to free the delegates for honest, transparent, respectful, and prayerful engagement. A predetermined pattern was designed to create an environment of trust and sharing that eschewed adversariality and combative posturing.

Here is how it worked: Each group or *circolo minore* had an expert facilitator, who was not a synod delegate and was therefore a non-voting member, whose job was make sure that the Spiritual Conversation Method[29] was faithfully adhered to. This method, dubbed "Conversation in the Spirit," was the bedrock for emulating a truly synodal way of proceeding. Its structure was sequential and repetitive: after introductions came the first silent prayer. This was followed by each of the dozen members of the *circolo minore* speaking in turn, under the direction of the facilitator, for a maximum of three minutes in response to one of a series of questions found in the module of the week (there were four modules: one for each week of the synod); this was understood as a reflection to be shared rather than argued over. No discussion was permitted at this point in the process.

This was followed by another period of silent prayer, during which the members were invited to ponder the "resonances" before a second round of reflections began, again with no discussion following.

After more silent prayer, a third round began that allowed for a free exchange of opinion, working toward identifying as a group the convergences and divergences that surfaced. Out of this emerged a draft report that was then read out by the rapporteur of the group to the plenary.

There were also opportunities for individuals to address the assembly. Concerted efforts were made to ensure that what was said at the table was accurately reflected in their submissions. As Austen Ivereigh, one of the twenty expert theologians enlisted to read all the reports and then synthesize them for the specifically commissioned group tasked with preparing the final synthesis or summary report of the Synod on Synodality, succinctly observed of the whole process: "The CiS [Conversations in the Spirit] method meant that the synod delegates could not move too quickly into a 'debate' mode, reiterating their own positions, without first listening to the reasoning that supported the positions of others. It allowed people to be vulnerable and hesitant. It's why confidentiality mattered and why the process needed time and patience."[30]

On the matter of confidentiality, it should be noted that although it is clear that the synod participants almost universally accepted the pope's injunction that they exercise a custody of the tongue and a fasting of the word, avoiding interviews, speaking only with high discretion about what was going on in the Paul VI *aula*, this emphasis caught many in the media off guard. As one of those present charged with covering the synod, this injunction was a problem. I understand that there are costs to speaking frankly, especially in an institution not hitherto known for its celebration of unhindered dialogue, and I appreciate the need for some serenity amid a babble of words, but not all journalists are hungering for sensation or mindless paparazzi driven by the next scandal.

Francis's belief that synodality could only be experienced in an atmosphere of mutual trust, with all the participants in the round-table discussions feeling free to share their hesitations and vulnerabilities in an environment enveloped in prayer, is entirely consonant with the Jesuit emphasis on deep listening as an integral part of any spiritual encounter. His sense that a steady flow of leaks to the scribblers of what the participants were saying would create a counter-environment to what he wanted, an environment in which would flourish fanciful speculation, willful invention, and the toxin of gossip, was not without empirical validation.

The synod was as much a spiritual undertaking as an intellectual one, and to some considerable degree, the special chemistry being created in the *aula* could be assured only if conditions of heightened discretion applied. Still, there was a price to pay, and Francis was prepared to pay it, although the cost was greater than he anticipated.

A vacuum was created: the conservative and ultraconservative press, whose presence in numbers and focused tenacity were much in evidence, hurried to fill it. At the daily press briefings, they pummelled the prefect of the Vatican's Dicastery for Communication, Paolo Ruffini, for clarifications around procedure, the wisdom behind synod decisions, and the politics behind the composition of commissions. They also barraged the daily synod delegate representatives—there were, on average, three or four different delegates at each briefing—with queries around such matters as the inalterability of divine Revelation, the wobbliness around church teaching on LGBTQ+ issues, and the prioritization of process over content to the detriment of Tradition, all designed to expose what these critics considered a hidden synod agenda to refashion the Catholic Church. Increasingly, they focused on the nature of *this* synod's status and whether the presence of so many laywomen and laymen drained the synod of its episcopal authority.

On this matter—the weakening of the synod's authority because it was no longer exclusively episcopal in its makeup— several of the senior synod delegates, cardinals and archbishops, were quick to repudiate the legitimacy of the allegation of diminished authority by noting that episcopal synods of the past all had non-bishop experts and advisors present as well as religious order superiors general, many with voting rights. So, Francis was not breaking with tradition in having delegates other than bishops present; he was simply expanding the membership to broadly represent the largest constituency of the church: its laity.

In contrast with the right-wing media, the progressive media remained steadfastly if frustratingly in the Bergoglio camp but had little to work with. Enter precisely the very thing the seal of confidentiality was intended to prevent: the gossip, the silly, the inconsequential. And so, we have a retired dicasterial cardinal leaving the *aula* in a huff; a celebrity bishop grumpy over inattention to his media expertise; a prominent Jesuit spiritual writer berated by an Eastern rite cleric of high rank who picks up his water bottle in holy dudgeon and changes tables.

Not the stuff of probing commentary.[31]

But over the weeks, things improved during the briefings: the delegates moved beyond the requisite and rhapsodic declarations of why synodality is so important to why they have been personally moved to think differently of being a synodal church as opposed to a magisterial one. They also moved beyond their cautious-in-content but upbeat-in-tone *ferverini* to speaking of the transformative nature of this synod in more open and refreshingly pertinent ways.

This is best illustrated by the press encounter with the military ordinary of Germany, Bishop Franz-Josef Overbeck of Essen. Although the problem of clericalism surfaced in many contexts at the synod—the inadequacies of priestly formation, the egregious disproportionality of respect and deference accorded clerics over their lay peers, the subservient role of women in leadership positions, emotional and sexual abuse by clerics of women and minors—the synod was not about clericalism or abuse per se, and some delegates felt that the issue of clericalism, although systemic and widespread, needed to be contextualized.

But the ravages of clericalism did surface publicly: in one case with Overbeck and in the other with Francis himself.

For some time, Roman anxieties over the direction of the German synod dominated the relationship between the two jurisdictions. The years-long concern in curial circles was much mitigated by frank conversations during meetings in Rome but not entirely allayed. The German synodal process was seen as too liberal, with few doctrinal guardrails, persistent dissension among some of the country's bishops, and a palpable fear that the "excesses" of the German synod process could derail the Rome Synod on Synodality.

That didn't happen. The Rome synod's integrity was respected.

So, when Overbeck spoke of the reality of the German church, its own four-year national synod, its very public debate around women *in* ministry and not just women *and* ministry, its fierce tensions between doctrine and enculturation—as well as the personnel challenges in his own diocese where, as bishop, he has presided over the funerals of some three hundred priests and the ordinations of a paltry fifteen—he pulled no punches.

The German synod was a synod of repentance: it started because of the catastrophic consequences of the clerical sex abuse tsunami. Overbeck commented that sitting on his desk back home is a dossier of allegations concerning a cardinal deceased by two decades. The bishop knows that his pastoral call for healing involves listening to the voice of survivors and ensuring that reconciliation and justice are secured. With a melancholy tone, he remarked that the "disaster is unending"— and he didn't mean only for his own diocese and ordinariate.

In the judgment of many reputable church historians, theologians, and canon lawyers, the ever-festering, ubiquitous, and morale-sapping reality of clerical sex abuse constitutes the greatest institutional and moral crisis facing Catholicism since the Reformation, and the German episcopate is facing the crisis head-on. Besieged by the angry, the disillusioned, and the alienated, the bishops have tried—and, I would argue, heroically—to grapple with the pastoral implications and to think innovatively about how to move forward.

The Roman synodal model is one way forward, but the German model is wrestling with a pressing moral urgency, and time is not a workable or credible option for them. Following the release of the Sauvé Report in France, the delayed awakenings to the issue in Italy, Spain, and Portugal, and the cascade of bankruptcies of many American dioceses, the Vatican strategies of redress and reform are slow in implementation, inconsistent, and woefully inadequate in effecting a substantive change in attitude.

When discussing the roots of clericalism—and clerical sex abuse is just one, if not the most egregious, example of clericalism—it makes sense to discuss, as I have argued before, where the incubation of clericalism and its attendant problems lies: the seminary.

Pope Francis may not be disposed personally to the eradication of seminary formation and its substitution by a more enlightened pastoral training outside the safe confines of physical, emotional, and intellectual enclosure, but he is ratcheting up his fiery critique of clericalism in all its manifestations. With his intervention on October 25, 2023, an intervention that surprised many by its intensity and timing, Francis lambasted clericalism

> as a whip, it is a scourge, it is a form of worldliness that defiles and damages the face of the Lord's bride; it enslaves God's holy and faithful people. And God's people, God's holy faithful people go forward with patience and humility, enduring the scorn, mistreatment and marginalization of institutionalized clericalism. And how naturally we speak of the princes of the church, or of episcopal appointments as career advancements! ... It is enough to go into the ecclesiastical tailor shops in Rome to see the scandal of young priests trying on cassocks and hats [birettas and Roman saturni] or albs and lace-covered robes.

It is a leitmotif of Francis's pastoral and, indeed, doctrinal commentaries to lament the misbehaviour of clerics—young and old, but increasingly young—who revel in a false exceptionalism, bedeck themselves with baubles, masquerade as holy vessels for all to see, who are bereft of the humility of Jesus, the High Priest, and who expect to be treated with reverence by virtue of their office. To that end, the biblical passage that provides the clearest warrant for Francis's righteous rage is the one in the Gospel of Saint Matthew where Jesus excoriates the religious leaders of his culture and time. The parallel with the pope's culture and time are crushingly obvious:

> Jesus said to the crowds and to his disciples, "The scribes and the Pharisees sit in Moses' chair; therefore, do whatever they teach you and follow it; but do not do as they do, for they do not practise what they teach. They tie up heavy burdens, hard to bear, and lay them on the shoulders of others; but they themselves are unwilling to lift a finger to move them. They do all their deeds to be seen by others; for they make their phylacteries broad and their fringes long. They love to have the place of honour at banquets and the best seats in the synagogues, and to be greeted with respect in the marketplaces, and to have people call them rabbi."[32]

Other biblical and spiritual sources throughout the centuries have similarly condemned those who preen and posture as holy—think of the religious hypocrites in Geoffrey Chaucer's *Canterbury Tales* or Giovanni Boccaccio's *Decameron*—so, Francis's harsh judgments are not atypical of reformists. The primary focus of the pope's accusations of religious hypocrisy is his own clerical tribe. We have seen his excoriations of cardinalatial cupidity before, his diatribes against self-serving and self-important prelates, and his increasingly vocal admonitions levelled at the seminary rectors and faculty in the training of young clerics who paid little heed to the quality and maturity of their candidates. This latest iteration is part of the continuum going back to the earliest days of his papacy.

But there is a touch of Girolamo Savonarola in his moral screeds, an echo of the righteous puritan judging his peers, and many of his hearers, those especially recognized as the intended targets of his holy venom, are resentful, with that resentfulness percolating not infrequently in the social media of the conservative anti-Francis faction. And with some justification. A steady stream of papal reprimands can create its own bromides pillorying this papacy for its moral failings.[33]

But then, no pope of the last millennium has been so quick to self-identify publicly and regularly as a sinner. And to mean it.

Such papal humility does not forestall his internal critics, however. Whether they think his contrite admission of personal sinfulness is a feint or an uncalculated instance of genuine humility certainly does not matter when it comes to his perceived unorthodoxy. This is particularly true when it comes to the questions raised by a group dubbed the "dubia cardinals."

Hovering over the synod, but especially active at its commencement, these cardinals post questions, or dubia, seeking clarity from the Supreme Pontiff. They were five in number and revolved around the role of divine Revelation, the increasingly widespread practice of blessing same-sex marriages, the nature of synodality as a "constitutive dimension of the Church," the sacramental ordination of women, and the discounting of repentance as a precondition for sacramental absolution.

In each case, the cardinals—all retired and no longer active—seek to pressure the pope to affirm traditional thinking by invoking the memory, theology, and magisterial writings of Saint John Paul II. He is the lodestar of their thinking and resistance. For them, John Paul embodies the healthy, firm, and continuous tradition Francis imperils with, as they see it, his reckless leadership.

With adroit Jesuit-tinged rhetorical skill and keenly nuanced thinking, Francis deploys the writings of the very same pope his critics religiously invoke to discredit him in his own responses to the dubia. A perfect illustration of this is his considered reaction to the vexatious question of women to the presbyterate:

> When St. John Paul II taught that we must affirm "defini-tively" the impossibility of conferring priestly ordination to women, he was in no way denigrating women and giving supreme power to men. St. John Paul II also affirmed other things ... He also stated that if the priestly function is "hierar-chical," it should not be understood as a form of domination but "is totally ordered to the holiness of the members of Christ" (St. John Paul II, *Mulieris dignitatem*, 27). If this is not understood, and practical consequences are not drawn from these distinctions, it will be difficult to accept that the priesthood is reserved only for men, and we will not be able to recognize the rights of women or the need for them to participate in various ways in the leadership of the Church.[34]

The current round of "dubia cardinals" consisted of two repeat interrogators. The first is Raymond Burke, the US bishop, canonist, and long-time Francis adversary who has held various positions in the Vatican, including on the Apostolic Signatura, the premier canon law tribunal. He has unceremo-niously been jostled about with dismissals, demotions, and reappointments, culminating with his being deprived of his

Roman accommodations and salary, but no matter where he ends up, he remains *the* burr in the papal saddle. Francis finally acted against Burke in late November 2023, when he deprived the American cardinal of his rent-free accommodation and subsidized salary in Rome as a consequence of his obduracy and increasingly flagrant attacks on the pope's orthodoxy. The other repeat signatory is Germany's Walter Brandmüller, who is out of step big-time with the vast majority of his fellow German bishops. The new signatories include Juan Sandoval of Mexico; former dicasterial prefect Robert Sarah of Guinea, whose confrontational indiscretions on matters of liturgy and church polity have earned him public papal rebukes; and Joseph Zen of Hong Kong, who has vigorously locked horns with Francis over the latter's efforts at rapprochement with the Republic of China and implicit cooperation with their invidious sinicization of religion.

He answered their questions but not to their satisfaction. That was not really possible, given that this interrogation of the pope was ecclesiastical theatre designed to embarrass Francis and to underscore for the traditionalist constituencies that they represented the signatories' devotion to the Holy, Catholic, Apostolic Church and that they stand at marked variance with the ministry of Peter now exercised by a Jesuit disruptor from the global South.

Francis knows how to outflank them. While they argue for Tradition, employing John Paul II, he responds in kind. Reacting to their emphasis on the "definitive statement," he provides the following kicker:

On the other hand, to be rigorous, let us recognize that a clear and authoritative doctrine on the exact nature of a "definitive statement" has not yet been fully developed. It is not a dogmatic definition, and yet it must be adhered to by all. No one can publicly contradict it and yet it can be a subject of study, as was the case of the validity of ordinations in the Anglican Communion.[35]

For Francis's critics, this is a crystal-clear example of Jesuitical or sophistical reasoning. The case for the ordination of women is closed, but it is not really closed. We have an official position to be adhered to and recognized for its binding quality, but at the same time we have been less than scholarly in making the kinds of theological distinctions essential in recognizing *both* the commanding power of traditional formulations *and* the openness needed for new insights and appropriate refinements. The papal responses to the dubia appeared with consummate timing. Garry O'Sullivan, editor and publisher of a recent monthly newspaper called the *Synodal Times*, observed in an interview that "the clowns who crafted and delivered the dubia handed Francis the ideal tool for recharging the momentum of the Synod after two exhausting years of preparation."[36]

Francis was helped in preparing his response by the new head of the Dicastery for the Doctrine of the Faith, the Argentine theologian Victor Manuel Fernández, an advocate of the "Francis Project" who was created a cardinal just five days before the Synod opened.

Although not quite what Francis had in mind when responding to the "dubia cardinals" on the matter of what constitutes "authoritative," the meditation on authority provided by Dominican friar Timothy Radcliffe in his synod spiritual talks is refreshingly pertinent:

Many lay people have been astonished during the preparation of this Synod to find that they are listened to for the first time. They had doubted their own authority and asked, "Can I really offer something?" But it is not just the laity who lack authority. The whole Church is afflicted by a crisis of authority. An Asian archbishop complained that he had no authority. He said, "The priests are independent barons, who take no notice of me." Many priests too say they lost all authority. The sexual abuse crisis has discredited us.[37]

Lost authority can only truly be reclaimed through authenticity of presence, through an open and not evasive or opaque recognition of institutional misdeeds and complicity, and through a creative engagement with prophetic witness, however that is embodied in one's unique context. In great part, this is what the synod is about, with its emphases on listening and encounter: the recovery of credible and life-giving authority.

One of the most volatile areas in which this is played out is ordination and women. Both immediately before, and also concurrent with, the synod were a series of events arranged by advocacy groups keen on promoting a deeper understanding behind the struggle for women and sacramental ministry. I attended a prayer vigil sponsored by such groups as Women's Ordination Conference, Women's Ordination Worldwide, Catholic Women's Council, and Catholic Network for Women's Equality (CNWE) that was held in a chapel of the Basilica di Santa Prassede—named, appositely, after a Roman woman who cared for the bodies of martyrs in the second century of the Common Era. The women who spoke did so with heartfelt conviction of the pain associated with not being permitted to live their call to orders and of being prevented from serving the church fully because of this exclusion. They were in Rome to remind the synod delegates, the dicasterial prefects, and the pontiff that, in the words of Mary Ellen Chown of CNWE, "we should add to Pope Francis's 'without prayer there is no synod' that without women there is no church."

Chown is armed with a graduate degree in theology, a lifetime of service as a mother and spouse working to make the church viable for ordinary Catholics, and a commitment to equity in an institution that often privileges its clerics and its reputation over justice. She made clear to me that this commitment is long-standing and unshakeable and is at the heart of CNWE's ministry:

> CNWE aims to advocate on behalf of women, and as such, we became aware of the case of a sexual abuse survivor who was taken by the Diocese of London, Ontario, to the Supreme Court of Canada so the Diocese might avoid a just settlement in a decades-long case that involved the Diocese misrepresenting what they knew. The Court thankfully ruled in favour of the survivor's right to a new settlement. I have also known women who have been beloved pastoral assistants in Catholic parishes and yet their positions have been terminated at the whim of a new priest ... I think there is a temptation for some new young clerics in North America to respond to the grave complexities of our world from a place governed by fear of uncertainty and resistance to change. It can be tempting to be reactive rather than reflective, to be nostalgic for some idealized, simplified version of Catholicism (that never truly existed), or to assume that the "people in the pews" can only be holy when clerics draw hard lines to proscribe their behaviour. A fine priest once told me that he was told by an older priest

that during his years of formation he would "learn to be a priest from the people."[38]

Chown's hope for a more equitable church is not an isolated sentiment from some alienated quarter of Catholicism. It is a global sentiment, as was made clear in the plenary assembly reports, which found eloquent expression in the press briefing speech by Ghanaian theologian Nora Kofognotera Nonterah, who declared with exuberant confidence that the church should sit at the feet of laywomen in Africa to come to a deeper knowledge of the spiritual fertility of living synodally: "I came to the synod with the hopes, the joys, the dreams, the anxieties, the lamentations, but also the resilience of the African women ... We need to give a preferential option for the laity in the educational fields of the church, like theology, canon law, the social teachings of the church, leadership ministry. This should become the norm and practice of a synodal church."

As is customary in a viscerally entrenched hierarchical church, where the press briefing delegates are called upon to speak in a sequence of office, rank, and gender, Nonterah had the last word. But she outshone all the prelates present with her clarity and gustily delivered address. She may have been the last in order of precedence, but in the order of vision and substance she was the first.

It is instructive to note that women—their status in the church, their gifts, their abuse at the hands of autocratic clerics, their indispensability to the church's daily governance—were discussed at some length. In its final summary, *Synthesis Report: A Synodal Church in Mission*, delivered at the end of the synod, the assembly asked "that we avoid repeating the mistake of talking about women as an issue or a problem. Instead, we desire to promote a Church in which men and women dialogue together, in order to understand more deeply the horizon of God's project, that sees them together as protagonists, without subordination, exclusion and competition."[39]

Many have heard these words, or their like, before. Many times. Patience is wearing thin, and hope is fading that efforts at reform will bear fruit—including more women in the critical formation of male candidates for the priesthood; women assuming ever more decision-making positions in chanceries, dicasteries (on this score, Francis has appointed more women to leadership roles than all previous popes combined), and diocesan marriage tribunals (canonical bodies set up to determine grounds for nullity); and women and the diaconate (in spite of two papal commissions mandated to provide theological, historical, and exegetical research of women and *diaconia*, no decision has yet been made).

But although this may be the case in many global jurisdictions—very often the result of hierarchical inertia, cultural incomprehension if not hostility, as well as the exhaustion of personnel given depleted resources, even when there is sympathy and a desire for change—the momentum for reform must not slacken. Francis understands the formidable antipathy to change, and the Synod on Synodality is his answer.

Once change is seen as an eruption of the Holy Spirit, a result of collective discernment and respectful listening, a product of profound prayer, a way of making the church a true servant of the Gospel of Love, as Cardinal Schönborn observed, then the fear of change will evaporate in the knowledge that nothing has been lost in the Tradition that is sacred, and much has been gained in the crafting of a church on the margins, a church of and for the poor.[40]

But the poor are not the only ones on the margins. Other constituencies feel that their inherent value and dignity as the baptized faithful have been historically sidelined. And they, too, call out for inclusion. Of their outstanding number, the plight of sexual minorities and the precarity of their lives in some political jurisdictions have been a constant in many of the preparatory consultations but did not surface in the *aula* in a way many LGBTQ+ Catholics had longed for.

Aware that it is easy for the church to keep the troublesome from breaking out of their peripheral status by retaining an understated and anodyne pastoral presence in their lives, activists like Mark Guevarra of Vancouver were determined to shatter that strategy by being in Rome at a parallel synod that provided a platform for their views and witness.

Guevarra has been in the trenches and is no neophyte in the struggle to get the Catholic Church to take LGBTQ+ issues to heart. Raised in a devout Filipino family, he is the product of Catholic schools and parishes that shaped the faith he treasures and lives. Following an undergraduate degree in religious studies at the University of British Columbia and a graduate degree in religious education at the University of St. Michael's College, University of Toronto, Guevarra moved to Edmonton to be with his life partner, a Presbyterian minister he had met while studying in Toronto. While in Alberta, he pursued further work in graduate theology at Newman Theological College, but it proved a mixed blessing. In an interview for lay students, he was asked to keep his sexual identity under cover because there were seminarians in his classes and, as he bluntly states, "they did not want me to 'infect' them." In addition, his proposal to write a thesis on the generativity and procreativity of same-sex marriage, given that Canada had recently passed same-sex marriage legislation, seemed like perfect timing. But his supervisor thought otherwise, aware of the topic's controversial nature and capacity to create dissension in the college.

Guevarra soon took on a position as a pastoral assistant in a large Edmonton parish with some two thousand families and revelled in the opportunities presented to be a creative and theologically rooted catechist. Still, his being gay was not seen by church officials as a boon but as an albatross.

The ministry was wonderful. I love parish life. I love seeing the seasons change. I love forming families in their faith, reintroducing them to their faith, rejuvenating their faith. At the time I was hired, it was an open secret that I was gay; sort of a sense of Clinton's "Don't ask, don't tell" prevailed.

We had a quick turnover of priests in our parish, and one of them was from Brazil. Actually, two of them were. The first said, well, some interesting things about Catholic schools that did not go down well, and the other hardly ever showed up at things. I would get calls from the parish secretary saying, "Father didn't show up at a funeral, or to a school liturgy, so will you cover?" Like his immediate predecessor, this priest moved on.

In time, I moved on to the historic St. Albert parish and worked with a very progressive priest with a community of diverse political and educational backgrounds, with enough money to engage in many outreach ministries. Emboldened by this, I decided to start an LGBTQ prayer group. I put up a poster at St. Joseph's College, University of Alberta. The chaplain insisted I take it down and find some other place—a basement somewhere else on the U of A campus, perhaps. Shortly thereafter, I was summoned with my pastor to a meeting with the archdiocesan chancellor that did not augur well for my employment. She repeatedly asked if I was gay and in a relationship, and I refused to answer, invoking human rights and the inappropriateness of the lifestyle query. I said that I wished to speak with her and my boss, Archbishop Richard Smith. For whatever reason, he declined, and she returned to her earlier line of questioning. All was brought to the inevitable conclusion a month later: I was fired because there was sufficient evidence to show that I was in fact gay and therefore incapable of teaching the church's sacramental theology.

So, I then posted my termination story, as anyone my age would do, on social media. It was 2018, after all. Within twenty-four hours, ten thousand people had read the post, and I was in rapid succession interviewed by the *New York Times*, *America*, CBC, CTV, Global, et cetera.

Time for some new discernment: I am now engaged in doctoral studies at the Graduate Theological Union (Berkeley), where I happened upon the document on synodality by the International Theological Commission, the theological foundation for this whole synodal process. I decided then that I want to spend the rest of my life learning about synodality, and more specifically, restorative justice practices with LGBTQ+ and the Catholic Church. Knowing that we have harmed people, how do we restore them? We can't restore them to an institution that's broken, so we have to transform this institution in the process.[41]

The archdiocesan chancellor did not say anything that could be construed as illegal or unethical. She was simply following a canonical reasoning that stipulates that an employee in the service of the church is not unreasonably expected to abide by its teachings and practices and that this employee's moral life should be in conformity with the stated position of the church. For instance, around the time this was unfolding in Edmonton, a similar event was at the centre of a national controversy in the United States. The Archdiocese of Indianapolis, Indiana, terminated a gay teacher at Cathedral High School because of his marriage to another man. Archbishop Charles Thompson's position was made explicit and non-negotiable in a statement published on the school's website: "Archbishop Thompson made it clear that Cathedral's continued employment of a teacher in a public, same-sex marriage would result in our forfeiting our Catholic identity due to our employment of an individual living in contradiction to Catholic teaching on marriage." This kind of problem has played out across numerous jurisdictions and does not admit of one easy solution. At the same time that the firing occurred at Cathedral High School, the local Brebeuf Jesuit Preparatory School issued its own statement, respectfully declining "the Archdiocese's insistence and directive that we dismiss a highly capable and qualified teacher due to the teacher being a spouse within a civilly-recognized same-sex marriage." Two distinctly different responses, with the archdiocese opting for the canonical approach and the Jesuits with the pastoral.[42]

Guevarra's unabated enthusiasm was echoed by Catholic gay media personnel who covered the synod with remarkable equanimity, given that their position was deemed by many of their conservative Catholic peers as misguided at best and demonic at worst. Although there are no recorded instances of outright homophobia in the *aula* or in the Stampa, gay-positive declarations were few and limited, in the end, to the platitudinous and generic.[43]

From the outset, Francis intended the synod as an assembly that was more faithfully representative of the Catholic demographic—preponderantly lay, disproportionately female in terms of actual practice, no longer Eurocentric, and more inclusive of other ecclesial communities in union with Rome—but he also intended the synod to be outward-looking, enjoining Catholics to attend to the greater challenges facing us all, including the continuing desecration of the planet.

So, although it had been briefly mooted before the synod began, on the Feast of Saint Francis of Assisi (October 4, 2023) the pope issued his second document on the ecological crisis, *Laudate Deum* (Praise God). He notes at the very beginning that the responses to climate upheaval afflicting our common home since the publication eight years earlier of *Laudato Si'* "have not been adequate, while the world in which we live is collapsing and may be nearing the breaking point" (section 2).

To that end, he reiterates many of his earlier fears, strengthened now in their intensity by the realities on the ground. Once again, he has done his homework:

All of Creation is integrated; our common home consists of all living companions: "Ocean waters have a thermal inertia and centuries are needed to normalize their temperature and salinity, which affects the survival of many species. This is one of the many signs that the other creatures of this world have stopped being our companions along the way and have become instead our victims" (section 15).

A human ecology serves as an alternative to the hegemonic technocratic paradigm:[44] "A healthy ecology is also the result of interaction between human beings and the environment, as occurs in the indigenous cultures and has occurred for centuries in different regions of the earth ... The great present-day problem is that the technocratic paradigm has destroyed that healthy and harmonious relationship" (section 27).

We have allowed vested powers and elites to profit while others languish because of our enslavement to a heartless and ruinous free market capitalism: "It continues to be regrettable that global crises are being squandered when they could be occasions to bring about beneficial changes. This is what happened in the 2007–2008 financial crisis[45] and again in the COVID-19 crisis. For 'the actual strategies developed worldwide in the wake of [those crises] fostered greater individualism, less integration and increased freedom for the truly powerful, who always find a way to escape unscathed' (Final document of the Special Assembly for the Pan-Amazonian Region [2019]" (section 36).

Papal social teaching around the principle of subsidiarity (first introduced in 1931 by Pope Pius XI—and invoked and expanded upon by John XXIII, Paul VI, John Paul II, Benedict XVI, and now Francis) remains a foundation stone for an equitable society: "The current challenge is to reconfigure and recreate [multilateralism], taking into account the new world situation" (section 37).

Papa Bergoglio's vision of an integral ecology is profoundly Franciscan, as previously discussed; the Umbrian friar's joy-infused celebration of the plenitude of Creation defines and directs the pope's thinking about our common home: "'The universe unfolds in God, who fills it completely ... there is mystical meaning to be found in a leaf, in a mountain trail, in a dewdrop, in a poor person's face.' The world sings of an infinite Love: how can we fail to care for it?" (section 65).

In *Laudate Deum*, Pope Francis continues to champion the poor, pleads for creative responses—no matter how quantitatively insignificant they may seem to our own eyes—to waste reduction, excoriates governments for their failure of nerve, denounces wealthy barons of industry with their scant regard for anything other than maximizing profits for their shareholders, and then links justice and social equality with a mite of mystical rapture.

Although there are many eco-theologians, scientists, and political activists in the Catholic Church in tandem with their like-minded secular counterparts who influence and in turn are influenced by Francis, the earlier-mentioned Irish philosopher-visionary John Moriarty strikes me as a thinker who presages the pope's Christo-cosmology and its integral ecology when he speaks of Christianity as a vast unity-in-multiplicity, uniting not only human beings but all species that have lived whether extinct or flourishing into an extraterritorial ecumenicity.

In keeping with this sentiment—if more prosaic and scholarly in its phrasing—is the plea from Conor Gearty, professor of human rights law at the London School of Economics, who sees in Francis's Vatican an agency that could just possibly save universalism in a time when

> Liberalism has run out of steam. For all its failings and fractures, the Church—led, of course, by a Pope from the Global South—can forge a new role, taking its place as the moral guardian of the equal rights and equal dignity of all the

peoples of the world, reaching across all divides—religious and political—to embrace and protect all those who suffer. Let's not let universalism disappear without lighting a candle.[46]

Francis has, with his commitment to synodality, lit a candle—a candle of hope, of possibility—a candle of reform that, if not extinguished by his successor, could effect profound change in the way Catholics live out their lives. In the process, he could make Rome, once the centre of an ecclesiastical empire, a treasured seat on the periphery, rooted in its identification with the poor—a beacon of human and spiritual harmony in a sea of dark turmoil.

Now *that* is disruption.

CONCLUSION

WHEN HE GAVE HIS homily on Corpus Christi Sunday in June of 2023, Father Bill Burke wanted it to be an invitation to his parishioners to take the fall Synod on Synodality to heart. This is *our* church, after all.

The pastor of St. Marguerite Bourgeoys parish in Cape Breton, Nova Scotia, has long been engaged in both administrative and pastoral ministry. A former director of the National Liturgy Office of the Canadian Conference of Catholic Bishops, fully bilingual (English and French), and with a long history of service to the Mi'kmaq, Burke is every inch a "Francis priest." That was in sharp evidence when he gave his Corpus Christi sermon.

He spoke of travelling to Florida some fifteen years ago with three Toronto priest-friends on what was purportedly a golf holiday. Given his embarrassing skills as a golfer, he knew that his culinary gifts were really the drawing card for his inclusion. At one point, they all trudged off to Sunday Mass in a church that was packed with thousands of worshippers. The homily did little for Burke, with its conservative political coloration, but the pastor's insistence that only Catholics in a state of grace were to receive communion, and then listing those who were to be excluded, really provoked him: the divorced, those living together without benefit of the sacrament of matrimony, those who are gay, those not opposed to abortion, those who have not gone to confession at least once in the past year.

For Burke, this is not a welcoming church, a church for the wounded and sinners, but a club of the saved, the elect, and in that, a desecration of authentic Catholic thinking. This was a church that excluded.

Just recently, Burke preached to his congregation, he was told a story by a friend from Alberta that provides a striking contrast in ecclesiologies with the Florida experience. The friend often babysits her grandniece; when this happens on a weekend, she and her husband will bring the child to Mass with them. On one occasion, when the dad came to collect his daughter, she said she wanted to go to Mass first. She then proceeded to ask him to accompany them, and although at first he demurred, he finally agreed. At communion, she took her father's hand and asked him to join her; once again, he reluctantly conceded. When he went up to the priest to receive communion, he said, *sotto voce*: "Father, I'll be fine with whatever you decide to do, but I need to be honest with you. It has been over twenty years since I have been at Mass." The priest held up the host and placed it in the palm of the man's hand, smiled, and said, "Welcome home."

This is the church that is the big tent, the field hospital, the sanctuary in a turbulent world. This is Francis's church.

Although Burke's natural instincts are in sympathy with

Bergoglio's, and although their pastoral sensibilities mesh, neither is operating in a spiritual vacuum. They are both theological descendants of the Second Vatican Council, spiritual sons of Roncalli.

For Francis, this has special significance, because like John XXIII, he is Peter and has primary responsibility for safeguarding the tradition and unity of the church. It's his job, after all.

He is acutely mindful of this divine charge, and his papacy, regularly denounced by his detractors as a catastrophic usurpation of the church's integrity, bears testimony to his overriding conviction that the church's theology must be relational rather than disembodied, its mode of inquiry and expression *a posteriori* (inductive) rather than *a priori* (deductive).

Emilce Cuda, an Argentine theologian appointed by Francis as secretary of the Pontifical Commission for Latin America, insists that Francis's pastoral theology is not pastoral theology as it is generally framed in North America, where pastoral is an adjective rather than a verb, a picture rather than a place:

> For Francis to be pastoral is to be *with* the people in *their* place. This is important to understand, because some people in the church—important theologians—they think "theological." What they fail to understand is that for those of us outside the Eurocentric orbit, for those on the peripheries, doing theology using philosophy as the *mediation*, or framework/ structure for mediating theological reflection and insight, is no longer viable. Theology is mediated by the lived wisdom of the people, and unlike liberation theology, with its emphasis on a preferential option for the poor, Francis prefers a preferential option *with* the poor. Theologians, the current doctors or teachers of the church, the professors on the balcony or

loggia creating their categories of understanding, must come down and live the realities of the poor and marginalized … The wisdom of God is not the exclusive preserve of those like you and me who went to university and obtained PhDs. No, no, no. It is not like that at all. It is not the experts acting in isolation but the entire people of God thinking and acting together that is the wisdom of God.[1]

The clearest formal or official statement on this way of doing theology was published immediately after the synod ended. It leaves no one in any doubt as to the way theology should be exercised in the contemporary world. On November 1, 2023, Francis issued his apostolic letter or motu proprio *Ad theologiam promovendam* (Promoting Theology),[2] and the latest paradigm shift entered Catholic consciousness.

It was issued in part as the pope's approval of the new statutes drawn up for the Vatican's Pontifical Academy of Theology, although it reflects current theological thinking in that it incorporates much of the methodological approach of the social sciences, and although it further develops Francis's perspective that theology must not remain secure in its intellectual citadel but be open to the world at the grassroots level.

Francis categorically states that "to promote theology in the future, we cannot limit ourselves to abstractly reproposing formulas and schemes from the past … [for] God has revealed himself as history, not as a compendium of abstract truths."

The document being a crystallization of much of his thinking around the role of theology, Francis is not shy in declaring that the science of theology is "called to a turning point, to a paradigm shift, to a 'courageous cultural revolution.'" Called, in fact, to become a "fundamentally contextual theology," by which he means a theology that must be "capable of reading and interpreting the Gospel in the conditions in which men and women live daily, in different geographical, social and cultural environments ... theology cannot but take place in a culture of dialogue and encounter between different traditions and knowledge, between religions, openly confronting all, believers and non-believers."

In addition, invoking the insight of the Italian thinker Antonio Rosmini, who argued that all knowledge is "oriented towards the Idea of Wisdom," Francis, with his fondness for emblematic symbols like the polyhedron, the pyramid, and the balancing dance of the Contraries or human and ecclesial tensions, is attracted to the "Idea of Wisdom [holding] Truth and Charity together internally in a 'solid circle,' so that it is impossible to know the truth without practising charity."

This papal summons to get theologians onto the streets, to be pioneers in effecting a cultural revolution, is not a diminishment of intellectual rigour or a departure from ecclesial connectedness but rather a clarion call for meaningful and credible witness. Theology in the marketplace need not mean that theology in the academy is to be abandoned. Rather, by being aware of Bernard Lonergan's shift of consciousness from a "classicist to historicist" model, Francis is committed to an enlivening theological enterprise rooted in the reality of the people, grounded in experience, not ideology, a science that is a way of life open to an endlessly unfolding culture of encounter.

Traditionalist theologians may find *Ad theologiam promovendam* a sad consolidation of the pope's woolly thinking, best exemplified by the commentary of Capuchin friar Thomas Weinandy, who sees it as "typical Pope Francis document—a great deal of high-sounding words that are very ambiguous. It is mostly bells and whistles ... There can be no authentic paradigm shift without being faithful to upholding and promoting what the Church has authentically taught through the centuries."[3]

But the disruptor Jesuit pope has done precisely that: inaugurate a paradigm shift by being faithful to the organic tradition. He has disrupted the established pattern of doing things as the premier occupant of the Vatican; he has disrupted the protocols that are the mainstay of institutional life on the Tiber; he has disrupted the way we see the church working in the world; he has disrupted the pattern of church priorities by centring the believing community on and with the poor; he has disrupted the settled questions by introducing a new perspective, replacing a magisterial with a synodal way of being church.

And he has managed to hold to the tradition he has sworn to protect as Peter by refusing to alter church teaching either by papal fiat or parliamentary consensus; by refusing to disregard forms of devotion or what sociologists now call popular religiosity; by refusing to dismiss the work of his predecessors and instead building on their scaffolding.

What the disruptor pope has disrupted is our spiritual and intellectual complacency, our foreclosure through fear of fresh ways of seeing the Gospel as the leaven of society, our ahistorical sense of the church that shields us from the reforming gusts of the Spirit.

The New Zealand Catholic theologian Christopher Longhurst, in reviewing *Ad theologiam promovendam*, believes that Francis's point that theology "cannot but take place in a culture of dialogue" implicitly recognizes that the "central presupposition of a theology of dialogue is that anyone can understand what is believed about God more deeply when they open themselves to the truth statements of all religions."[4]

As we saw earlier, when Francis spoke to the joint session of Congress in Washington, DC, in September 2015, celebrating four American moral prophets, Thomas Merton was one of them. In his life as pope, Bergoglio has come by a different route to share the comprehensive embrace of a culture of dialogue articulated by Merton in his diary *Conjectures of a Guilty Bystander*:

> the more I am able to affirm others, to say "yes" to them in myself, by discovering them in myself and myself in them, the more real I am. I am fully real if my own heart says *yes to everyone*. I will be a better Catholic, not if I can *refute* every shade of Protestantism, but if I can affirm the truth in it and still go further. So, too, with the Muslims, the Hindus, the Buddhists, etc. This does not mean syncretism, indifferentism, the vapid and careless friendliness that accepts everything by thinking nothing ... If I affirm myself by denying all that is Muslim, Jewish, Protestant, Hindu, Buddhist, etc., in the end I will find that there is not much left for me to affirm as a Catholic and certainly no breath of the Spirit with which to affirm it.[5]

In his struggle to contain "all divided worlds," Merton realized that he needed to evolve even further beyond healing the rifts in Christianity and to affirm and not refute the truth in Judaism, Islam, Hinduism, Buddhism, et cetera. And this is precisely what Pope Francis has done in his papacy, the fruit of his culture of genuine encounter and dialogue.

The Jesuit disruptor, the *pontifex maximus*, is a bridge to a greater and encompassing unity.

ACKNOWLEDGEMENTS

EVERY AUTHOR IS INDEBTED to a multitude of people while making a book: interlocutors aplenty, a supportive publisher with its cohort of diligent and affirming editorial personnel, scholarly peers engaged in similar undertakings, querying critics and enthusiastic students, and those folk who share a passionate interest in the subject. I owe them all a goodly measure of thanks for their diverse contributions during the four years of this work's unfolding.

But some in particular deserve special mention: my daughters Sarah and Alexa Higgins for their professional expertise as editor and researcher respectively; Anne-Louise Mahoney, whose detailed familiarity as editor with the subject matter and astute editorial eye were treasured boons; my colleague and friend, Dr. David Sylvester, President and Vice-Chancellor of St. Michael's College, University of Toronto, who created a position for me at the university, provided me with an office, and arranged for some research monies to assist in the travel, interview, and research phase; and my rabbi friend, Dr. Yosef Wosk, whose spiritual and intellectual affinity with Francis resulted in many enlightening conversations, a great deal of moral support, and much appreciated financial funding.

NOTES

INTRODUCTION

1. Blaise Pascal, *Pensées*, as quoted in *Sublimitas et miseria hominis*, an apostolic letter by Pope Francis published on June 19, 2023. The English translation title is *The Grandeur and Misery of Humankind*.

2. Reeves was a polymath in his own right: winner of the Italia, Drainie, and Masaryk Awards, author of the Sump and Coggin detective mysteries, competitive long-distance runner, poet, and composer of several motets and oratorios. I had a long association with Reeves researching, writing, and narrating several documentaries for his CBC Radio *Celebration* program.

3. Apostolic letter *Sublimitas et miseria hominis* of the Holy Father Francis on the Fourth Centenary of the Birth of Blaise Pascal, June 19, 2023, vatican.va/content/francesco/en/apost_letters/documents/20230619-sublimitas-et-miseria-hominis.html.

4. Jansenism often gets a bad press for its reputation for moral inflexibility and theological rigidity, but Gemma Simmonds, a senior research fellow at the Margaret Beaufort Institute of Theology at Cambridge University and a British sister of the Congregation of Jesus, identifies some aspects of Jansenism that actually anticipate progressive Catholic practices of the post–Second Vatican Council: "the Jansenists were remarkably forward-looking in some respects, at the forefront of social and political radicalism, championing the rights of the lower clergy, the emancipation of slaves and the restoration of civil status to Jews and Protestants [Huguenots]. They fostered stronger roles for the laity in the

church, especially women, and emphasized the need to return to original sources—including Scripture—in theology and the liturgy, and advocated the greater use of the vernacular in the Missal [liturgical book used for the celebration of Mass]." "Blaise Pascal: Forged in the Night of Fire," *Tablet*, July 1, 2023, 5.

5. Michael W. Higgins, "Jacqueline et Blaise: Le coeur a son ordre," *Celebration*, CBC Radio, May 19, 1985.

6. Jorge Mario Bergoglio in Silvina Premat, "L'attrattiva del cardinale," *Tracce* 6 (2001): 34.

CHAPTER 1

1. Eamon Duffy, *Saints and Sinners: A History of the Popes* (New Haven, CT: Yale University Press, 1997), preface.

2. P. G. Maxwell-Stuart, *Chronicles of the Popes: The Reign-by-Reign Record of the Papacy from St. Peter to the Present* (London: Thames and Hudson, 1997), 6.

3. Michael W. Higgins, *Stalking the Holy: The Pursuit of Saint Making* (Toronto: Anansi, 2006), 180.

4. Robert A. Ventresca, *Soldier of Christ: The Life of Pope Pius XII* (Cambridge, MA: Belknap Press of Harvard University Press, 2013), 156.

5. Michael W. Higgins and Douglas R. Letson, *My Father's Business: A Biography of His Eminence G. Emmett Cardinal Carter* (Toronto: Macmillan, 1990), 104.

6. Brocard Sewell, *The Vatican Oracle* (London: Duckworth, 1970), 10.

7. Fr. Rolfe, *Hadrian the Seventh* (Harmondsworth: Penguin, 1982), 137.

8. Colm Tóibín, "The Bergoglio Smile," *London Review of Books* 43, no. 2 (21 January 2021).

CHAPTER 2

1. Paul Vallely, *Pope Francis: The Struggle for the Soul of Catholicism* (London: Bloomsbury, 2015), 19.

2. Michael W. Higgins and Douglas Letson, *The Jesuit Mystique* (Toronto: Macmillan, 1995), 142.

3. Higgins and Letson, *Jesuit Mystique*, 73.

4. A Jesuit provincial has responsibility for an ecclesiastical region composed of Jesuits known as a Province. He is appointed by the General of the Order in Rome following consultation with the members of the designated region. They submit a *terna* or list of three names for consideration by the general, but the latter is not obligated to restrict his choice to these names.

5. Jimmy Burns, *Francis: Pope of Good Promise* (New York: St. Martin's Press, 2015), 135–36.

6. Michael W. Higgins and Douglas R. Letson, eds., *Soundings: Conversations about Catholicism* (Toronto: Novalis, 2000), 88.

7. I am indebted to Bergoglio biographer Austen Ivereigh for alerting me to Campbell-Johnston's subsequent change of mind when the British Jesuit before he died "realized he had been wrong about Bergoglio's stance during the dirty war, as he recognized publicly more than once (and told me personally) because he hadn't at the time grasped the difference between the very different contexts of El Salvador and Argentina." Email exchange with author, April 13, 2024. Recent historical research into newly opened archives for the purpose, which led to the multi-volume *La verdad los hará libres: La Iglesia Católica en las espiral de violencia en La Argentina 1966–1983*, published in 2023, confirms the far more textured, measured, and nuanced response of the church during the "dirty war" than is the generally accepted popular view of ecclesiastical complicity at worse and overt non-resistance to the regime at best.

8. Burns, *Francis*, 173.

9. Austen Ivereigh in *The Great Reformer: Francis and the Making of a Radical Pope* (2014) makes a highly persuasive case for Bergoglio's complicated and adept relationship with his country's rulers by asserting his refusal to capitulate to pressure, by recognizing his skillful and compassionately executed strategy of helping scores of people escape the ruthlessness of the generals, and by helping the Jesuits at the time avoid the ideological polarization justifying the violence both of left-wing guerrillas and the military dictatorship seeking to eradicate them. The many transitions in the Bergoglio life trajectory are more continuous than discontinuous, his patience often misconstrued as passivity, his firm decision-making often the product of protracted discernment rather than a blunt exercise of power. In other words, Pacelli to Roncalli is too summary and categorical a liberal soundbite.

10. Antonio Sparado, SJ, "A Big Heart Open to God: An Interview with Pope Francis," *America: The Jesuit Review*, September 30, 2013.

11. Michael Collins, *Francis: Bishop of Rome* (Collegeville, MN: Liturgical Press, 2013), 51.

12. Fifth General Conference of the Latin American Episcopate, Concluding Document, 61, 65. ltrr.arizona.edu/~katie/kt/misc/Apercida/Aparecida-document-for-printing.pdf. Italics added.

13. Vatican Press Office official English translation release, February 2013.

14. Alberto Melloni, "How to Elect a Pope," *Tablet*, April 24, 2021, 4.

15. Gerard O'Connell, *The Election of Pope Francis: An Inside Account of the Conclave That Changed History* (Maryknoll, NY: Orbis, 2019), 226–27.

16. Vatican Press Office, Papa Francesco March 2013 speeches.

CHAPTER 3

1. John Paul II, "Address at the Seminary of Rome," *L'Osservatore Romano*, March 5–6, 1984, 6, as quoted in Patrick Granfield, *The Limits of the Papacy: Authority and Autonomy in the Church* (New York: Crossroad, 1987), 184.

2. J. M. R. Tillard, *The Bishop of Rome* (Wilmington, DE: Michael Glazier, 1983), 115.

3. John R. Quinn, *The Reform of the Papacy: The Costly Call to Christian Unity* (New York: Herder and Herder, 1999), 180.

4. As drawn from my chapter "Padre Pio: Saint and Stigmatic," in *Stalking the Holy*, 122.

5. André Vauchez, *Francis of Assisi: The Life and Afterlife of a Medieval Saint* (New Haven, CT: Yale University Press, 2012), 335.

6. Jack Costello, SJ, interview for the "The Jesuit Mystique," *Ideas*, CBC Radio One, writer and researcher Michael W. Higgins, producer Bernie Lucht, 1994–95.

7. Jack Costello, SJ, "Ignatian Spirituality: Finding God in All Things," *Grail: An Ecumenical Journal* 8 (March 1992): 27–29.

8. Ignatius of Loyola, *A Pilgrim's Journey: The Autobiography*, trans. Joseph N. Tylenda, SJ (Collegeville, MN: Liturgical Press, 1985), 38–39.

9. This is explored in greater detail in the chapter "Jesuit as Spiritual Director," in Higgins and Letson, *Jesuit Mystique*.

10. W. W. Meissner, SJ, *Ignatius of Loyola: The Psychology of a Saint* (New Haven, CT: Yale University Press, 1992), 108.

11. David Lonsdale, SJ, "The Spiritual Exercises: A Popular Path to Personal Wholeness," *International Minds: The Quarterly Journal of Psychological Insight into International Affairs* 2, no. 2 (Winter 1990–91): 13.

12. George E. Ganss, SJ, trans., *The Spiritual Exercises of Saint Ignatius Loyola* (St. Louis, MO: Institute of Jesuit Sources, 1992), 21.

13. Higgins and Letson, *Jesuit Mystique*, 83.

14. Higgins and Letson, *Jesuit Mystique*, 83.

15. André Brouillete, SJ, "The Ignatian *Magis*: Spirituality and Growth," *Canadian Jesuits*, no. 1 (2021): 23. jesuits.ca/stories/the-ignatian-magis-spirituality-and-growth.

16. Pape François, *Entretiens avec les Jésuites* (Roma: Editions Parole et Silence/La Civiltà Cattolica, 2019), 16.

17. Pape François, *Entretiens*, 38.

18. Bernard Lonergan, "Dimensions of Meaning," in *Collected Works of Bernard Lonergan*, vol. 4: *Collection* (Toronto: University of Toronto Press, 1993), 245.

19. Gordon A. Rixon, "Dwelling on the Way: Pope Francis and Bernard Lonergan on Discernment," *Irish Theological Quarterly* 84, no. 3 (2019): 310–11.

20. Lonergan, "Dimensions of Meaning," 238.

21. Thomas Merton, "Barth's Dream and Other Conjectures," *Sewanee Review* 73, no. 1 (Winter 1965): 3.

22. Austen Ivereigh, "Pope Francis 'Meets' Thomas Merton: Austen Ivereigh Imagines Their Conversation," *Tablet*, December 12, 2018.

23. Thomas Merton, *Conjectures of a Guilty Bystander* (New York: Doubleday/Image, 1968), 21.

24. Christopher Pramuk, "God Accompanies Persons: Thomas Merton and Pope Francis on Gender and Sexual Diversity," *Merton Annual* 28 (2015): 85–86.

25. Thomas Merton, *The School of Charity: Letters on Religious Renewal and Spiritual Direction*, ed. Patrick Hart, ocso (New York: Farrar, Straus and Giroux, 1985), 337.

26. Pope Francis, *Desiderio desideravi* (2022), section 54, vatican.va/content/francesco/en/apost_letters/documents/20220629-lettera-ap-desiderio-desideravi.html.

27. Thomas Merton, "Letter to Dom Francis Decroix," *The Hidden Ground of Love: The Letters of Thomas Merton on Religious Experience and Social Concerns*, ed. William H. Shannon (New York: Farrar, Straus and Giroux, 1985), 157.

28. *L'opposizione polare*, as translated by Barry Hudock and quoted in Massimo Borghesi's *The Mind of Pope Francis: Jorge Bergoglio's Intellectual Journey* (Collegeville, MN: Liturgical Press Academic, 2018), 114.

29. Joseph Quinn Raab, *Opening New Horizons: Seeds of a Theology of Pluralism in Thomas Merton's Dialogue with D. T. Suzuki* (Eugene, OR: Pickwick, 2021), 147.

30. Pope Francis, "Address of the Holy Father to a Joint Session of the United States Congress," Washington, DC, September 24, 2015.

31. Paul J. Griffiths, "The Future of Ukraine: A Dissent," *Commonweal* (September 2022), 53.

32. Myroslaw Tataryn, "Vatican Diplomacy or Gospel Solidarity?," *Go, Rebuild My House* (blog, Sacred Heart University), April 26, 2022.

33. Tim Parks, "The Pope's Many Silences," *New York Review of Books*, October 20, 2022, 70.

34. There has been considerable debate over the use of the word "fraternal" and "brothers all" or *Fratelli tutti*, given their masculine provenance. Various

alternatives have been advanced to replace "brotherhood" with "siblinghood," but the linguistic squabbles, though legitimate, shouldn't derail the content of the encyclical. Given the pope's grounding in Romance languages, he is not automatically sympathetic to the reservations of the English speakers. He took the title of his enycyclical from St. Francis's own words.

35. Some of this analysis appeared in various commentaries I wrote for the *Globe and Mail* following the publication of *Fratelli tutti*.

CHAPTER 4

1. James Martin, SJ, *Building a Bridge: How the Catholic Church and the LGBT Community Can Enter into a Relationship of Respect, Compassion, and Sensitivity* (New York: HarperOne, 2018), 29.

2. Pontifex Maximus is one of the many titles ascribed to the office of the papacy.

3. Anthony Spadaro, SJ, "A Big Heart Open to God: An Interview with Pope Francis," *America: The Jesuit Review*, 30 September 2013. Italics added.

4. Giulia Evolvi, "Is the Pope Judging You? Digital Narratives on Religion and Homosexuality in Italy," LGBTQs, *Media and Culture in Europe* (Abingdon-on-Thames: Routledge, 2017), 149.

5. David Gibson, *The Rule of Benedict: Pope Benedict XVI and His Battle with the Modern World* (New York: HarperOne, 2007), 317.

6. Michael Cassabon, "Love Should Be at the Heart of the Vatican's Views toward Same-Sex Unions," *Globe and Mail*, March 27, 2022.

7. Joshua J. McElwee, "Pope Francis Meets Jeannine Gramick, US Sister Known for LGBTQ Ministry," *National Catholic Reporter*, October 17, 2023, ncronline.org/vatican/vatican-news/pope-francis-meets-jeannine-gramick-us-sister-known-lgbtq-ministry.

8. Christopher Lamb, "View from Rome," *Tablet*, December 18/25, 2021, 51.

9. Joan Grundy, "Don't Let Vatican Same-Sex Ruling Erase That We Are All Original Blessings," *Waterloo Region Record*, March 23, 2021, op ed page.

10. Paddy Agnew, "The Francis Process: Moving from a Minor to a Major Key?," *Studies: An Irish Quarterly Review* 104, no. 415 (Autumn 2015): 284–85.

11. Gerry O'Hanlon, "The Joy of Love—*Amoris laetitia*," *Furrow* 67, no. 6 (June 2016): 333.

12. John Montague, private email correspondence with the author, December 31, 2022.

13. Charles J. Reid Jr., "Same-Sex Relations and the Catholic Church: How Law and Doctrine Have Evolved, 1820–2020," *Journal of Law and Religion* 34, no. 2 (August 2019): 234.

14. Paul Elie, "Pope Francis Supports Same-Sex Civil Unions, but the Church Must Do More," *New Yorker*, October 25, 2020.

15. James Alison, "How to Recognise a Tantrum," *Tablet*, March 27, 2021, 7.

16. Robert McElroy, "Cardinal McElroy Responds to His Critics on Sexual Sin, the Eucharist, and LGBT and Divorced/Remarried Catholics," *America*, March 2, 2023.

17. Paul Lakeland, "God Can't Bless Sin: True, but …," *Go, Rebuild the Church*, Sacred Heart University Ecclesial Reform blog, March 24, 2021.

18. Francis, Angelus Prayer, March 21, 2021, press.vatican.va/content/salastampa/en/bollettino/pubblico/2021/03/21/210322a.html.

19. The ruling and the address would be superseded on December 18, 2023, by the Dicastery for the Doctrine of the Faith with its Declaration *Fiducia supplicans* (The Supplicating Trust) on the pastoral meaning of blessings. The declaration, with the approval of the pope, stipulates conditions whereby those couples in irregular situations (divorced and remarried without a decree of nullity) and same-sex couples may request an ordained minister to bless them. The canonical and liturgical requirements for such a benediction must include clear recognition that the church's teaching on marriage is in no way compromised. The blessing is to be understood by all participating parties in the following light: "even when a person's relationship with God is clouded by sin, he can always ask for a blessing, stretching out his hand to God, as Peter did in the storm when he cried out to Jesus, 'Lord, save me!' (Mt. 14:30). Indeed, desiring and receiving a blessing can be the possible good in some situations … Any blessing will be an … invitation to draw ever closer to the love of Christ" [section 43]. In other words, blessings are a conduit of grace, a welcome into God's forgiving embrace, and not a reward for a settled, undisturbed, and complacent piety.

20. The interview was published in English as Pope Francis and Fernando Prado, *The Strength of a Vocation: Consecrated Life Today* (Washington, DC: USCCB, 2018).

21. Both the John Jay College Report—*The Causes and Context of Sexual Abuse of Minors by Catholic Priests in the United States, 1950–2010* (Washington, DC: USCCB, 2011)—and Philip Jenkins's *Pedophiles and Priests: Anatomy of a Contemporary Crisis* (New York: Oxford University Press, 1996) are generally referenced for their argument of relative parity of abusing Roman Catholic priests with other professional equivalents, but their methodology and statistical sources are hugely controverted by other authors and data-tracking bodies, principally Bishops Accountability (bishop-accountability.org). The total number of victims and abusers

remains shockingly volatile, as evidenced by a cascading number of national episcopal reports that have taken a full disclosure approach following decades of restricted access. Celibacy in and of itself is not a predictor of abuse, but it can be and has been used as a cover for abusive behaviour. Suffice it to say that the reputational damage to the church remains a depressing constant.

22. This discussion on Nouwen, priesthood, spirituality, and sexuality is explored in depth in *Genius Born of Anguish: The Life and Legacy of Henri Nouwen* (Mahwah, NJ: Paulist Press, 2012) and *Impressively Free: Henri Nouwen as a Model for a Reformed Priesthood* (Mahwah, NJ: Paulist Press, 2019), both co-authored by Michael W. Higgins and Kevin Burns. In addition, there are three articles I wrote on Nouwen: "Priest, Prophet, Mentor, Misfit—Henri Nouwen," *Commonweal*, December 5, 2016; "Henri Nouwen: An Obituary," *Tablet*, October 5, 1996; as well as "Henri Nouwen, Thomas Merton, and Donald Nicholl," in *Turning the Wheel: Henri Nouwen and Our Search for God*, ed. Jonathan Bengston and Gabrielle Earnshaw (Maryknoll, NY: Orbis, 2007).

23. Works such as *The Wounded Healer: Ministry in Contemporary Society*; *Gracias: A Latin American Journal*; and *The Return of the Prodigal Son: A Story of Homecoming*.

24. Philip John Bewley, "Queer Catholics as Living Human Documents: Henri J. M. Nouwen, Self-availability and the Therapeutic Turn in Dutch Catholicism" (research thesis, University of Wollongong, Australia, 2022), 112, 116.

25. Luigi Gioia, "Pain and Hope of Compromise," *Tablet*, January 28, 2023.

26. Andrew Buechel-Rieger, "Out at Mass: Pope Francis, Liturgical Formation, and LGBTQ People" (paper presented at the Pope Francis Conference: Pope Francis and the Future of the Church—Prospects and Challenges for Renewal, St. Mark's College, University of British Columbia, May 5, 2023).

CHAPTER 5

1. David Owen, "Annals of Geography: Promised Land," *New Yorker*, February 8, 2021.

2. Thomas Merton, "Letter to Barbara Hubbard," February 16, 1968, in *Witness to Freedom: The Letters of Thomas Merton in Times of Crisis*, sel. and ed. William H. Shannon (New York: Farrar Straus Giroux, 1994), 74–75.

3. *On Heaven and Earth: Pope Francis on Faith, Family, and the Church in the Twenty-First Century*, by Abraham Skorka and Jorge Mario Bergoglio, trans. Alejandro Bermudez and Howard Goodman (New York: Random House, 2013), consists of conversations on numerous topics, but those on

religion and science, faith and reason, are especially germane. The original Spanish edition (*Sobre el Cielo y la tierra*) appeared three years before Bergoglio's election as pontiff.

4. John McCarthy, SJ, "Science and Religion: A Dance of Beauty and Truth," in *Looking to the Laity: Reflections on Where the Church Can Go from Here*, ed. Anne Louise Mahoney (Toronto: Novalis, 2021), 107.

5. Although the majority of the encyclical is the product of Benedict's labours and intellectual preoccupations, it would never have been published under the seal of the current pontiff were he not in agreement. It constitutes a nice marriage of the theology professor and the chemistry teacher.

6. Pope Francis in conversation with Austen Ivereigh, *Let Us Dream: The Path to a Better Future* (New York: Simon and Schuster, 2020), 31.

7. Although it is understandable that Francis would revert to Guardini— the original subject of his abandoned doctoral research—to provide a workable thesis around the petty tyrannies and insufficiencies of technology, the absence of any mention of the more immediate, and in some instances deeper analysis of technology, by such richly Catholic thinkers as Marshall McLuhan, Charles Taylor, and fellow Jesuit Walter Ong is surprising.

8. Although Francis does not identify by name individuals or countries that have fallen short of serious fiscal reform, his mention of the 2007–2008 financial crisis, indicating that it provided an opportunity "to develop a new economy, more attentive to ethical principles, and new ways of regulating speculative financial practices and virtual wealth," applies with particular force to the United States and President Barack Obama. The president had dispatched his treasury secretary, Timothy Geithner, to Canada to find out why Canada weathered the financial crisis so much better than most other countries. His conclusion: limited and highly regulated banks. Such a national practice would have been too radical for the American barons of commerce, and Obama failed to rise to the opportunity.

9. Robert M. Doran and John D. Dadosky, eds., *Collected Works of Bernard Lonergan*, vol. 14: *Method in Theology* (Toronto: University of Toronto Press, 2017), 221, 223.

10. Brian Grogan, SJ, *Finding God in a Leaf: The Mysticism of Laudato Si'* (Dublin: Messenger, 2018), 39–40.

11. John Moriarty, *Invoking Ireland, Ailiu Iaith n-hErend* (Dublin: Lilliput, 2005), 183.

12. Brendan O'Donoghue, ed., *A Moriarty Reader: Preparing for Early Spring* (Dublin: Lilliput, 2013), 290.

13. Michael W. Higgins and Seán Aherne, eds., *Introducing John Moriarty in His Own Words* (Dublin: Lilliput, 2019), xx.

14. Pierre Teilhard de Chardin, as quoted in "Pierre Teilhard de Chardin:

100th Anniversary, Program One: Teilhard the Man," *Ideas*, CBC Radio One, initially aired in January 1981.

15. Pierre Teilhard de Chardin, as quoted in "Pierre Teilhard de Chardin: 100th Anniversary, Program Four: Teilhard the Mystic."

16. On his trip to Mongolia prior to the Synod, Francis spoke glowingly of Teilhard, who he said was often misunderstood. Indeed, the pope quoted from Teilhard's *La Messe sur le Monde*, saying that he had seen in some powerful way a connection between the Eucharist and the world of matter. Ample evidence of this Jesuit pope championing a Jesuit scientist who spent his life under Roman suspicion and Jesuit censure.

17. Francis and Ivereigh, *Let Us Dream*, 5–6.

18. Nolan Scharper, "Where the Sacred and the Profane Intertwine," *Generation Laudato Si': Catholic Youth on Living Out an Ecological Spirituality*, ed. Rebecca Rathbone and Simon Appolloni (Toronto: Novalis, 2023), 79.

19. Scharper, "Where the Sacred and the Profane Intertwine," 80.

20. Simon Appolloni, "Engendering a Canadian Catholic Conversation about Care for Our Common Home," in *Looking to the Laity*, ed. Mahoney, 91.

CHAPTER 6

1. As quoted in Michael W. Higgins, "The Laity and the Hour of the Lord," *Grail: An Ecumenical Journal* 3 (September 1987): 26.

2. As quoted in Higgins, "The Laity and the Hour of the Lord," 26.

3. Margaret Hebblethwaite, "Towards a New Theology of the Laity," *Tablet*, June 15, 1985.

4. This work—its genesis, controversy and transforming impact on Catholic thinking—are explored in some depth in my book *The Church Needs the Laity: The Wisdom of John Henry Newman* (Mahwah, NJ: Paulist Press, 2021).

5. John Henry Newman, *On Consulting the Faithful in Matters of Doctrine*, ed. John Coulson (London: Collins, 1986), 63.

6. Newman, *On Consulting the Faithful*, 106.

7. Catherine Mulroney, "Lay Women in the Church," in *Looking to the Laity: Reflections on Where the Church Can Go from Here*, ed. Anne Louise Mahoney (Toronto: Novalis, 2021), 45.

8. George B. Flahiff, "Ministries of Women in the Church" (intervention delivered at the Synod of Bishops in Rome, October 11, 1971).

9. Robert Lebel, "The Role of Women in Family Ministry and the Life of the Church" (intervention delivered at the Synod of Bishops in Rome, October 14, 1980).

10. Louis-Albert Vachon, "Male-Female Reconciliation in the Church" (intervention delivered at the Synod of Bishops in Rome, October 3, 1983). See also Michael W. Higgins and Douglas R. Letson, "Canadian Particpation in Episcopal Synods, 1967–1985," *Historical Studies of the Canadian Catholic Historical Association* 54 (1987): 145–57.

11. Alfonso P. Suico, "Reframing Reproductive Rights: Pope Francis's Genius of Women as a Paradigm of Conversation between Filipina Women and Church Leadership" (PhD diss., Santa Clara University, 2022), 166.

12. Michael G. Lawler and Todd A. Salzman, "Pope Francis Brings Nuance to Notion of Complementarity," *National Catholic Reporter*, May 29, 2015, ncronline.org/news/theology/pope-francis-brings-nuance-notion-complementarity. Enthusiasm for John Paul II's thinking on sexuality has not been widespread—in fact, resistance to his often hard-line teaching on the subject has succeeded in obscuring the immense value of his social justice writings, the jewel in the Wojtyla papacy. Even so, a significant minority of conservative Catholics have wholeheartedly embraced the Theology of the Body with some surprising results. I recall a panel I was on with a distinguished Catholic scholar when she announced that Pope John Paul II understands a woman's orgasm better than any woman. The host of the program at the time, TVOntario's Mary Hynes, and I were rendered speechless. My interlocutor, with a taste for the philosophical, clearly meant the pope's understanding was grounded in the abstract.

13. Sacred Congregation for the Doctrine of the Faith, Declaration Inter insigniores on the Question of Admission to Women to the Ministerial Priesthood, October 15, 1976, vatican.va/roman_curia/congregations/cfaith/documents/rc_con_cfaith_doc_19761015_inter-insigniores_en.html.

14. A perfect example of the text's less than luminous prose and lucidity of argument is the following: "To move from this position to the necessity of ordaining women is to impose, for the most part unreflectively, a monadic logic upon a Trinitarian and covenantal equality. Equal monads are qualitatively indistinct; their differentiation is quantitative only." Carter neither talked nor wrote like this.

15. Gerald Emmett Cardinal Carter, *Do This in Memory of Me: A Pastoral Letter upon the Sacrament of Holy Orders* (Toronto: Archdiocese of Toronto, 1983), 53.

16. Cardinal Carter, interview with Janet Somerville and Grant Jahnke, *Catholic New Times*, February 12, 1984.

17. As excerpted in Michael W. Higgins and Douglas R. Letson, *My Father's Business: A Biography of His Eminence G. Emmett Cardinal Carter* (Toronto: Macmillan, 1990), 189–90.

18. A perfect example of this renaming and reconfiguration in Canada

can be seen with the morphing of Catholics for Women's Ordination into Catholic Network for Women's Equality.

19. Tina Beattie, "Pope Francis, Sex and Gender," *Tablet*, December 17, 2022, 12.

20. Pope Francis in conversation with Austen Ivereigh, *Let Us Dream: The Path to a Better Future* (New York: Simon and Schuster, 2020), 68.

21. John Lahr, "Acting Up: Emma Thompson's Third Act," *New Yorker*, November 14, 2022, 60. It would be a mistake to think that Francis's view of women as the compassionate agents of human suffering is a benighted old-fashioned view easily rendered redundant by contemporary feminism and gender theory. Like Emma Thompson, he knows that the ones who will do the enabling work that men often neglect or forsake are the women and, it should be said, his view of complementarity is not a minority view within large sections of the Catholic laity, including women. Margaret Karram is president of the Focolare Movement, an ecclesially approved entity that is open to women and men and to Christians of all persuasion; also known as the Work of Mary, it was founded by Chiara Lubich in 1943 as a radical way of uniting humanity in its diversity, listening in dialogue, praying in common, and dedicated to acts of charity. Speaking of her own work and that of other Focolarini, Karram observes in an interview for *Jerusalem Cross: Annales Ordinis Equestris Sancti Sepulchri Hierosolymitani* (2022–23): "The president of the Focolare Movement will always be a woman, a sign that underlines the importance of women in the Church and their enriching and truly complementary role. Women have a different capacity to love and suffer than men, they have a different sensitivity and can do much to transmit the faith, to 'give life' spiritually. Today's world, tired of speeches, needs vital experiences that are realized in the patience of waiting. Physiologically, women are more oriented towards fecundity than efficiency. Pope Francis emphasizes this, without wanting to clericalize women, and his pontificate is a great hope in this field." To be sure, this is not Emma Thompson's thinking, but it is instructive to see this surprising alignment of view.

22. John Henry Newman, *Certain Difficulties Felt by Anglicans in Catholic Teaching* (London: Longmans, new impression, 1900), 2:79.

23. Fintan O'Toole, "A Moral Witness," review of *Yours, for Probably Always: Martha Gellhorn's Letters of Love and War, 1940–1949*, edited by Janet Somerville, *New York Review of Books*, October 8, 2020, 29.

CHAPTER 7

1. In his magisterial biography of Pope John, *John XXIII: Pope of the Council* (New York: HarperCollins, 1984), Vaticanologist and biographer

Peter Hebblethwaite notes that although Siri was overheard to have made this comment, he later retracted it during the beatification process of Pope John and admitted that his judgment was in error. It would be Pope Francis who would actually raise John to the altars, canonizing him at the same time he sainted Pope John Paul II.

2. Daniel O'Leary, *Dancing to My Death: With the Love Called Cancer* (Dublin: Columba, 2019), 112.

3. This case and others are studied in some detail in Michael W. Higgins and Peter Kavanagh, *Suffer the Children unto Me: An Open Inquiry into the Clerical Sex Abuse Scandal* (Toronto: Novalis, 2010).

4. Higgins and Kavanagh, *Suffer the Children.*

5. John Cornwell, *Church Interrupted: Havoc and Hope—The Tender Revolt of Pope Francis* (San Francisco: Chronicle Prism, 2021), 130.

6. Austen Ivereigh, *Wounded Shepherd: Pope Francis and His Struggle to Convert the Catholic Church* (New York: Henry Holt, 2019), 136.

7. One former chancellor of the Newark archdiocese and one-time priest president of Seton Hall University, John Petillo, told me that McCarrick's proclivities and activities were common knowledge in clerical circles, but that firm evidence never surfaced, or at least when concerns were raised, they were discounted as malicious gossip or as accusations without empirical foundation. So, matters festered for years enveloped in a conspiracy of silence.

8. "By eliding the sex abuse imbroglio with the credibility of Francis's pontificate, Archbishop Viganò has raised the ante. This isn't simply a *cri de coeur* by a former bishop-diplomat enraged by Vatican corruption; it isn't simply his *revanche* for past demotions or frustrated ambitions. It is his *j'accuse.*" Michael W. Higgins, "The Radical Change Needed for the Catholic Church to Survive," *Globe and Mail*, September 4, 2018.

9. Some twenty years ago, while attending an international meeting of rectors and presidents of universities influenced by Thomas Aquinas, I spent some time in conversation with the dean of the Faculty of Medicine at the Catholic University of Lyon, who was both a priest and a hematologist. He was also the person in charge of sex abuse allegations against clerics for both the Archdiocese of Lyon and the Diocese of Angers. When I remarked that the number of allegations against abusing clerics seemed paltry compared with many other European jurisdictions, he observed that because of the doctrine of *laïcité* so beloved of the French post-1907, with its clear demarcation of state and church, whenever an accusation arose, he simply handed it over to the local judiciary to handle, thereby freeing the church from any legal entanglement. All seemed to be well; the state authorities would proceed with the investigation. But it isn't quite what it appears, as the Sauvé Report uncovers.

10. Michael W. Higgins, "The Hard Truth of Sexual Abuse in the Catholic Church Is Demoralizing. But We Must Confront It," *Globe and Mail*, October 10, 2021.

11. Vanier fell under Philippe's influence almost from the moment he first met him in 1947. Throughout the 1950s, Vanier cemented his relationship with and dependence on Père Thomas, initially as a student of his esoteric Thomism but eventually as an initiate in his secret society of Gnostic libertines glossed as devout votaries of Mary and her son. No less a French Catholic luminary than Jacques Maritain judged Philippe's Marian spirituality "mad," writing in a letter to Charles Journet that "his mannerism of wanting to make the Holy Virgin her Son's bride infuriates and shocks me." Michael W. Higgins, "A 'Toxic Nucleus' within the Church: The L'Arche Report Confirms the Worst about Vanier," *Commonweal*, May 3, 2023.

12. Full disclosure moment: I wrote a commissioned biography of Jean Vanier, *Logician of the Heart* (Collegeville, MN: Liturgical Press, 2016), and was completely blindsided by the allegations, the history of sexual and emotional manipulation by Vanier, as well as the sordid history of Thomas Philippe and his ecclesiastical coven. The commissioners of the L'Arche Report note that "the biographers of the Vanier parents—Georges and Pauline [Canada's vice-regal couple]—and of Jean himself, have *only h*ad access to the outward, expurgated part of the historical documentation, without the possibility of access to all the archives (J. Vanier's Personal Archives, the Archives for the Congregation for the Doctrine of the Faith, etc.)." The Philippe apparatus ensured continued promotion of the brand, and there was too much invested in the image of living sanctity to allow for any kind of serious investigative biography. Outside the elect, the toxic nucleus, there would be only controlled, expertly fashioned, portraiture. Publishers, scholars, editors, and biographers worked *with* this image. There was insufficient scrutiny, no hermeneutic of suspicion, and if there were concerns, they were put on hold in the face of a juggernaut of media construction. But it wasn't all fraudulence. Behind the patina of holy serenity there was a turbulent struggle, many Vanier moments of genuine empathy and compassion, penetrative insights into suffering and the human ache for unconditional love. So very much undone by a parallel life of sexual and emotional abuse rooted in a world of mystical perversity.

13. Andrew Coyne, "The Shame of Residential Schools Must Be Worn by All—Not Just Historical Figures," *Globe and Mail*, June 4, 2021.

14. Tim Lilburn, "In the Time of Extreme Heat, in the Time of the Discovery of Unmarked Graves at the Sites of Residential Schools," an

unpublished text sent to me and quoted in my article "Après Kamloops, le Déluge: Institutional Church, Indigenous Oppression and the Catholic Intellectual Tradition," *Merton Annual* 34 (2021): 80. Italics added.

15. Harry Lafond in conversation with Elaine Enns and Ched Meyers, "The Church Must Change Its Thinking about Indigenous People," *Sojourners*, August 2022, 36.

16. Tanya Talaga, "Will Accountability Ever Come in the Catholic Church and the Canadian Government?," *Globe and Mail*, July 8, 2021.

17. Jane Barter, Doris M. Kieser, and Daryold Winkler, "Missed Opportunities and Hope for Healing: Reflections of an Indigenous Catholic Priest—Interview with Daryold Winkler," *Journal of Moral Theology* 12, no. 1 (2023): 77.

18. Kelsi-Leigh Balaban, "The Pope Comes to Treaty Six: An Interview with Emily Riddle (nehiyaw, Alexander First Nation)," in *Calls to Action Accountability: A 2022 Status Update on Reconciliation*, ed. Eva Jewell and Ian Mosby (Toronto: Yellowhead Institute, Toronto Metropolitan University, 2022), 35.

19. Donald Bolen, "The Papal Apology and Seeds of an Action Plan," *Journal of Moral Theology* 12, no. 1 (2023), 38.

20. James Baldwin, *Go Tell It on the Mountain* (New York: Knopf, 1953).

21. "*Terra nullius* (literally: no one's land) is a term that attempts to explain how Europeans often justified their seizure of Indigenous lands … While the 'law of the first taker' existed in Roman Law, it generally applied to things like wild animals … the term *terra nullius* is of quite recent origin and we should be cautious about assuming that there is a single, common legal principle underlying European expansion in the New World. However, it cannot be doubted that the term … does point to a historical reality, namely that Europeans, because of their own limited understandings of agriculture, technology, property, and culture, often did see Indigenous land as being essentially unused and therefore free for the taking. That these same Europeans often seized these lands without the consent of the land's rightful owners was a profound injustice." *The "Doctrine of Discovery" and* Terra Nullius: *A Catholic Response* (Ottawa: Concacan, 2016), 7. cccb.ca/wp-content/uploads/2017/11/catholic-response-to-doctrine-of-discovery-and-tn.pdf.

22. Irenic because of the kerfuffle over the meaning of a word that the pope used when in Edmonton. Tanya Talaga and others objected strenuously to the pope's comment that the Vatican would "conduct a serious investigation into the facts of what took place in the past," implying that the multiple and intensive investigations already conducted, including especially the TRC Report of 2015, might have been deficient. The Vatican

clarified by saying that the word investigation was "lost in translation," as the word he used in the original Spanish text was *search*. Certainly, nerves have been frayed by some rebarbative articles published in various media outlets, including most noticeably the *New York Post*, questioning the historical methodologies employed by Indigenous advocates, the scholarly validity of oral history, and the paucity of written records. The atmosphere around the topic of legitimate historical scholarship has become malodorous in several circles, and Francis stumbled into it.

23. Nicole Winfield, "Indigenous Leaders Hope Vatican's Repudiation of Oppressive Colonial Concepts Leads to Real Change," Associated Press, March 30, 2023.

24. Jean-Pierre Fortin, "Indigenous Witness, Christian Confession: Decolonization as Integral Component of Pope Francis's Theology of Mercy" (paper presented at the conference Pope Francis and the Future of the Church: Prospects and Challenges for Renewal, St. Mark's College, University of British Columbia, May 4–6, 2023).

25. Frederick Bauerschmidt, "After Christendom: Catholicism in a More Secular Future," *Commonweal*, May 19, 2022, 38.

26. Vatican News, "It Was a Genocide against Indigenous Peoples," July 30, 2022, vaticannews.va/en/pope/news/2022-07/pope-francis-apostolic-journey-inflight-press-conference-canada.html.

27. In a private email correspondence with Michael Swan, a veteran reporter for the country's premier Catholic diocesan newspaper, the *Catholic Register*, I was told that although he was able to report the pope's answer to the question in his first bit of reportage, "thereafter, in follow-up stories and in my summary of the trip the word 'genocide' was excised from my stories. At weekly budget meetings (where reporters and editors review possible stories to pursue for the next edition), *no* story regarding the most remarkable statement any pope had made since the Catholic Church began teaming up with European royalty on colonial projects was given a green light" (July 5, 2023).

28. Cassidy Caron, "The Pope's Comments on Genocide Marked a Turning Point for Canada," *Globe and Mail*, August 26, 2022.

29. As quoted in Michael Swan's unpublished essay "Confessing Genocide: A Catholic Journalist Confronts Our Residential School Legacy."

CHAPTER 8

1. What an irony it would be if a Jesuit pope presided over a major schism. Jesuits have been, since their inception in the sixteenth century, especially loyal to the pope, many of them taking a fourth vow of fealty

to the pontiff. But Francis also knows that the Jesuit spirit is a pioneering spirit. You take risks in spiritual leadership, and he is poised for the wager.

2. Francis Spufford, interview by Peter Stanford, "Grace under Pressure," *Tablet*, February 20, 2021, 11.

3. Brian Doyle, *One Long River of Song: Notes on Wonder* (New York: Little, Brown, 2019), 224.

4. As quoted in Phil Christman's "A Change of Hart?," *Commonweal*, October 10, 2022, 45.

5. Christian Wiman, *He Held Radical Light* (New York: Farrar, Straus and Giroux, 2018), 83.

6. Pope Francis, Address at the ceremony commemorating the fiftieth anniversary of the institution of the Synod of Bishops, October 17, 2015, vatican.va/content/francesco/en/speeches/2015/october/documents/papa-francesco_20151017_50-anniversario-sinodo.html.

7. Quoted from an address given at Santa Clara University in 2015 and referenced in Rita Ferrone's "From Lived History to Legacy: Vatican II at Sixty," *Commonweal*, December 15, 2022, 9.

8. Paul Vallely, *Pope Francis: Untying the Knots* (London: Bloomsbury, 2013), 184–85.

9. The Ordinary synods are scheduled to be held at specifically determined intervals, are universal rather than regional in their focus, are primarily pastoral in emphasis, and are distinctly contemporary rather than historical in their hermeneutical lens. Extraordinary synods have greater urgency driving them and, though highly limited in their number and constitution by comparison with the Ordinary synods, are more explicitly theological and ecclesiological in their nature. But they are no less potent for that. As I indicated earlier, the 1985 Second Vatican Council Anniversary Extraordinary synod was a watershed moment in the life of the post-conciliar church, and we are still living out the consequences of that 1985 assembly to this day. Special synods are geographically limited and specific to a church in a particular region: Africa, America, Asia, Europe, Oceania, the Netherlands, Lebanon, and Amazonia; they are designed to respond to specific geo-religio challenges and internal church crises.

10. Michael Czerny, SJ, "Towards a Synodal Church," *La Civiltà Cattolica*, January 25, 2021.

11. Austen Ivereigh, *Wounded Shepherd: Pope Francis and His Struggles to Convert the Catholic Church* (New York: Henry Holt, 2019), 89.

12. Newman, *On Consulting the Faithful*, 106.

13. This is a highly edited precis of my book-length essay on Newman, *The Church Needs the Laity*.

14. John Henry Newman, *Apologia pro Vita Sua*, ed. Martin J. Svaglic (Oxford: Oxford University Press, 1967), 226.

15. Joseph W. Tobin, "The Long Game: Pope Francis's Vision of Synodality," *Commonweal*, June 1, 2021, 26. Tobin is one of Francis's sturdy and insightful allies. A former superior general of a religious order—the Redemptorists—he came to his position as a bishop with an extensive background of global travel and with a keen missionary sensibility. Francis is fond of bishops who know something of the larger world, have the "smell of the sheep" about them, and recognize the value of the margins to evangelization. His appointment of Robert Prevost as head of the Dicastery of Bishops in Rome confirms the papal trend to draw on leaders who have extensive field experience (Prevost worked for years as a missionary in Peru) and are possessed of a geopolitical perspective that is not Eurocentric but global (Prevost was at one time the head of the Augustinians). Tobin's passionate advocacy of the Francis project on synodality is shared by several bishops worldwide—Cardinals Basil Cupich and Robert McElroy in the United States, Archbishops Paul-André Durocher and Donald Bolen in Canada, Cardinals Mario Grech of Malta and Jean-Claude Hollerich of Luxembourg are essential or core Bergoglians—but it would be a wishful leap to suggest that their number constitutes the majority of the current episcopate. Most are not overtly resistant, only cautious and worried. Men of the standard clerical formation of their time, many appointees of previous popes, temperamentally inclined to preserve what they have rather than wager on an uncertain future, conservers rather than innovators, they look on the Francis papacy with a mighty dollop of reserve sometimes spilling over into trepidation. They are potentially for turning. But there is also a minority—and they *are* a minority—whose opposition not only to synodality but to the Francis pontificate is fierce and reactionary. And they are not for turning. Without exception, however, during the daily press briefings at the Synod on Synodality, the president delegates, dicasterial cardinals, archbishops, and bishops who had been at previous synods, spoke uniformly of their genuine pleasure in arriving at the synod without the outcomes determined in advance. Regardless of their personal theological leanings, to a prelate they all affirmed the superiority of the revolutionized Bergoglio synod model. One cannot help but observe that this was, in its way, a repudiation of the previous model—without their actually saying so—because it respected their right to contribute in an open and free manner, cognizant of the fact that the proposals of the synod were not prescripted and their involvement accordingly empty and formulaic. Tobin was especially vocal in his support for the new, open way of being a synod.

16. Cardinal Schönborn, interview by François Vayne, *Jerusalem Cross: Annales Ordinis Equestris Sancti Sepulchri Hierosolymitani* (2021–22), 3–4. Schönborn was a peritus at the 1985 Extraordinary synod and has been a regular at every synod since being ordained a bishop. At a press briefing, he reminded the media and other guests present that Europe is no longer the centre of Catholicism, and that if faith, hope, and charity don't increase because of this Synod on Synodality, then the synod was in vain. In this, he echoed the concluding remarks made at the Second Vatican Council. He also made one of the more stunningly pertinent remarks of any of the synod delegates at the Synod on Synodality when he observed in the context of the continuing Russia–Ukraine conflict, compounded by the Hamas–Israel war, that a distinguished political scientist remarked to him that if the UN Security Council operated in as honest and transparent a way as the synod, with emphasis on deep listening and mutual respect, then the stalemates that prevent effective peace-making would be overcome.

17. The priest-psychologist and spiritual writer Henri Nouwen reminds us in his work *Lifesigns: Intimacy, Fecundity, and Ecstasy in Christian Perspective* (New York: Doubleday, 1986) that "the word 'school,' which comes from 'schola' (meaning: free time), reminds us that schools were originally meant to interrupt a busy existence and create some space to contemplate the mysteries of life" (49). But Nouwen, variously a Yale and Harvard professor, lamented that the *schola* had become a space wherein productivity, quantifiable success, and achievements that could be measured according to an index of meaning actually hostile to the genuine fecundity of mind and spirit at the heart of the school's origin. The synodal process, as conceived by Francis and the Bergoglians, is a recovery of the *schola* as a setting for fertile Holy Spirit–generated free time.

18. Daniel E. Flores, "Closeness and the Common Journey: Synodality as an Expression of the Church's Responsiveness to Christ," *Commonweal*, June 20, 2022, 31. The synod experience—global, fully representative, diverse, inclusive—can be a template of conciliation, peace, and depolarization for the nations. Our fraught earth, ravaged by our failure at stewardship; our fraught politics, damaged by hyper-partisanship and incendiary rhetoric; and our fraught interfaith relations, seeded with suspicion and ignorance, can all benefit by seeing a church community coming together to discern and pray *as* a community, offering an antidote to the enervating malaise that weighs so heavily on the human family.

19. Catherine E. Clifford, "The Remedy of Synodality," *Go, Rebuild My House* (blog, Sacred Heart University), September 15, 2021,

sacredheartuniversity.typepad.com/go_rebuild_my_house/2021/09/
the-remedy-of-synodality.html.

20. Numerous organizations prioritizing women in the church—their
status, their exclusion from sacramental/ordained ministries, their minimal
presence in leadership positions in the majority of dioceses—have taken
up the challenge to speak boldly and forthrightly when responding to the
invitation to engage in consultations in the first phase of the synodal process.
Spirit Unbounded, Root and Branch, Women's Ordination Conference, to
name but a few (and it should be noted that membership is not limited to
women), all planned various interventions throughout the duration of the
synod with the hope that the call to discern and listen is not ecclesial spin
but a genuine invitation to share in the freedom of the Spirit.

21. Cardinal archbishop of Vienna and a former Benedictine abbot,
Groër was accused of having molested young seminarians while in charge
of a prominent Marian shrine. His leadership as archbishop of Vienna was
undistinguished—a mediocre mind and non-charismatic personality, Groër
had the ill fortune to succeed one of the greatest European churchman of
his time, Franz König—but it was not his personality that was the problem.
When he refused to respond to the charges of abuse—neither refuting
the accuracy of the charges nor at any time admitting guilt and seeking
forgiveness—he alienated hundreds of thousands of Austrian Catholics
(they have still not recovered their former strength as a national church),
and his resistance to accountability spurred groups of Catholics to move
into protest mode, as the Vatican was more than dilatory in its response
to a heightened credibility crisis in the Austrian church. With most of the
hierarchy increasingly vocal over its unhappiness with Groër, and with lay
people formally disaffiliating in hitherto unprecedented numbers, John Paul
II was finally persuaded to act. Further analysis of the Groër affair, other
European scandals, and their many North American parallels can be found
in Higgins and Kavanagh, *Suffer the Children.*

22. North American Working Group, *Doing Theology from the Existential
Peripheries* (report of the North American Working Group members: William
T. Cavanagh, DePaul University; Meghan J. Clark, St. John's University;
Darren Dias, University of St. Michael's College; Bradford E. Hinze, Fordham
University; Stan Chu Ilo, DePaul University; Thomas M. Landy, College of
the Holy Cross; Thomas Lynch, St. Augustine's Seminary; Jennifer Owens-
Jofré, University of San Diego; and Jaime L. Waters, Boston College), 9.
drive.google.com/file/d/1obYU6RVaCweuCSdPjAxbJslh-uBD9mcP/view.

23. "Globally, participation exceeded all expectations. In all, the Synod
Secretariat received contributions from 112 out of 114 Episcopal Conferences

and from all the 15 Oriental Catholic Churches, plus reflections from 17 out of 23 dicasteries of the Roman Curia besides those from religious superiors, from institutes of consecrated life and societies of apostolic life, and from association and lay movements of the faithful. In addition, over a thousand contributions arrived from individuals and groups as well as insights gathered through social media thanks to the initiative of the Digital Synod. These materials were distributed to a group of experts: bishops, priests, consecrated men and women, lay men and lay women, from all continents and with very diverse disciplinary expertise. After reading the reports, these experts met for almost two weeks together with the writing group, composed of the General Relator (Cardinal Jean-Claude Hollerich, SJ of Luxembourg), the Secretary General of the Synod (Cardinal Mario Grech of Malta), the Undersecretaries (Sister Nathalie Becquart, XMCJ and Bishop Luis Marín de San Martín, OSA) and various officials of the Synod Secretariat, plus members of the Coordinating Committee. This group was finally joined by the members of the General Council. Together they worked in an atmosphere of prayer and discernment to share the fruits of their reading in in preparation for the drafting of this Document for the Continental Stage." General Secretariat of the Synod, *Enlarge the Space of Your Tent*, 4. synod.va/content/dam/synod/common/phases/continental-stage/dcs/ Documento-Tappa-Continentale-EN.pdf. The gestation of this document is mind-numbing in its thoroughness. The results, understandably, are uneven: deadly prose peppered with moments of luminous poetry, incisive insights sharing space with banal summaries, breadth of range commentary dancing respectfully around issues of compelling local concern, and although the conventional clerical sensibility is not absent in the composition, full marks for producing a document that successfully captures the scope and intensity of the submissions and doing so fairly.

24. "Almost all reports raise the issue of full and equal participation of women: '*The growing recognition of the importance of women in the life of the Church opens up possibilities for greater, albeit limited, participation in Church structures and decision-making spheres*' (Brazil). However, the reports do not agree on a single or complete response to the question of the vocation, inclusion and flourishing of women in Church and society. After careful listening, many reports ask that the Church continue its discernment in relation to a range of specific questions: the active role of women in the governing structures of Church bodies, the possibility for women with adequate training to preach in parish settings, and a female diaconate. Much greater diversity of opinion was expressed on the subject of priestly ordination for women, which some reports call for, while others consider

a closed issue." It remains a peculiarity of the discussion around women that in some fundamental way it is anomalous. Why should gender be a determinant of full inclusion? Why do we have women in/and the church when men in/and the church is a given? The deeper cultural-historical-anthropological dimensions of this discussion have yet to be fully explored. The biblical appears to be consigned to the margins, the ontological and canonical enjoying privileged priority, the ecumenical sidelined. There are many signs that Francis understands the stakes involved and that they are high: after all, in his position as Bishop of Rome, he exercises the Petrine ministry of unity. And he also understands that we live in a time when there has been a fundamental shift of consciousness, which his fellow Jesuit Bernard Lonergan identified as a shift from a classicist to a historicist consciousness, and that this shift is epoch shaking. Time, prudence, trust, and meaningful encounter are the way forward if the very structures of the church are not to be permanently sundered. Hence, the need for synodality that embodies those very qualities and virtues.

25. A careful parsing of this passage from the *Instrumentum laboris* reveals the key concepts shoring up the synodal approach: listening deeply, walking together, with real people in mind. In other words, pastoral attentiveness to the concrete rather than preoccupation with the abstract world of legal and dogmatic niceties and formularies; communion as a lived encounter; meaningful participation rather than passive reception.

26. Interview with the author conducted in the Office of the President of St. Jerome's University, Waterloo, Ontario, September 27, 2023, following Archbishop Bolen's public address at the St. Jerome's Centre Catholic Experience Lectures: "The Wounds of the Past, Truth-Telling and a Future of Hope: The Doctrine of Discovery and the Path of Reconciliation."

27. At past synods, the media would be invited on one occasion only per synod into the *aula del sinodo* as *auditores* only. That is, as listeners and not as participants. The reasoning behind this gesture of bracketed inclusion was to allow us the opportunity to see the synod dynamic in action. Predictably, the action was controlled and uninspiring. The joke circulating among the press folk that when the pope was present, he seldom appeared engaged and spent most of the time reading his breviary—for, after all, the outcome was already determined—was certainly not cynical. On the three occasions when I was present, the pope was fully occupied with his reading—whatever it was—while the delegates droned on. Not the most riveting theatre.

28. There was a kerfuffle over the exclusion of German this time. Some of the delegates saw it as a snub, given the strained relationship that existed

in several quarters over the radicality of the German synod—a four-year intensive process that opened up an array of the most contentious issues roiling the church. Certainly, there were concerns raised, and certainly, frank conversations were held in Rome with the German episcopate, but the German delegates at the Synod on Synodality were committed to the process as defined and played by the rules. The Secretariat and the Sala Stampa played down the mini-controversy by saying that all the German delegates were fluent in several languages, English specifically, and therefore could be assigned to a number of linguistic groups. I suspect that this is true, but diluting the German presence by spreading them about, thereby ensuring that they did not function as one determined congregate of like-minded participants, also played its role.

29. Although this method is traced to the early church dynamics found in the evangelist Luke's Acts of the Apostles when he speaks of the Council of Jerusalem and how the assembly worked through the touchy and potentially divisive issue of whether Gentile converts needed to be circumcised, it has been incorporated subsequently in a wide variety of ways. For instance, the Society of Jesus attached great importance to reviving the method for its 36th General Congregation in 2016, and as Christina Kheng, a theologian who teaches at the East Asian Pastoral Institute in Manila, makes clear, "similar approaches were also gaining traction in the wider Church, such as in the continental and national ecclesial assemblies and councils occurring just before the Synod 2021–2024 ... When the *Vademecum [Handbook] for the Synod on Synodality* was released in September 2021 it could be said that myriad creative videos and other training resources on the Spiritual Conversation produced spontaneously by people all over the world attested to its positive reception and broad-based traction." "The Method Is the Message: Method of Spiritual Conversation," in *The People of God Have Spoken: Continental Ecclesial Assemblies within the Synod on Synodality*, ed. Myriam Wijlens and Vimal Tirimanna, CSsR (Dublin: Columba, 2023), 25.

30. Austen Ivereigh, "How the Synod Will Change the Church," *Tablet*, November 11, 2023, 5.

31. Synod delegates who may have had some hesitation at and resistance to the pope's requirement that contact with the media be highly restricted did come around to see it the pope's way. Canadian theologian Catherine Clifford was one such convert to the kind of intelligent discretion the pope was calling for in relation to the press; in an interview with me, conducted midway during the synod (October 16), she observed with historical sensitivity that "I do think that the request for discretion is important so that the conversations around the table take place in camera, giving

the people the freedom to speak. Let me put this in context. I have heard things said this week that may be silly but were for me highly encouraging. These are things that, when I was interviewing for my first job in the 1990s, were highly contentious. I was quite fearful that someone would ask me my views on homosexuality and about women's ordination. Those were the litmus tests of orthodoxy, and it was forbidden to question the magisterium's position on these matters. I could say, well, of course I will teach accurately the teaching of the magisterium, but you know, they haven't been well received, and they haven't been convincing, and they are not very strong theological positions. So, we have gone from living through decades of a magisterium that tried to put a lid on all these issues to finally having in Francis a leader who is willing to risk creating a space for a free-wheeling discussion of *everything*. Everything. And that is nothing short of remarkable." For me, existing *extra aula*, I had a few challenges because I was contracted to provide on-site commentary no matter what obstacles. And so, I filed several articles and columns for the Canadian, British, and Irish press. Some of what appears here was first mentioned in these dispatches from Rome: "Pope Francis Shakes the Ground beneath His Detractors, Yet Again," *Globe and Mail*, September 27, 2023; "My Expectations for the Coming Synod on Synodality? Simple Really—It's Destined to Be Both a *Bousculade* and a *Galimafrée*," *Synodal Times*, October 5, 2023; "The Vatican Gathering Signals a New Approach for the Catholic Church," *Globe and Mail*, November 1, 2023; "The Secretive Synod," *Tablet*, November 4, 2023; "Refreshing Candour," *Synodal Times*, November 9, 2023.

32. Matthew 23:1–7. The biblical commentary—*Liturgy and Life Study Bible* (Collegeville, MN: Liturgical Press, 2023)—provides the original context for Jesus's denunciation with some historical and theological context: "While the tradition of a deep opposition between Jesus and the Pharisees is well founded, this speech reflects an opposition that goes beyond that of Jesus' ministry and must be seen as expressing the bitter conflict between Pharisaic Judaism and the church of Matthew at the time when the gospel was composed. The complaint often made that the speech ignores the positive qualities of Pharisaism and of its better representatives is true, but the complaint overlooks the circumstances that gave rise to the invective. Nor is the speech purely anti-Pharisaic. The evangelist discerns in his church many of the same faults that he finds in its opponents and warns his fellow Christians to look to their own conduct and attitudes" (1568).

33. The most curious, frequently irreverent, and unconventional of Vatican correspondents is the redoubtable Robert Mickens. A decades-long observer of three papacies, and an unreconstructed gadfly on the body of

settled ecclesiastical opinion, Mickens finds Francis's regular denunciations of clerical perfidy a bit contradictory: "Francis dislikes the puritans of the church, but he is every bit the unbending moralist. For instance, his treatment of Cardinal Giovanni Angelo Becciu, a one-time *sostituto* in the Vatican Secretariat of State who was charged with embezzlement, abuse of office, conspiracy, and witness tampering, is unfair. Even before the final court judgment, he publicly humiliated Becciu, accusing him of stuff without giving him the chance to present his side of the story. This is what the Dicastery for the Doctrine of the Faith used to do, and we know Francis has changed that. He took away Becciu's voting rights as a cardinal, and I could understand that if he was created a cardinal by John Paul II or Benedict XVI, but he was Francis's creation. [The court sentencing of Cardinal Becciu for crimes of embezzlement and related financial improprieties was released on December 16, 2023: five years, six months imprisonment and a fine of eight thousand euros.] He also booted Benedict's private secretary, Georg Gänswein, out of his digs and told the Ratzinger acolyte to get a job. He is right to be upset with those he knows are two-faced and plot against him but, again, he is the one who famously said: 'Who am I to judge?'" Robert Mickens, interview with the author, October 17, 2023.

34. Vatican News, "Pope Francis Responds to Dubia Submitted by Five Cardinals," unofficial working translation, October 2, 2023, vaticannews.va/en/pope/news/2023-10/pope-francis-responds-to-dubia-of-five-cardinals.html.

35. "Pope Francis Responds to Dubia."

36. Garry O'Sullivan, interview with the author, October 4, 2023.

37. Timothy Radcliffe, OP, "Synod Retreat Meditation: 'Authority,'" Vatican News, October 2, 2023, vaticannews.va/en/church/news/2023-10/synod-retreat-meditation-authority.html.

38. Mary Ellen Chown, interview and email correspondence with the author, October 15, 2023.

39. XVI Ordinary General Assembly of the Synod of Bishops, First Session (October 4–29, 2023), *Synthesis Report: A Synodal Church in Mission*, synod.va/content/dam/synod/assembly/synthesis/english/2023.10.28-ENG-Synthesis-Report.pdf.

40. In *To the Margins: Pope Francis and the Mission of the Church* (Maryknoll, NY: Orbis Books, 2018), philosopher and social activist Andrea Riccardi speaks of Francis's option for the poor as "Pope Bergoglio's Gospel Geopolitics or simply *geotheology*. This is not something impromptu or pragmatic; it comes from lived conviction and the depth of the church" (4).

41. Mark Guevarra, interview with the author, October 16, 2023, Rome.

42. The canonical approach is frequently, although not always, formulaic,

categorical, and explicitly in full alignment with official teaching. The pastoral approach, in contrast, without spurning official teaching, is contextual and subtle in its application. Given Pope Francis's general teaching on ministry to the marginalized—frequently open to criticism by his detractors for being Jesuitical—you can see his pastoral sensibility stretched to the breaking point. But he always opts to include rather than exclude.

43. The *Synthesis Report* states with crushing blandness and generality that "in different ways, people who feel marginalized or excluded from the Church because of their marriage status, identity or sexuality also ask to be heard and accompanied. There was a deep sense of love, mercy and compassion felt in the Assembly for those who feel hurt or neglected by the Church, who want a place to call 'home' where they can feel safe, be heard and respected, without fear of being judged." Altogether worthy, for sure, and a welcome departure from the canonical strictures and narrow theological discourse of recent papacies, but surely not quite enough. As yet another demonstration of the unpredictable and pastorally charged interventions of Francis, he balanced the benign but theologically safe distancing of the synod from substantive and reformative engagement with such hot-button issues as same-sex marriage and blessings by actually staging a meeting with Sister Jeannine Gramick, co-founder of New Ways Ministry, a once-censured Catholic outreach body committed to dialogue and reconciliation specifically with gays and the Catholic Church. Gramick has been delated, investigated, and calumniated and yet has remained a loyal Catholic much admired by Francis, who has written to her commending her valour and mission. She appeared first in chapter 4 of this book. This is her welcome reprise. By meeting with her and representatives of New Ways Ministry and Bondings and their media reps at the synod, Francis once again signalled his approval of Catholic gay outreach—he has consistently done likewise with James Martin, SJ—in spite of institutional timidity. This is a perfect illustration of Francis, in Peter Warrian's phrase, "ragging the puck."

44. The notion of the technocratic paradigm that Francis critiques is drawn from his study of Romano Guardini. Coupled with his sensitivity to Indigenous Peoples and their tragic intergenerational traumas created by centuries of oppressive colonization, as well as his reverence for their spirituality, connectedness with the harmonies of nature, and respect for the wisdom of their Elders (all on abundant display during his Canadian pilgrimage in 2022), Francis has an integrated approach different in kind from the other global voices on our climate calamities.

45. One of the major global bankers and thinkers in the area of economics, politics, morality, and society who has written and spoken

approvingly of Francis's approach to this matter is Canadian Mark Carney, former governor of both the Bank of Canada and the Bank of England, author of *Value(s): Building a Better World for All* (Toronto: Signal, 2021), and a committed Roman Catholic (he was once voted the first of the top one hundred Catholics in the United Kingdom).

46. Conor Gearty, "Who Will Stand for Universalism?," *Tablet*, November 11, 2023, 7. Gearty is not unaware of Catholicism's sorry history, just acutely aware of the current and tragic paucity of credible moral leadership in an increasingly anti-liberal democracy world: "when the Catholic Church wielded temporal power it was a cruel beast: all those Crusades and pogroms against infidels (especially, of course, the Jews). But with the loss of its physical power has come spiritual strength, a power of critique that transcends the ideology of the day, whether it be nationalism, communism or (to the point at the present moment) liberalism."

CONCLUSION

1. Emilce Cuda, interview with the author, October 16, 2023, at the office of the Pontifical Commission for Latin America in the Palazzo di San Callisto.

2. Francis, apostolic letter *Ad theologiam promovendam*, November 1, 2023, vatican.va/content/francesco/it/motu_proprio/documents/20231101-motu-proprio-ad-theologiam-promovendam.html.

3. As quoted in an email correspondence with the editor in "*Ad theologiam promovendam*: A Brief Guide for Busy Readers," *Pillar*, November 6, 2023.

4. Christopher Longhurst, "Pope Francis' New Relational Theology," *La Croix International*, November 7, 2023, 2.

5. Merton, *Conjectures*, 144.

INDEX

© Sarah Higgins

MICHAEL W. HIGGINS is President and Vice-Chancellor Emeritus, St. Jerome's University in the University of Waterloo; Basilian Distinguished Fellow in Contemporary Catholic Thought, St. Michael's College in the University of Toronto; and Distinguished Professor of Catholic Thought Emeritus, Sacred Heart University, Connecticut. He is the author of numerous books, including the award-winning *Heretic Blood: The Spiritual Geography of Thomas Merton*, co-author of the national bestseller *Power and Peril: The Catholic Church at the Crossroads*, and a regular contributor on Vatican affairs for the *Globe and Mail*. He has also been a CBC radio documentarian and film consultant. He lives with his wife, Krystyna, in Guelph, Ontario.